Luminos is the Open Access monograph publishing program from UC Press. Luminos provides a framework for preserving and reinvigorating monograph publishing for the future and increases the reach and visibility of important scholarly work. Titles published in the UC Press Luminos model are published with the same high standards for selection, peer review, production, and marketing as those in our traditional program. www.luminosoa.org

Ginseng and Borderland

Ginseng and Borderland

*Territorial Boundaries and Political Relations between
Qing China and Chosŏn Korea, 1636–1912*

Seonmin Kim

UNIVERSITY OF CALIFORNIA PRESS

University of California Press, one of the most distinguished university presses in the United States, enriches lives around the world by advancing scholarship in the humanities, social sciences, and natural sciences. Its activities are supported by the UC Press Foundation and by philanthropic contributions from individuals and institutions. For more information, visit www.ucpress.edu.

University of California Press
Oakland, California

Suggested citation: Kim, Seonmin. *Ginseng and Borderland: Territorial Boundaries and Political Relations between Qing China and Chosŏn Korea, 1636–1912*. Oakland: University of California Press, 2017. doi: https://doi.org/10.1525/luminos.36

Cataloging-in-publication data is on file with the Library of Congress.
ISBN 978-0-520-29599-5
e-ISBN 978-0-520-96871-4

CONTENTS

ILLUSTRATIONS AND TABLES

FIGURES

MAPS

TABLES

ACKNOWLEDGMENTS

This book is indebted to many teachers, colleagues, and friends who have supported me for all these years. I have waited for this opportunity to express my long-delayed gratitude to them.

At Duke University, Professor Sucheta Mazumdar has trained me patiently in critically reading, thinking, and writing. Her question of why a Korean student should study Chinese history has led me to this path of exploring the Korean agency in Qing history. Professor Kären Wigen has provided full support at every stage, from taking her graduate classes to completing my dissertation to publishing this book. I am deeply grateful for her steadfast confidence in my work for all these years. At Korea University, Professor Pak Wonho inspired me to study Ming and Qing history. His reading seminar was the most valuable training in learning how to read Chinese documents.

Professor Peter Perdue has encouraged my project from its early stages to this present version of the book manuscript. This book would have been impossible without his staunch support of my project and his motivating scholarship on Qing history. Professor Nam-lin Hur has supported my research in many ways, especially by inviting me to his research project at the University of British Columbia and to workshops and conferences in Canada, Korea, and China. Professor Mark Elliott showed interest in my work since the early stages and has inspired me to explore Qing and Chosŏn relations into a new direction. Professor Wen-hsin Yeh has provided valuable advice for this publication. I would like to thank all of them for sharing their precious time and knowledge with me, and making this book possible.

Friends and colleagues have read various stages of the manuscript to help make it a publishable version. My special gratitude goes to Professor Adam Bohnet, who has shown his friendship and support by taking the time to read the entire

ix

manuscript and giving me useful advice and comments. Professor Saeyoung Park also read the manuscript and helped polish the key arguments and narratives. I am grateful for her never-ending confidence in my project. Professor Koo Bumjin helped me avoid errors by reading the introduction and providing valuable comments. Professor Kim Hyong-Chong generously shared with me his unpublished book manuscript, which allowed me to improve and mend many parts of the fifth chapter of this book.

Portions of this book have been presented at various conferences and workshops in the United States, China, and Hong Kong. Professors Evelyn Rawski, Pamela Crossley, Richard von Glahn, Kirk Larsen, and Yuanchong Wang have asked important questions and made valuable comments on different stages of the work. Professors Ding Yizhuang, Liu Xiaomeng, and Zhao Zhiqiang have not only given me the opportunity to present early versions of this work in Chinese, but have also provided valuable comments and advice. Professors Loretta Kim and Chang Yuenan invited me to their conferences, where I was able to further enhance my arguments.

At the Research Institute of Korean Studies of Korea University, Professor Cho Sungtaek made an excellent environment for scholarly projects and academic networking. This book is hugely indebted to his vision and passion for Korean studies. Professors Kim Munyong, Park Heonho, Kang Sangsoon, and Jung Byungwook have guided me with integrity and generosity. Professor Park Sang-soo has supported my career and research in every possible way. The graduate students who attended our weekly reading seminar of Manchu and Chinese documents have inspired me with their passion and hard work. I am especially grateful to Dr. Lee Sun-ae, who has led the seminar for many years with dedication and expertise.

Executive Editor Reed Malcolm at the University of California Press has patiently answered each and every one of my questions and has helped me revise the manuscript. Keila Diehl and Hanna Siurua polished and edited my early writings into this publishable version. Their professional expertise and personal support helped me endure the long and painful revision phase. Lee Seungsu produced beautiful maps for this book, and Choi Soonyoung edited the bibliography and glossary. I am thankful that their friendship is imprinted in these pages.

Generous support from the following institutions helped me to conduct research and complete the book: Duke Graduate School; the AAS China and Inner Asia; the Center for Chinese Studies at the National Central Library in Taiwan; and Keimyung University, Korea University, and the National Research Foundation in Korea. Most of all, the Laboratory for the Globalization of Korean Studies of the Academy of Korean Studies in Korea provided me financial support to finish the book manuscript and contributed a subsidy for publication (AKS-2013-LAB-2250001).

Some material in chapter 2 appears in "Ginseng and Border Trespassing between Qing China and Chosŏn Korea," *Late Imperial China* 28, no. 1 (2007): 33–61, and is used with the permission of Johns Hopkins University Press. The Korea University Library, the Kyujanggak Institute for Korean Studies at Seoul National University, and the Korean Christian Museum at Soongsil University have given me generous permission to use their illustrations and maps in this book.

Finally, I would like to thank my parents, who have waited patiently for their youngest daughter to finish her long stay abroad and for her professional career to be fully pursued. My brothers and sisters in Korea and in the United States have supported me for the past years by making me smile during the hardest times. I hope that they will discover how far I am in my career after reading this book. Lastly, my deepest gratitude is reserved for Lee Hun, my husband and colleague. His knowledge and support made it possible for me to complete this book. It is his unwavering faith in my work that has kept me from giving up.

Citations of Asian-language books and articles observe the following conventions: the pinyin romanization system for Chinese, the Hepburn system employed by the Library of Congress for Japanese, and the McCune-Reischauer romanization system for Korean. Manchu words and names are transcribed according to the Möllendorff system. Chinese, Japanese, and Korean names are transcribed surname first, in the traditional order. Chinese transliterations of Manchu personal names are written with dashes, for example "Mu-ke-deng."

Terms in Chinese, Japanese, Korean, or Manchu are marked C., J., K., or M. respectively. If not specified, the word is assumed to be Chinese.

Citations from the *Ming Shilu*, *Qing Shilu*, *Chosŏn Wangjo Sillok*, *Tongmun Hwigo*, and *Pibyŏnsa tŭngnok* give the date in terms of reign year, lunar month, and day.

NOTE ON WEIGHTS AND MEASURES

1 *liang* = 1.3 ounces or 37 grams

   liang is used for both currency and weight, for example, 1 *liang* of silver; 1 *liang* of ginseng

1 *jin (16 liang)* = 1.3 pounds or 0.6 kilograms

1 *li* = 0.36 miles or 0.5 kilometers

1 *mu* = 0.16 acre or 0.06 hectare

1 *xiang (15 mu)* = 2.4 acres

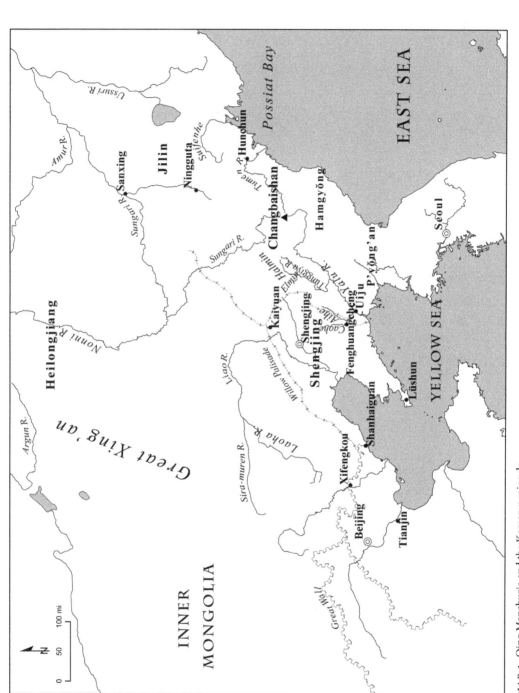

MAP 1. Qing Manchuria and the Korean peninsula.

Introduction

In 1745, the Shengjing military governor (*jiangjun*), Daldangga, wrote to the Qianlong emperor (r. 1736–95) to propose building a guard post at the mouth of the Yalu (K. *Amnok*) River. The suggested place was Mangniushao, a sandbank located where the confluence of two tributaries of the Yalu River, the Caohe and the Aihe, flowed into the mainstream of the Yalu. These tributaries, both originating in Changbaishan (K. *Paektusan*), also led to the Halmin and Elmin areas, the biggest ginseng preserve in Shengjing. Daldangga's predecessors had tried to protect the ginseng mountains (*shenshan*) in their jurisdiction by building outposts and stationing soldiers on the land routes around the area, but the waterways were poorly guarded and open to illegal poachers. Eager to improve the security situation in the Shengjing area and to tighten the management of ginseng production in particular, Daldangga emphasized the necessity of a guard post on the waterways; without one, people could easily build boats, transport food grains, and approach the prohibited ginseng preserves. He was concerned that, without a guard post, it was impossible to prevent, among other things, illegal ginseng poaching. Trained naval forces in Lüshun could be mobilized and stationed at Mangniushao, added Daldangga, and for their living they could cultivate the empty land available near the Yalu River.[1]

However, it was not his emperor or his rival officials in Beijing who severely objected to the military governor's idea; it was the Chosŏn court that urged the Qianlong emperor to reconsider the proposal and eventually succeeded in persuading him to drop the plan for an outpost on the Yalu River. Even though Qing officials confirmed that the sandbank was located within Qing territory, the Chosŏn repeatedly insisted that the two countries had long prohibited any settlement or cultivation in the vast area, as wide as a hundred *li*, between the Willow Palisade and the Yalu River. The Chosŏn king, Yŏngjo (r. 1724–76), lauded the ban as "a well-designed plan by the virtue of the imperial court [K. *hwangjo*]" to prevent contacts between Qing and Chosŏn people and thus eliminate any chance of trouble with the "small country" (K. *sobang*). Rejecting the Shengjing military governor's proposal for a new guard post to protect the ginseng mountains, the Qianlong emperor finally decided to acquiesce to the Chosŏn king's insistence that the land near the Yalu River should remain empty and not be opened to soldiers or civilians. The eighteenth-century Qing emperor agreed to keep his territory north of the Yalu River in the state that the Chosŏn king preferred.[2]

The Shengjing military governor's proposal for a guard post on the Yalu River was eminently reasonable in order to protect the Manchurian treasure and the imperial estate. But despite his full awareness of this, and even after confirmation that the sandbank was located within Qing territory, the Qianlong emperor decided to favor the Chosŏn request and reject the opening of the Yalu River to settlement. Why did the Qing emperor accept the Chosŏn king's request over the Manchu official's proposal? What empowered the "small country" of Chosŏn to persuade the "imperial court" to change its plans to protect its lands? This study seeks to find answers to these questions through the lens of ginseng, whose roots are entangled between the Qing and the Chosŏn and which reveals the peculiar nature of the two states' territorial boundaries and political relations.

The jurisdiction of the Qing Shengjing military governor overlapped roughly with today's Liaoning Province in China. It was also the sacred birthplace where Nurhaci (1559–1626) had raised himself from the leader of the Jianzhou Jurchens to the khan of the Aisin Gurun, also known as the Later Jin (*Jinguo, Houjin*); his son Hong Taiji (1592–1643) consolidated the Manchus, the Mongols, and the Han Chinese into the Qing empire. Even after its 1644 conquest of China proper, the Qing never lost its strong interest in Manchuria, including Shengjing, Jilin, and Heilongjiang. The Manchu homeland was to be preserved from the Han Chinese, because it was arguably the place where the Manchu ethnic identity and military prowess—the "Manchu way"—were maintained. In addition to the political and cultural significance of Manchuria, the land's natural resources had huge economic value, since they had provided the Manchu ancestors with the material wealth to develop their own state and eventually establish the Qing empire. Pearls, sable, and ginseng, all growing in the rich mountains and rivers in Manchuria, were widely called the three treasures of the northeast. Of the three, ginseng was widely available in the Jianzhou Jurchen territory and was also the most valuable commodity in trading with the Ming. Well aware of the commercial value of this root, the Qing court paid special attention to protecting the ginseng monopoly until the 1850s through strong restrictions that allowed only people holding official permits to enter ginseng-producing mountain areas in Shengjing and Jilin. When he proposed the erection of a guard post on the Yalu River, the Shengjing military governor sought only to be loyal to his emperor by preventing illegal poachers from accessing the ginseng crop and arrogating the profits of the imperial court.

It was their special interest in ginseng that had led the Manchus to be involved with Chosŏn Korea from the very beginning of their history, because this precious root was primarily available in the region near Chosŏn territory. Throughout the years from the initial rise of the Jurchens in Liaodong to their conquest of China proper, the issue of Korean trespassers poaching for ginseng and hunting animals north of the Yalu and Tumen (K. *Tuman*) Rivers was a constant source of trouble between the Aisin Gurun/Qing and the Chosŏn. Illegal Korean incursions into Qing territory brought the Chosŏn court nothing but trouble, in the form either of Manchu armies' attacks or of fines levied by the exasperated emperor on the Chosŏn king. In order to avoid conflicts with the great country, the Chosŏn punished illegal crossing severely and forbade its people to approach the Yalu and Tumen Rivers. The Chosŏn kings wanted to have the areas around the two rivers empty and off-limits, and so did the Qing emperors. The Manchus built the Willow Palisade, gates, and outposts to curb Han Chinese traffic into the northeastern region; the Qing emperors further told the Chosŏn court to reinforce its guards on the Yalu and Tumen Rivers and to prohibit Korean subjects from approaching the ginseng-producing mountains in Qing territory. Accordingly, the Yalu and Tumen Rivers as well as Changbaishan, as part of the sacred Manchu birthplace, were restricted and closed off from civilian access. The Qing, then, was motivated by the goal of securing its profits from ginseng, while the Chosŏn sought to avoid conflicts over the root with its strong neighbor; but the two countries settled on the same solution of clearing the sensitive areas near the two rivers. They pursued different aims through this policy, but for both it was ginseng that led them to reach the solution.

There is no doubt that considerable powers were required in order to keep people out of the vast territory near the Yalu and Tumen Rivers, where lucrative ginseng and fertile land were widely available. It was not equal relations between the Qing and the Chosŏn that enabled them to achieve this feat; rather, it was the asymmetrical tributary relationship that led the two countries to pursue the same solution and to endure the problems caused by the restriction of access to the area. The Chosŏn found that an empty buffer zone between the two states was more effective in preventing trespassing and subsequent troubles with the Qing. In order to persuade the Qing emperors to keep the land near the Yalu River uninhabited, the Chosŏn, interestingly, emphasized their asymmetrical relationship. The Koreans insisted that the benevolent rulers of the great country should embrace the inferior subjects of the small country, and therefore the Qing emperor should do the Chosŏn king a favor. The Qing was convinced by this argument. Since the

Chosŏn suggestion of banning settlement near the Yalu River corresponded to Qing restrictions on entry to Manchuria, and since Korean loyalty to the suzerain court was proved by its regular dispatch of tributary envoys, the Qing emperor was willing to accept the Chosŏn request. In this way, the Qing special interests in ginseng and Manchuria, as well as the tributary relations between the Qing and Chosŏn courts, contributed to the creation of an empty stretch of land between the two countries.

By examining the contacts and conflicts over ginseng in the region of the Yalu and Tumen Rivers and Changbaishan, this book explores the territorial boundary between the Qing and the Chosŏn and the asymmetrical tributary relationship between the two states. It discusses the process by which the two countries recognized and managed their separate realms through an analysis of the Qing policy regarding Manchuria, the Qing-Chosŏn tributary relationship, and the two states' ideas about territory and sovereignty. The Yalu and Tumen Rivers and Changbaishan were a place where the special Qing interests in Manchuria were well revealed, and it was also a location at which the Qing and the Chosŏn clashed and negotiated their respective claims to land and authority. Through the lens of the Qing-Chosŏn boundary, this study examines the ways in which Qing imperial authority sought to safeguard the special status of Manchuria within the empire while protecting its economic interests in the region's natural resources and maintaining the old relationship with its neighbor. Finally, by exploring the efforts of the Chosŏn to preserve its territory and sovereignty within the asymmetrical relationship with its more powerful neighbor, the study seeks to highlight the Chosŏn agency in the formation and development of the Qing empire.

MANCHURIA, KOREA, AND GINSENG

Recent studies of Qing history—most notably those studies that fall under the umbrella term of "New Qing History"—have cast light on the centering of the Manchus in the Qing period by exploring a variety of themes, including ethnicity, cultural diversity, empire, and ruling ideology.[3] Among various elements and topics related to Manchu distinctiveness, the Qing northeast has a special importance. As earlier studies have pointed out, Manchuria was the homeland of the Manchus and thus held very different meanings for the Ming and the Qing, respectively. While the Liaodong region during the Ming period was a place where different groups of people interacted and prepared the ground for the rise of the Jurchens-cum-Manchus, the Qing northeast was carefully preserved in order to maintain the Manchus' difference and separation from other ethnic groups. During the Ming period, as well as in the early twentieth century, Manchuria was a site of "the interacting migrations of peoples and cultures" and, therefore, a "reservoir" where people gathered.[4] The Liaodong region under Ming rule was a typical zone of "between-ness" and "transfrontier-ness," where ethnic distinctions between the Han Chinese and the Jurchens were not clear-cut.[5] Contrary to this trend, Qing Manchurian policy sought to keep contact among people to a minimum and to protect local ethnic groups from Han Chinese cultural and economic influence— strategies aimed at maintaining this vital region as a reserve for Manchu identity and power.

Many studies written in Chinese have examined the Qing northeast, not necessarily sharing the scholarly interests of the New Qing History in the area of Manchu distinctiveness.[6] Their discussions of Qing policy in the northeast have mainly focused on the Willow Palisade (*liutiaobian*) and the restriction policy (*fengjin*), the specific institutions that the Qing court reinforced in Manchuria until the late nineteenth century. The Willow Palisade was built to divide Manchuria into three regions with distinct physical and cultural characteristics: a region of Han Chinese settlement in Fengtian, a Manchu preserve to the northeast, and land belonging to various allied Mongol princes. This physical barrier was designed to control people's movements in the region and especially to limit Han Chinese immigration to Manchuria.[7]

The Qing court sought to preserve its native homeland from its Han Chinese subjects as a strategy to maintain its ethnic identity and military prowess in this restricted region. Furthermore, natural resources in Manchuria were strictly controlled as a state monopoly. Throughout the Qing years, the state endeavored to restrict access to areas of Manchuria that contained economically profitable and politically critical natural resources. The eastern part of the Willow Palisade, in particular, was designed to exclude civilian exploiters from Shengjing and China proper from access to ginseng, furs, and pearls. This restriction policy was "economically motivated to aid a politically privileged group," namely, the Manchus.[8] The nature of the Manchu relationship to Manchuria changed over time, as Qing power expanded from the northeastern margin to China proper. However, the special interest of the Manchus in their sacred birthplace never diminished. As the Qing state consolidated its rule in the economically rich regions of China proper, the significance of Manchuria tended to shift from material concerns to the cultural preservation of the old Manchu traditions.[9] After the 1644 conquest and during the Kangxi era, the Qing developed a deliberate state policy to preserve, encourage, and prescribe hunting and gathering culture. The purpose of the Qing policy in Manchuria was not merely immediate material sustenance but rather "imperial foraging," as David Bello puts it, which was intended to embody and maintain Manchu identity in Qing Manchuria. Given that the practice of archery and the activities necessary for foraging required isolated spaces, the closing of Manchuria was an appropriate strategy for Qing imperial foraging.[10] In fact, the Qing efforts to define "the nature of the empire's frontiers" continued until the late nineteenth century. As Jonathan Schlesinger explains, the three

Manchurian treasures—pearls, sable, and ginseng—were the primary items gifted by early Manchu rulers to their neighbors and followers, representing "a form of intimacy characteristic of Manchu rule." The Qing court monopolized the three precious Manchu treasures after the 1644 conquest, because it needed them not only as commercial items but as symbolic objects of Manchu ethnicity. "The nature of this demand insisted upon authenticity, so that ginseng, pearls, and furs had to be produced the right way and gathered by the right people."[11] As such, the policy of conservation of Manchurian resources reflected the unique position of the northeastern region under Qing imperial rule.

These explorations of the special position of the northeastern region and its natural resources in the Qing empire can be richly complemented by proper attention to Korean history and its connection to Manchuria. In her recent study, Evelyn Rawski correctly stresses the significance of Manchuria and the Korean peninsula for the purpose of "de-centering China from the perspective of the periphery rather than from the core." She discusses Chosŏn Korea as well as Edo Japan in the context of "the geopolitical boundary of China's northeast Asian frontier," an approach that challenges the conventional narratives of national history and further highlights the Chosŏn agency in the development of the Qing empire.[12] Her analysis of the contemporary debates between Chinese and Korean scholars over Koguryŏ (C. *Gaogouli*) shows that the close connection of Manchuria to the Korean peninsula has been the defining factor in Chinese-Korean relations. Scholars of Chinese-Korean history have long emphasized that the triangular relationship among China, Manchuria, and Korea had special importance in East Asian international relations. As long as Manchuria was contested, Gari Ledyard states, stable Sino-Korean relations were impossible, and even internal Korean stability could not be maintained. This lesson was well proven in the early seventeenth century, when the rise of the Manchus radically changed the relationship among China, Manchuria, and Korea.[13] In fact, the history of the Jurchen chieftain Möngke Temür (K. *Tong Maengga Chŏmmoga*; C. *Mengtemu*) in the early fifteenth century also provides a good example of the crucial role of Korea's connection to Manchuria in the development of Chinese-Korean relations. This figure, who was revered as the forefather of the Manchu imperial family by the eighteenth-century Qing court, was in fact the leader of just one tribal group among many that competed with one another between the Ming and Chosŏn states. The saga of Möngke Temür is, above all, evidence of the close relationship between the Manchus and the Koreans.[14] As Kenneth Robinson describes, various forms of contact between the Jurchens and the Koreans in the fifteenth to sixteenth centuries showed that the Chosŏn northern region was "an economic frontier, linguistic frontier, status frontier, environmental frontier, trans-boundary frontier."[15]

Of the three Manchurian treasures, ginseng holds the greatest significance for an examination of the special connections between the Manchus and Manchuria, as well as the political relations between Qing China and Chosŏn Korea. The early Manchu state initially depended for its very existence on the natural resources produced in Manchuria, of which the most important was ginseng. Many scholars have shown that Nurhaci was active in the ginseng trade with the Ming, which strengthened economic ties between the Liaodong region and China proper. Military power was not the only basis on which Nurhaci was able to rise and build the Manchu state: he acquired his economic strength from the ginseng trade.[16] Most studies have emphasized that in contrast to previous dynasties, which had no system of rule for ginseng production, the Manchus developed detailed regulations for ginseng prior to the 1644 conquest. The specific content and scope of these regulations changed over time, but the primary concern was to secure sufficient amounts of ginseng for imperial expenses and state revenue. A select group of people working for the imperial court and other imperial families were allowed to collect a given amount of ginseng; people without official permits were prohibited from accessing the ginseng-producing mountains; and traffic through Shanhaiguan, Tianjin, Lüshun, and other ports on the Yalu River was regulated to limit illegal transportation of and trade in ginseng. The Qing court maintained strict controls on all aspects of ginseng collection, transport, and marketing well into the nineteenth century, since the ginseng monopoly was an important way of preserving the traditions of the early Manchu state.[17] Accordingly, some studies estimate that during the eighteenth century ginseng profits still accounted for a substantial portion of Qing government revenue.[18] For the Manchu rulers, as Van Jay Symons points out, "it was crucial to have independent sources of income to assure the financial stability of the ruling house."[19]

Ginseng was only one of the three treasures of Manchuria, and only one of many goods that have at different times been imported and exported from Manchuria. However, it appears more frequently than nearly any other good in the sources related to Qing-Chosŏn relations, whether as a vital diplomatic good provided by the Chosŏn court, as an important monopoly of the Qing court, or as an attractive target for smugglers. Extremely slow to mature, much valued as a medicinal root, but also small and light and easy to transport, it was chronically subject to overharvesting. The high value of ginseng inevitably brought both smugglers and legitimate ginseng diggers ever deeper into remote territories that would otherwise have been of limited concern to the Qing and Chosŏn courts. Eventually, it shaped, more than any other product, Qing-Chosŏn relations as well as Qing policy for the northeastern region.

Japanese scholarship has paid close attention to the connection between Qing Manchuria and Chosŏn Korea.[20] Inaba Iwakichi and Imamura Tomo, in particular, have highlighted the significance of ginseng in Chinese-Korean relations.[21] While explaining that Korean ginseng was primarily paid to the Chinese emperors as tribute and therefore symbolized the hierarchy between China and

Korea, Imamura also emphasizes that ginseng was the primary reason for illegal crossings and poaching between China and Korea.[22] The rich natural resources, combined with the close connections and interactions between the Koreans and the Jurchens, invited ginseng exploiters from both sides to the Yalu and Tumen Rivers. The area south of the Yalu River, where the Chosŏn court decided to abolish Korean settlement and cultivation by the mid-fifteenth century, had produced a good amount of ginseng and therefore attracted Jurchen poachers. After the Manchus moved to China proper, the Changbaishan region was preserved as the Manchu birthplace, but its abundant production of ginseng encouraged Korean exploiters to risk their lives to intrude into it. As long as Korean exploiters continued to harvest ginseng in Qing territories, Qing ginseng policy could not be only a matter of domestic politics and economy, narrowly applied to Manchuria; it had to be discussed as part of foreign relations with the Chosŏn. For this reason, ginseng has played an important role in Qing-Chosŏn relations.

TRIBUTARY RELATIONS AND BOUNDARIES

It is actually the theory of tributary relations, not the idea of Manchu distinctiveness or Korean connections to Manchuria, that has long dominated the historiography of Chinese-Korean relations. The conventional understanding of the tributary relationship between the two, based on John K. Fairbank's interpretation, has emphasized the Sinocentric worldview, or "the Chinese world order," in Qing foreign relations.[23] The Fairbank model became overwhelmingly influential in studies of China and Asia, not only in US academia but in China and Korea as well. Many scholars of Qing history, however, have challenged this essentialized interpretation of China's foreign relations and stressed that the definition of China has been ever-changing, dependent on China's current relations with its neighbors.[24] Recent studies of the Qing relationship with nomads on its own northwestern margin highlight the variety of ways in which the Qing dealt with its neighbors, including political marriages, religious patronage, commerce, diplomacy, and war.[25] Nicola Di Cosmo states that the tribute trade in the northwest "was not a system, but rather a political, ritual, and economic environment that enabled the Qing to interact with native peoples."[26] As Peter Perdue puts it, tributary relations in the Qing period were therefore "a kind of intercultural language, serving multiple purposes for its participants."[27] Diversity in Qing foreign relations is also found in the court's contacts with various countries in Southeast Asia. Anthony Reid emphasizes that "each of China's relationships with neighboring countries was unique and these relations changed radically over time; none can be said to have been understood in the same light on both sides."[28]

Among the many neighbors of China, the Chosŏn, in particular, has long maintained a reputation as the preeminent and ideal tributary. Proponents of the Sinocentric thesis have stressed that political powers in China and Korea have always maintained markedly hierarchical relations with one another and that the Chosŏn court dutifully preserved the practice of paying tribute to the Qing emperors during the period from 1637 to 1895.[29] However, recent studies of Korean history have begun to explore a new way of looking at Qing-Chosŏn relations from the perspective of Manchu distinctiveness. In contrast to the Sinocentric understanding, which tends to erase stories of the violent beginnings of Qing-Chosŏn history, this new research highlights the history of conflict and tensions under the disguise of tributary rituals. Anti-Manchu sentiment was prevalent at the Chosŏn court and was expressed in various ways, including the movement for a "northern expedition" (K. *pukpŏl*) to avenge the Manchu invasions and the establishment of a shrine for the Ming emperor in memory of his support for the Chosŏn against the Japanese invasions. As a way of overcoming the shame of their submission to the Qing and of dealing with a crisis of legitimacy, the Chosŏn literati began to claim that they were the last true heirs to the Ming and Chinese culture and, indeed, to civilization itself, which they believed the Manchus took away from China.[30] As Kye Seung explains, "Even though the Manchus ruled China, the Chosŏn elites lived in an imaginary Ming order, [by means of which] they [prolonged] Ming times under the reality of Manchu dominance."[31] The Chosŏn elites privately despised the Manchus as barbarians, even though the Chosŏn court continued to participate in the same tribute practices with the Qing that it had engaged in with the Ming. The practice of paying tribute and receiving rewards—although maintained for centuries between China and Korea—had notably different implications at different times.

Appreciation of Manchu distinctiveness in Qing history can also be traced back to a new understanding of the status of the Chosŏn in the Qing world order. By challenging the conventional placement of the Chosŏn among the societies of the southeastern crescent,[32] Ku Pŏmjin stresses instead that Qing policies concerning Chosŏn affairs showed some similarities with those concerning Mongolia, Xinjiang, and Tibet in the northwest. While the Ryukyu and Vietnam, two other southeastern crescent societies, built a peaceful relationship with the Qing after the 1644 conquest, the Chosŏn joined the Qing imperial order as a result of violent wars. The Qing emissaries visiting the Chosŏn were, in fact, selected from among bannermen, not Han civil officials, and the same practice was followed for imperial envoys dispatched to the northwestern region of the empire. In addition, the copperplate "Map with a Complete View of the Imperial Territories" (*Huangyu quanlan tu*), made in 1719, displayed the place names of China proper in Chinese characters but those of Manchuria and Korea in Manchu script.[33] All these features demonstrate that Qing-Chosŏn relations under Manchu rule differed from those of the preceding era.

Among the various issues that affected the two countries, their geographical adjacency—and the consequent debates over the movement of people—was
a defining characteristic of Qing-Chosŏn relations. In fact, the name of the river
between the respective realms of the Manchus and the Koreans, *Yalu*, means "the
boundary between two fields" in the Manchu language.[34] After the first Manchu
invasion of Korea in 1627, Hong Taiji articulated a territorial division in their peace
agreement with the Koreans, saying, "We two nations have now established peace.
From today onward, let us each respect this agreement, each should observe the
territories [*geshou fengjiang*], and refrain from disputing small matters and excessive requirements."[35] The Aisin Gurun/Qing and the Chosŏn were separated by
the Yalu and Tumen Rivers, an agreement that the two states mutually recognized.
Despite Hong Taiji's statement, however, the Qing-Chosŏn boundary would be
subject to debate from the beginning to the end of their relations. Scholarly discussions of the Qing-Chosŏn boundary have largely focused on two related events:
the 1712 investigation of Changbaishan, and the surveys of the Tumen riverhead
in the 1880s. The Kangxi emperor sent his Manchu official, Mu-ke-deng, to investigate the Changbaishan region together with Chosŏn officials, and they set up a
stone stele at a place that they estimated to be the origin of the Yalu and Tumen
Rivers. By the late nineteenth century, however, Korean immigrants north of the
Tumen River argued that they actually lived in Chosŏn territory because there
were two different Tumen Rivers. This debate over the Tumen riverhead—and
thus the exact location of the Qing-Chosŏn territorial boundary—led the Qing
and the Chosŏn to launch two surveys of the region in 1885 and 1887.

Gari Ledyard has analyzed in detail the dispatch of the Kangxi emperor's emissary Mu-ke-deng, his joint survey of the mountain ranges with Chosŏn officials,
and the discussions that took place at the Chosŏn court after the survey; however, his analysis is situated in the context of the history of Korean cartography.[36]
Andre Schmid explores the survey in the wider historical context of Korean territoriality and sovereignty, emphasizing "the territorial limits of the Qing empire together with the rather ambiguous, and contested, position of the Chosŏn
within that empire."[37] By connecting the investigation of 1712 with the boundary
debates of the 1880s, Schmid reveals an active interaction between nationalist
and prenationalist discourses on Korea's spatial understanding. Earlier investigations of Changbaishan had already developed Korean ideas about territorial
sovereignty, and the later debates over the Kando territory show that late nineteenth-century Chosŏn officials used the same vocabulary of sovereignty as had
early eighteenth-century Korean scholars.[38]

Scholars of China and Korea have examined these events in detail, but they
still contest the boundaries and claim territorial losses suffered by one or the
other side. Zhang Cunwu argues that the Kangxi emperor and his Manchu official were ignorant about history and geography: they did not know that the

Tumen River, where the Jurchens had lived, should be part of Qing territory, and they were unaware of the fact that Chosŏn territory was limited to areas south of Changbaishan, not demarcated by the rivers on the mountaintop. These mistakes on the part of the emperor and his man led to a substantial loss of Qing territories, Zhang argues, since the Chosŏn had always sought to expand north of the Tumen River and took advantage of the 1712 investigation of Changbaishan for territorial extension.[39] Li Huazi explains that the survey of 1712 confirmed the Yalu and Tumen Rivers as the Qing-Chosŏn boundary, but its failure to identify the correct location of the Tumen riverhead brought on a series of territorial debates and diplomatic conflicts in the late nineteenth century.[40] Yang Zhaoquan and Sun Yumei discuss in detail the Qing-Chosŏn boundary surveys of the 1880s, noting that after the inspections, Korean immigrants and the Chosŏn court agreed that there was only one Tumen River. Korean immigrants in Qing territories changed their hairstyles and clothing and were registered as Qing subjects. In 1909, China and Japan reached an agreement that the Tumen represented the Chinese-Korean boundary. In spite of such clear historical evidence, Yang and Sun argue, some Korean scholars and newspapers have raised false claims on the Kando territory north of the Tumen, an area that has always been "an inseparable part of China's territory since the ancient time," where "various nations [gezu renmin] in China, such as the Manchu, Han, Korean, Mongol, and Hui peoples, have developed together."[41]

Equally, some Korean scholars have insisted that the Chosŏn lost its northern territories as a result of the surveys and agreements of the nineteenth century.[42] However, Kim Hyŏngjong criticizes such Korean claims on the northern lands as a nationalist argument and instead stresses the need for a more careful analysis of the processes involved in the Chinese-Korean boundary investigations of the 1880s on the basis of relevant documents issued by the Qing and Chosŏn courts.[43] Recent Korean studies have, in fact, considered the 1712 investigation in the context of the Chosŏn court's and elites' perceptions of their territory. Kang Sŏkhwa explains that for the eighteenth-century Chosŏn, the investigation of Changbaishan did not necessarily imply clear demarcation of the boundary with the Qing; instead, the Koreans saw it as official confirmation by the Qing that the south of Changbaishan was Chosŏn territory. Only after the erection of the stone stele on the mountaintop, nearly a hundred years after Hong Taiji's statement that "each should observe the territories," did the Chosŏn court finally begin to pay delayed attention to its northern provinces.[44] By analyzing a variety of Korean maps, Pae Usŏng has also examined how the Chosŏn court and literati understood their northern provinces after the 1712 investigation and how the Koreans described the geography of the boundary in visual images. The eighteenth-century Chosŏn had increasing interest in Qing Manchuria as well as in its own northern provinces, and it sought to import new geographic knowledge from China. As Pae Usŏng points out, some

Korean maps from this period, evidently influenced by Qing geographic references, are a reflection of Korean conceptions of territories and boundaries, which were shaped by their understanding of Qing-Chosŏn relations and the place of the Chosŏn in the world.[45]

The responses of the Chosŏn court and literati to the 1712 Changbaishan investigation show that a seemingly unexceptionable statement—"The Yalu and Tumen Rivers serve as the Chinese-Korean boundary"—was not taken for granted by the courts or the people of the Qing and the Chosŏn, and that therefore their ideas about territoriality require more careful scrutiny. Since Nurhaci and Hong Taiji built the Jurchen/Manchu state, the Aisin Gurun/Qing and the Chosŏn agreed that the Yalu and Tumen Rivers separated the two states. However, the exact ways in which their spatial realms and limits of rulership were to be conceived, managed, and enforced were open to interpretation. Furthermore, their discussions about how to control the movement of people in the areas near the Yalu and Tumen Rivers and how to maintain security at the boundary varied depending on the specific locations and contexts of their concerns. The Qing-Chosŏn conversations about their shared boundary had always followed the norms and rhetoric of the tributary relationship; however, their ideas about how to protect and maintain their territories and sovereignty, masked by the words of the tributary relationship, were not the same. The ways in which the Qing and Chosŏn courts discussed and managed the Yalu and Tumen Rivers and Changbaishan in the eighteenth century differed from those in the late nineteenth century, when the two states' relations were undergoing significant change. Consequently, the nature of the Qing-Chosŏn boundary needs to be explored within the specific context of Qing-Chosŏn relations, which were distinct from Jurchen-Chosŏn relations as well as from the Chinese-Korean relations of modern times.

TERRITORIALITY AND SOVEREIGNTY

The debate over the Mangniushao guard post in 1745 provides an excellent illustration of the respective conceptions and practices of territory and sovereignty of the Qing and the Chosŏn. Conventional studies have explained restrictions on access to the boundary (C. *bianjin*; K. *pyŏngŭm*) and the creation of the empty space (C. *outuo*; K. *kut'al*) at the Yalu River as an outcome of either Qing imperial benevolence toward the inferior Chosŏn court or the two states' negligence in securing the boundary. As for the failed attempt to erect a guard post on the Yalu River, Zhang Cunwu, Li Huazi, and Zhang Jie and Zhang Danhui all contend that the emperor's well-intentioned decision became a misguided precedent that constrained Qing efforts to open up the Yalu River and invited only confusion regarding the boundary with the Chosŏn. As a consequence, they argue, the Qing lost control over its own territory, while the Chosŏn succeeded in protecting its territory against the Qing.[46] Sun Chunri explains that the empty space was a good reflection that the Qing imposed a tolerant policy in the Qing-Chosŏn boundary and respected the concerns of the Chosŏn in many aspects.[47] In contrast, Inaba Iwakichi has described the empty land as a result of undefined boundaries, claiming that "the boundaries at that time were not a clear line but something similar to a zone." Inaba further argues that Hong Taiji endorsed the uninhabited zone at the boundary as a way of protecting his territory from Korean trespassing and that the Qianlong emperor's decision to reject the Mangniushao post was not only due to "the favor of the emperor in Beijing" but also related to "the capability of the Chosŏn" to safeguard their territory.[48]

As for the guardpost at the Yalu River, Pae Usŏng addresses the particular nature of Qing and Chosŏn ideas about their boundaries and territories. The primary strategy of the Chosŏn in boundary negotiations with the Qing was to emphasize the hierarchical nature of their tributary relations and to remind the great country of its obligation to protect the small country. As Pae points out, "Today it is generally considered unacceptable for a modern nation-state to solve issues related to territorial boundaries through petitions to its neighbor."[49] The two states agreed that the imposition of an uninhabited zone at the boundary neither undermined Qing imperial authority nor violated the territorial sovereignty of either party; instead, both concluded that the restrictions on access to the boundary would prevent people from trespassing and eventually help protect their territories and relations. This idea of territory and sovereignty cannot be fully explained only by the rhetoric of the tributary relationship, such as imperial benevolence toward a small tributary state. The creation and maintenance of an empty space at the boundary should be seen as a reflection of Qing and Chosŏn conceptions and practices of territorial boundaries, which differ from those that we find among modern states.

The history of Siam provides a useful example of how different conceptions and practices of territory and sovereignty emerged, confronted, and negotiated with each other. Nineteenth-century Siam experienced a clash between its traditional ideas about boundaries and those of the British. While the modern boundary, as the British understood it, lay between neighboring countries, the boundary of sovereign authority in premodern Siam was well inside the margins. If modern boundaries must be clear-cut and leave no space between states, premodern margins of states were often "a thick line with a broad horizontal context," "ambiguous and overlapped." Therefore, "sovereignty and border were not coterminous. . . . The political sphere could be mapped only by power relations, not by territorial integrity."[50] Different conceptions of boundaries are also found in nineteenth-century Japan. Bruce Batten explains that the boundaries of modern societies refer to clearly demarcated lines, whereas premodern societies such as Tokugawa Japan had zonal frontiers with poorly defined territorial limits.[51] David Howell has also explored Japan's transition to a modern state by analyzing the transformation of the Ainu ethnicity and its boundaries. While the Tokugawa shogunate treated its peripheries, such as Hokkaido and the Ryukyu Islands, as something between a subordinate part and an independent entity, the Meiji government claimed full sovereignty over these areas and therefore "redefined Japan's political boundaries in terms of Western notions of international laws."[52] The cases of Siam and Tokugawa Japan demonstrate that a country's conceptions and practice of boundaries can be different at different times and that new ideas about territory and sovereignty reflect changes in relations with its neighbors.

In order to clarify the nature of Qing-Chosŏn territorial boundaries and political relations, it is useful to refer to the various terms for boundaries that have been applied to different times and places.[53] Bradley Parker and Lars Rodseth define a border as "a legally recognized line, fixed in a particular space, meant to mark off one political or administrative unit from another—a boundary between sovereign polities such as states and empires." "Frontier" is different from "border," because the former is "a vaguely defined boundary—a region rather than a line, and a zone of transition between two core areas."[54] Jeremy Adelman and Stephen Aron put forward the terms "borderland" and "bordered land" in an effort to revise old frontier narratives: "While frontiers are cultural meeting places where geographic and cultural borders were not clearly defined, borderlands were zones of interaction and rivalry among empires and contested boundaries between colonial domains." With the rise of modern nation-states, the fluid and inclusive space of borderland became the more bounded and territorialized space of bordered land.[55] In the context of imperial China, Peter Perdue points out that the term *bianjiang* was frequently used to mean both a broad zone (*bian*) and a defined border (*jiang*). This term shows "a consciousness both of remote zones beyond the realm of orderly rule, and the awareness of the need to construct fortified borders to defend against attacks by rival states."[56]

Throughout their long relationship, the Qing and the Chosŏn agreed that the Yalu and Tumen Rivers constituted the boundary between them. The boundary was not necessarily vaguely defined, given that the two states tried to conduct a field survey, as shown by the 1712 Changbaishan investigation, and also dispatched soldiers to patrol the riverbanks, as suggested by the debates over the Mangniushao guard post at the Yalu River. However, their efforts to investigate and control the boundary, though similar to those of modern states, did not make their territorial limits into clearly drawn lines. The exact location of the Tumen riverhead remained unclear largely because of the Chosŏn court's reluctance to clarify it; the vast expanse of land at the Yalu River was kept off-limits and empty by the agreement between the two states. The Qing-Chosŏn boundary thus had features of both a vague zone and a distinct line. Some parts of the boundary were clearly demarcated; other parts, especially the upper Tumen River, remained unclear. The nature of the Qing-Chosŏn boundary was shaped by the deliberate plans and mutual agreement of the two states for the purpose of protecting the territory and rulership of each.

In order to stress the particular characteristics of the Qing and Chosŏn conceptions and practice of boundary and sovereignty, this study differentiates the Qing-Chosŏn borderland from the Jurchen-Chosŏn frontier as well as from the modern Chinese-Korean border. "Frontier" refers to an undefined zone between distinct political or social entities, such as the Jurchen tribes and the Chosŏn or the Jurchens and the Ming, whose power relations were often asymmetrical, with one being more powerful and tending to extend its influence over the other. "Border" is a defined boundary between two neighboring powers, such as modern China and Korea, a product of the emergence of the nation-state with its attendant consciousness of sovereignty and territory. "Borderland," the term I use to denote the nature of the boundary between the Qing and the Chosŏn, includes features of the frontier and of the border.[57] "Borderland" in this book refers not to the concrete strip of land between the two countries but to the significance of this area as a zone of demarcation, a site at which the two neighbors encountered one another and clashed but nonetheless recognized their mutual boundary. Beyond the specific meanings and contexts of frontier, borderland, and border, "boundary" in this study is a general term for the territorial limits of a country, and "trespassing" means a violation of a neighboring country's territory.

· · ·

This book explores the ways in which the Qing-Chosŏn borderland was managed under the dual principles of Qing restrictions in Manchuria and the Qing-Chosŏn tributary relationship. The special status of Manchuria in the Qing empire and the attendant constraints on entry to the region, together with the active agency of the Chosŏn court within its asymmetrical relationship with the powerful Qing, created an uninhabited stretch of land at the Yalu River and unclear territorial claims on the upper Tumen River. These two defining features of the Qing-Chosŏn borderland were the source of persistent confusion and disagreement regarding the two neighbors' territorial sovereignty over the next century. First, the study explores the transition from frontier to borderland, which took place in the early seventeenth century. It then analyzes three topics in close detail to highlight the characteristics of the Qing-Chosŏn borderland: the 1712 investigation of Changbaishan, control of areas to the north of the Yalu River, and the Chosŏn embassy's trade at the Fenghuangcheng gate. Finally, it examines the process through which the Qing-Chosŏn borderland was replaced by a border, as the two states faced a new political situation in the late nineteenth century.

The first chapter, "From Frontier to Borderland," addresses the early history of Qing-Chosŏn relations. By the late fourteenth century, various groups of Jurchen tribes had settled near the Yalu and Tumen Rivers and the Changbaishan mountains. Ming authority beyond the Liaodong region was largely symbolic; the Chosŏn established its own hierarchical relationship with the Jurchens and shared with the latter the territory and its natural resources, most notably ginseng. By the end of the sixteenth century when the Jianzhou Jurchens emerged, the triangular relations among the Ming, the Chosŏn, and the Jurchens were no longer maintained, and their unclear frontiers were in need of redefinition. As a result of its two military campaigns against Korea in 1627 and 1637, the Aisin Gurun/Qing successfully imposed a hierarchical tributary relationship on the Chosŏn and agreed to make the Yalu and Tumen Rivers the boundary between the two. The Manchus were no more the uncivilized "wild people" but rather became the rulers of the imperial court; the Koreans, on the other hand, were no longer allowed to cross the rivers in search of ginseng and animals. Manchuria and its natural resources came to belong exclusively to the Manchus, a monopoly that remained intact until the mid-nineteenth century.

Manchuria in general, and the special interest in ginseng in particular, largely defined Qing policy in the northeastern region and shaped Qing ideas and plans for its boundary with the Chosŏn. The second chapter, "Making the Borderland," explains that the Kangxi emperor's interest in Changbaishan was part of his efforts to preserve Manchuria and its ginseng for the Manchus only. Commercial profits from Manchuria's natural resources and its political significance as the Qing court's sacred birthplace granted Changbaishan special status in the Qing empire. Korean trespassing for the purpose of ginseng poaching in Qing territory prompted the Kangxi emperor to launch the investigation of Changbaishan as well as of the Yalu and Tumen Rivers. The investigation left an unclear area on the upper Tumen River. This outcome enabled the Qing emperor to demonstrate his imperial authority at the margins of his empire, while the Koreans received confirmation of Chosŏn territorial sovereignty over areas to the south of the Yalu and Tumen Rivers. Chapter 3, "Managing the Borderland," shows that the ginseng monopoly continued to define Qing restrictions in the northeast as well as the boundary with the Chosŏn throughout the eighteenth century. The Yongzheng and Qianlong emperors initially agreed with their Manchu officials who sought to build a military guard post on the Yalu River in order to strengthen security in the ginseng-producing preserves. However, the Qing emperors eventually decided to clear the vast territory to the north of the Yalu River and to maintain the empty buffer zone that separated the Qing realm from that of the Chosŏn. This uninhabited and restricted land made the Qing-Chosŏn boundary a thick demarcating line. Chapter 4, "Movement of People and Money," describes the unexpected ways in which the empty space at the boundary attracted people and goods and became a meeting place between local Qing people and Chosŏn visitors. The gate into Qing territory was officially opened to the Chosŏn tributary embassy, and Korean merchants took advantage of the enforced vacuum at the boundary to increase opportunities for trade with the Qing. As a consequence, the tributary relations disruptively commercialized the Qing-Chosŏn borderland.

Until the end of their tributary relations in 1895, the Qing court stressed the inferior status of Chosŏn Korea in order to demonstrate the emperor's prominence and legitimacy as the Son of Heaven. The Chosŏn government, in turn, used this relationship to protect its territory, sovereignty, and commercial profits. The Chosŏn court relied on the rhetoric of the tributary relationship in every discussion with the Qing. When the Kangxi emperor sent his emissary to investigate the Changbaishan mountain range, the Chosŏn court complimented the emperor on his care for the small country, on the one hand, but intentionally left the source of the upper Tumen River unclear, on the other. During a series of efforts on the part of the Yongzheng and Qianlong emperors to strengthen security at the Yalu River, the Chosŏn court again employed the language of the tributary relationship and eventually succeeded in preventing Qing soldiers from approaching Chosŏn territory. The development of trade in the area near the Yalu River was the direct result of regular and frequent visits by Korean embassies to Beijing. The Chosŏn king was not intimidated into letting the Qing court rule his country. Instead, by repeatedly stressing the fundamental principle of the tributary relationship— namely, the great country's unlimited benevolence toward the small country—the Chosŏn court actually endeavored to secure the Qing empire's recognition of Chosŏn authority in Korea.

As long as the Qing court saw a complementarity between the empty space at the Chosŏn boundary and its policy of restricting entry to Manchuria, the potential of confusion over territorial limits and the concrete difficulties in boundary control were not a serious concern. That the origin of the Tumen River was left unclear, that the vast terrain between the Willow Palisade and the Yalu River remained off-limits and uninhabited, and that Korean merchants were actively engaged with Qing merchants in Fenghuangcheng were not overly threatening to Qing-Chosŏn relations. In fact, a certain level of confusion and ambiguity was acceptable if it served the asymmetrical relations between the two countries. Chapter 5, "From Borderland to Border," traces the changes that took place at the Qing-Chosŏn boundary in the nineteenth century. After centuries of exploitation, wild ginseng became scarce in Manchuria; instead, people multiplied and occupied the land. A massive influx of Han immigrants circumvented Qing restrictions and settled in the supposedly restricted areas of Manchuria, including those at the Chosŏn boundary. Later, increasing numbers of Korean immigrants crossed the Tumen River in order to inhabit Qing territory. Before, the ambiguity inherent in the empty space between the great country and the small country had been endured and perhaps even respected. But it was no longer acceptable in the late nineteenth century, when the two countries had to redefine their relations based on the modern international order. The Qing-Chosŏn borderland was eventually transformed into a clear border.

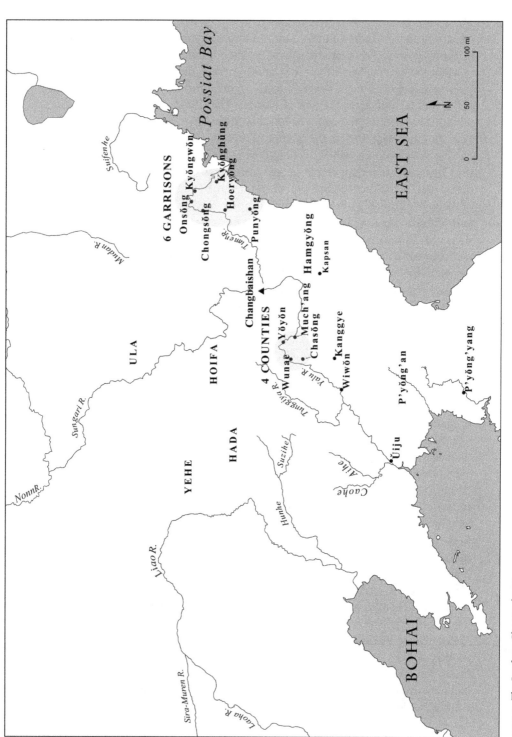

MAP 2. The Jurchen-Chosŏn frontier

From Frontier to Borderland

In the summer of 1595, Nurhaci received a three-day visit from a Ming official and a Korean interpreter who had come to Fe Ala to discuss Jurchen transgressions into Chosŏn territory that had happened three years earlier.[1] At the time of these transgressions, Nurhaci had complained to the Chosŏn court that when Korean soldiers arrested Jurchens for poaching ginseng in Chosŏn territory, they beheaded and even skinned them as punishment. In response to Nurhaci's complaint, the Chosŏn king, Sŏnjo (r. 1567–1608), had asked the Ming general, Yang Hao, who was in Korea at the time to deal with the Japanese invasion, to send the Jianzhou Jurchens a letter stating firmly that "the boundaries [K. *ponggang*] under heaven should be clearly demarcated and therefore you should not dare to covertly communicate with Koreans without the permission of the Heavenly Court [K. *chŏnjo*]."[2] Three years later, when Nurhaci received his visitors in Fe Ala, he admitted that he still sought revenge for the Korean soldiers' excessive behavior. But he also added that "since the Ming persuaded the Chosŏn to send an official to me, I hope to maintain a friendly relationship with you." He blamed the twenty-seven Jurchens who had violated Chosŏn territory for risking their own lives and promised that in the future Jurchen trespassers would be most severely punished at his own hand. Then he treated his Korean guests to a good meal.[3]

Nurhaci had to put up with his own people being treated as "barbarous wild people," but his successor, Hong Taiji, did not tolerate such humiliation in his relations with the Ming or the Chosŏn. After establishing his superior standing to the Chosŏn with the successful military campaign of 1627, the khan of the Aisin Gurun began to press the Chosŏn to stop Koreans from entering Jurchen territory to collect ginseng. In his letter to the Chosŏn king Injo (r. 1623–49) in 1633, Hong

Taiji complained that ginseng poaching by Koreans caused significant damage to the Jurchen ginseng trade:

> The price of ginseng used to be set at sixteen *liang* per *jin*. However, you are now saying, "Since we Koreans do not use ginseng, we can pay only nine *liang* per *jin*. If you Jurchens do not agree with this price, we will not trade." You are simply breaking your previous promise for the purpose of letting the price fall. You say that Koreans do not use ginseng. Then what makes your people collect useless ginseng by trespassing on and stealing from our land?[4]

By analyzing the incidents of trespassing and the competition for ginseng between the Aisin Gurun and the Chosŏn, this chapter addresses the transition of the Jurchen state to the Qing empire from three perspectives. First, the history of the Jurchens needs to be discussed in terms of their dual relations with the Ming and the Chosŏn, each of whom they had been subservient to and dependent on, both politically and economically. Ming authority had reached beyond China proper to Liaodong and the Korean peninsula, so both the Jurchens and the Koreans had paid tribute to the Ming emperor. While serving the Son of Heaven, the Chosŏn court simultaneously strove to subjugate the Jurchens under its own influence. It was, in fact, trade relations that enabled the Ming and the Chosŏn to control the Jurchens. The underdeveloped economy of Jurchen society made it very dependent on commercial exchanges with the Ming Chinese and the Chosŏn Koreans, who in turn used trade as a means of curbing the unruly Jurchens. Unexpectedly, however, the resulting close economic ties helped the Jurchens grow beyond the reach of the Ming and the Chosŏn, eventually breaking up their triangular relationship.

Second, this chapter emphasizes that ginseng came to hold different meanings as the Jurchens transformed themselves into the Manchus. Ginseng used to be just one of many commercial items that the Jurchens traded with the Ming Chinese for products from China proper. Later, as the commercial value of ginseng rose, the areas where it grew became more important for Jurchen society, politics, and diplomacy. Ginseng became the symbol of the Jurchens themselves, as well as a physical marker to indicate the limits of Jurchen territory. When Hong Taiji founded the Qing dynasty and defeated the Chosŏn, he enforced the Qing monopoly on ginseng production at the Chosŏn boundary. After having established clear suzerainty over the Chosŏn court, the Qing was able to forcefully prohibit Koreans from harvesting ginseng in the areas near the Yalu River and the Changbaishan area in a manner that had previously been impossible.

Lastly, this chapter describes the transformation of the Jurchen-Chosŏn frontier to the Qing-Chosŏn borderland. The Liaodong region under Ming rule offers a typical case study of a frontier at which the ethnic lines between people were not clearly defined. The establishment of the Aisin Gurun, however, put an end to the tolerance for such vagueness at the Liaodong frontier. Hong Taiji sought to build a country whose boundaries with its neighbors were clearly marked. Nonetheless, he did not manage to establish a clear line between Chosŏn territory and his own; instead, his successors inherited a borderland, a site of more pronounced demarcation but still with a certain ambiguity.

THE LIAODONG FRONTIER AND GINSENG

During the Ming dynasty, various Jurchen groups lived scattered throughout a vast region stretching from the Heilongjiang River in the north to the Liaodong and Korean peninsulas in the south, and from Shanhaiguan in the west to the East Sea in the east. This region, better known to contemporary readers as Manchuria,[5] is surrounded by three mountain ranges: the Great Xing'an in the west, the Lesser Xing'an in the north, and Changbai in the east. The Argun River flows from the northwest of the Great Xing'an Mountains, passing Inner Mongolia to meet the Heilongjiang and merging with the Ussuri River to flow into the Sea of Okhotsk. The Heilongjiang divides Manchuria from Russia, and the Tumen serves as its boundary with Korea.[6] This huge region is also divided into four zones by geographic features and primary economic characteristics. The first zone is the lower Liao River plain, a region with rich and fertile soil suitable for agriculture and primarily populated by Han Chinese. This plain is linked to northern China by Shanhaiguan at the eastern end of the Great Wall. The second zone is the western steppe of the Liao River (*Liaoxi*), the area near the Great Xing'an range and the western part of Jilin and Liaoning. It is a semiarid region, with twelve inches of precipitation per year. This region is the home of pastoral nomads, who originated on the Mongolian steppe but later established a close relationship with the farmers of the Liao River plain. The third and largest zone includes the heavy forests bordering Korea and Siberia, where the local people developed a mixed economy of stock raising and agriculture. Hunting fur-bearing animals was also an important business in the forest areas near the mountain ranges. Lastly, there is a maritime coastal zone in the far north, near the Heilongjiang and the Ussuri. This northern region has rich land, but its severe winters allow only hunting and fishing, not agriculture.[7]

Another name for the Jurchen homeland was Liaodong, literally meaning "east of the Liao River." The geographical boundaries of Liaodong had, in fact, changed over time, reflecting the historical development of relations between the people in China proper and those living on the frontier. During the Warring States period (403–221 BCE), when the Yan dynasty established an administrative site in Liaoyang and sought to check raids by the local people, the name Liao indicated the contemporary Liaoning Province. In 668, when the early Tang ruler subjugated the Koguryŏ, one of the three kingdoms in Korea, the northeastern frontier, in addition to the northern part of the Korean peninsula, was put under the control of the Andong commander (*Andong duhufu*). At this point, Liaodong encompassed a broad swath of the northeast frontier beyond Shanhaiguan, not just the narrow district of Liaodong. When the Liao (916–1125) and successive Jin (1114–1234) dynasties ruled this area, the name Liaodong became widely used to indicate a broad region comprising three contemporary northeastern provinces. During the Yuan period (1206–1391), the name Northeast (*Dongbei*) first came to signify not only a geographical direction—the northeast of the center—but also a region with its own characteristics and significance. Under Ming rule, the Liaodong frontier was set apart from China proper by Shanhaiguan and was therefore often called "east of the pass" (*guandong*), "outside the pass" (*guanwai*), or "east of the Liao River" (*Liaozuo*).[8] The Liaodong frontier discussed in this chapter generally refers to the southern part of Manchuria.

Of the many natural resources available in Liaodong, the most prominent was ginseng. Growing between 30 and 48 degrees north latitude, it is found in Changbaishan, Jilin, and Heilongjiang in China, in present-day Primorsky Krai in Russia, and throughout the entire Korean peninsula. It is all the more valuable when found in the wild, where it grows much more slowly than cultivated ginseng.[9] Ginseng lives indefinitely, with only its leaves dying at the end of every season. After the leaves die, a bud scar is left on the neck of the root; this marker serves as the basis for estimating the plant's age. Age is the defining factor in determining the value of ginseng: the older it is, the more expensive it will be.[10] The shape of the plant is another important characteristic. The significant resemblance of ginseng to the human figure, especially the torso and legs, gave it names such as "man-shaped root" or "man-root." *The Annotated Collections of Materia Medica* (*Bencao jing jizhu*), a Chinese medical book written in the late fifth century, emphasizes the visual similarity of ginseng and the human body as the key element of the root's medical efficacy: "Ginseng is also called the mysterious root [*shencao*] or the energy of the earth [*tujing*]. . . . The one that resembles the human figure is particularly miraculous [*youshen*]."[11] Folklore holds that the more the root resembles a human shape, the more potent its healing properties and the greater its worth.[12]

The medical efficacy of ginseng has a long reputation in East Asia.[13] It is well known that the first emperor of the Qin dynasty, who sought longevity and immortality, dispatched a group of three thousand young men and women to the mountains of a remote eastern area that produced the "divine herb." This area was later assumed to have been located either in Japan or on Cheju Island in Korea, and the herb they were searching for was ginseng. Taoism and Buddhism, both having great influence, considered the medical effects of ginseng a great mystery. An early Chinese medical book, the *Compendium of Materia Medica* (*Bencao gangmu*), introduced the medical potency of ginseng in this way:

> In order to test for the true ginseng, two persons walk together, one with a piece of ginseng root in his mouth and the other with his mouth empty. If at the end of three

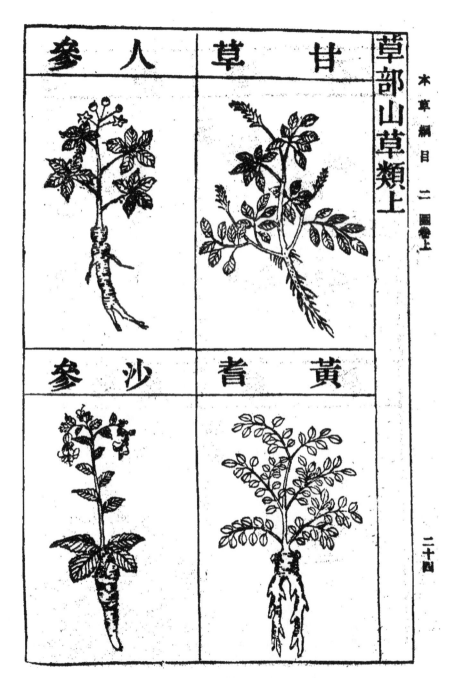

FIGURE 1. Ginseng. From Li Shizhen, *Bencao gangmu* (*Compendium of Materia Medica*), (Taipei: Shangwuyin shuguan, 1968), *juan 2, tu, juan shang*, 24.

to five *li*, the one with ginseng in his mouth does not feel himself tired, while the other is out of breath, that is genuine ginseng root.[14]

By the seventeenth century, knowledge of ginseng's medical efficacy had also spread to Europe via Jesuit missionaries. Notably, the French priest Pierre Jartoux (1680–1720), who accompanied an imperial tour to Manchuria, reported on the antifatigue properties of ginseng as "a sovereign remedy for all weakness occasioned by excessive fatigues either of body or mind."[15]

Due to its medical efficacy, mysterious age, rarity, and physical features, ginseng has always been a favorite subject of folktales and legends.[16] According to these tales, ginseng can transform itself into a human being or an animal such as a tiger or a bird. Ginseng is believed to have various means of self-protection in order to evade discovery by humans, such as the ability to multiply the number of plants that look similar to it. Folktales also connect ginseng to tigers, which are thought to protect the roots, a story that makes sense because ginseng and tigers are the two symbols of Manchuria.[17] All of these legends about ginseng's medical efficacy and extreme rarity demonstrate the high respect ginseng has commanded over the centuries.

By the Song period (960–1126), the ginseng consumed in China proper came largely from the area of Shangdang in Shanxi or from the Korean peninsula. It was not until the Liaodong people founded the Liao and Jin dynasties that Liaodong ginseng became more widely known. The Jurchens lived in the areas surrounded by deep forests—in particular Changbaishan—where ginseng mostly grew, so they gathered it to pay as taxes or to trade. Especially during the Jin dynasty, ginseng gathering was extended to the areas of Kaiyuan and Liaoyang. When the Mongols defeated the Jin in 1234 and the Jurchen trade in ginseng also declined, ginseng consumers in China proper had to depend on the Korean supply.[18] Later, in the Ming period, ginseng from Shangdang was overexploited and replaced with roots from Liaodong, which were considered to have higher medical potency. Manchurian ginseng subsequently achieved its greatest fame during the Ming and Qing periods, and all the state policies regarding ginseng production, collection, and trade were directed at this region.[19]

THE JURCHENS IN MING CHINA'S NORTHEAST

When the Ming dynasty defeated the Mongols and claimed China proper, Liaodong was largely occupied by Jurchen and Mongol populations.[20] The Ming distinguished between three groups of Jurchens—the Wild Jurchens, the Haixi Jurchens, and the Jianzhou Jurchens—but collectively called them "wild people" (*yeren*).[21] The Wild Jurchens, whose name arguably came from their inferior cultural status vis-à-vis the two other groups, included various tribes such as the

Hūrha, the Weji (or Udike), and the Warka. The Haixi Jurchens were named after the Sungari (Songhua) River, which was previously called the Haixi River. They were scattered south of the Heilongjiang, east of the Nonni River, and along the various tributaries of the Sungari River, where the Mongols' cultural influence remained strongest.[22] The last group, the Jianzhou Jurchens, occupied the area near the Mudan River, Ningguta, Sanxing (Yilan), and Changbaishan, making their living through pearl and ginseng gathering, spinning, and weaving. They mixed with Han Chinese and Koreans and were therefore more exposed to agriculture and a sedentary lifestyle.[23]

The Jurchen populations in Liaodong were placed under the loose control of the Ming regional military commission of Liaodong (*Liaodong duzhihui shisi*), which was established in Liaoyang after the Ming armies defeated the Mongols in Liaodong in 1371.[24] The Ming authorities established Jurchen guards (*wei*) and posts (*suo*) and granted Jurchen tribal rulers a variety of official titles, such as regional military commissioner (*duzhihuishi*) and battalion commander (*qianhu*), along with certificates (*luyin*) that allowed these individuals to visit Beijing to pay tribute. The Jianzhou Jurchens were one of the early Jurchen groups who were incorporated into the Ming guard and post system in 1403.[25] The local peoples living along the Heilongjiang, Sungari, and Ussuri Rivers, falling outside the jurisdiction of the Liaodong military commission, were put under the Nurgan regional military commission (*Nurgan duzhihui shisi*), which was established in 1409. After the first quarter of the fifteenth century, however, the Nurgan military commission existed in name only. By the late sixteenth century, the number of Jurchen guards and posts under the Liaodong military commission had increased to as many as 384 guards and twenty-four posts.[26]

The Liaodong Frontier Wall (*bianqiang*) served as the physical barrier separating the Liaodong military commission from the areas outside of its control. The wall stretched from Shanhaiguan to Kaiyuan and southward to the Yalu River, with a total length of two thousand *li* and the shape of the roman letter *M*. The western side of the wall was built first, with the purpose of fending off the Uriangkha (*Wuliangha*) and other Mongol tribes; the eastern length was built later to control the Jianzhou and Haixi Jurchens. Seven passes (*kou*) and ninety-two posts (*bao*) were built along the wall for the purpose of designating areas for Han Chinese, Mongols, and Jurchens and to protect China proper from the frontier tribes. Each group of Mongols and Jurchens was assigned a specific location and a time for its visit to Ming territory.[27] In fact, as Inaba Iwakichi has pointed out, it is doubtful whether the Ming authorities were truly capable of ruling the whole area in which they granted titles; it is more likely that Han Chinese had largely lived in the areas between Fushun, Qinghe, and Lianshanguan, so the Ming people considered Lianshanguan "a boundary between the civilized and the uncivilized."[28] As this remark explains, the presence of Ming guards and posts did not necessarily mean that the Ming had full authority over the Jurchens or Mongols in the area. Instead, the tribal leaders presented tributes and followed the proper rituals at the Ming court in exchange for receiving official titles, which in turn provided them with access to Ming markets and commercial privileges. Beyond the Liaodong Frontier Wall lay the outside of the Ming realm (*bianwai*), and the wall was a visible indicator of the limits of Ming power in Liaodong.[29]

The primary reason for Jurchen and Mongol recognition of Ming authority in Liaodong was the economic benefits that accompanied the tributary relationship with the Ming. Every year, a thousand Haixi Jurchens and five hundred Jianzhou Jurchens traveled to Kaiyuan to present to the Ming emperor their local products, including horses, sable skins, gyrfalcons, wax, walrus teeth, and ginseng.[30] In return, they were awarded silk and gifts, whose amounts depended on their ranks and official titles. These presents from the Ming court were usually more valuable than the tributes offered by the Jurchens, so the Jurchen rulers were able to realize huge profits from their visits to Beijing. By the late sixteenth century, the presents were given in silver, not in kind, an important change that brought even more benefits to the Jurchen visitors and thus further fueled competition among tribal rulers for an invitation from the emperor.[31]

Private trade at frontier markets was another type of economic benefit that the Jurchens enjoyed as a result of their relationship with the Ming. Since the number of Jurchen visitors to Beijing and the value of the Ming presents they received were always limited, the Jurchens wanted access to markets near their residence. The first market for the Jurchens was opened in Ming Liaodong in 1405. It was often called the "horse market" (*mashi*) or "timber market" (*mushi*), although trading items also included Chinese iron products and agricultural tools, Jurchen ginseng and furs, and Mongol horses and oxen.[32] By the end of the Ming era, there were a total of fourteen such markets, of which those in Guangning, Kaiyuan, and Fushun were the biggest. Each tribal group was assigned a specific place to trade.[33] All of these markets were built at strategically important passes along the Liaodong Frontier Wall; they were placed near fortresses, with city walls and a watchtower, and in locations where grass and water were available for animals. Special "officials of the horse market" (*mashiguan*) were appointed to three-year positions and commissioned to manage the trade. Able to speak both Chinese and local languages, these officials were usually appointed from among local tribal leaders and were given a Ming title. The Ming thereby sought to regulate the duration of the markets; for example, once a month for five days in Kaiyuan, and twice a month for five days each time in Guangning. However, by the mid-sixteenth century, such regulations were not respected at all. The Kaiyuan market, for instance, was open every three days or even every other day, and the number of visitors was not limited.[34]

It was Manchurian natural resources that the Jurchens brought to the markets for trading with Ming Chinese. Starting with the reign of Chenghua (1465–87), an increasing number of records attest to Jurchen leaders visiting the Ming court and paying tribute in furs. As the popularity of and demand for furs increased among Han Chinese, the Ming Board of Rites assigned a certain amount of fur tributes to officials in Liaodong, who checked the Jurchen visitors and allowed them to proceed to Beijing only after their fur tributes had been approved. Chinese demand for furs grew to the point that the Ming court decided to prohibit lower-class people from wearing furs. At the end of the Ming period, fur consumption continued to increase; the Ming court was estimated to use ten thousand sable pelts and sixty thousand fox pelts per year.[35] In addition to furs, Liaodong ginseng was very popular, and by the late Ming period it became the most sought-after Jurchen product at the markets. As ginseng prices continued to go up in the late sixteenth century, the Ming court directed the Liaodong commissioner to take responsibility for ginseng tributes to Beijing. This move pushed Han Chinese to go and collect ginseng in Jurchen land. Strong complaints from the Jurchens about Han Chinese ginseng exploiters led the Ming court and the Liaodong commissioner to give up their attempt to collect ginseng in Jurchen territory, but Han Chinese trespassing for ginseng remained one of the main reasons for Ming-Jurchen conflicts.[36]

China's high demand for furs and ginseng led to rapid growth in the number of Jurchen merchants and to substantial changes in the tribal societies. The development of frontier markets allowed the Ming authorities to amass a significant amount of tax revenue, a big portion of which was in turn gifted to Jurchen visitors. Kim Kujin's analysis of Ming records of tax collection in Liaodong shows that the value of commodities traded at frontier markets totaled 21,000 to 24,000 *liang* of silver.[37] Ming officials in Guangning spent 4,500 *liang* of silver from 1599 to 1601 on various presents for Jurchen visitors, such as textiles, foodstuffs, salt, and iron products; by 1605, this amount increased to 17,400 *liang* of silver. The increasing wealth of Jurchen merchants caused social differentiation among the local tribes.[38] As a result, "competition for the privilege of accessing [Ming] markets led to struggles among the Jurchens, conflicts that became worse when the Ming intervened to play one tribal ruler against another."[39] The rise of Nurhaci provides a good example of how rivalries for commercial profits led to the unification of local tribes at the Liaodong frontier.

THE JURCHENS IN CHOSŎN KOREA'S NORTH

The Jianzhou Jurchens in Liaodong benefited from their contacts with another sedentary neighbor—Chosŏn Korea (1392–1910). Chosŏn T'aejo Yi Sŏnggye (r. 1392–98) was born and raised in Kyŏnghŭng, where his ancestors had served the Yuan as local officials. As *Songs of Flying Dragons* (K. *Yongbi ŏch'ŏn'ga*) mythologizes, Yi Sŏnggye's great-grandfather and grandfather mingled with the Jurchens, both in trade and in war, and Yi Sŏnggye himself achieved his military reputation after defeating Nahacu's Mongol armies in Liaodong.⁴⁰ When he established the Chosŏn dynasty, many Jurchen tribes scattered to live around the Yalu and Tumen Rivers. Unlike the Ming division of the Jurchens into the Wild, the Haixi, and the Jianzhou, the Chosŏn called them by Jurchen names, such as Uriangkha (K. *Ollyanghap*), Odori, and Udike.⁴¹ The Uriangkha and the Odori used to live at the convergence of the Sungari and Mudan Rivers, also known as Ilan Hala or Sanxing; later, when one of the tribal leaders, Ahacu, led his people to move to the upper Suifenhe, the Ming Yongle emperor (r. 1403–24) appointed him the Jianzhou Guard commander.⁴² In 1424 Ahacu's grandson, Li Manzhou, settled at the Tunggiya River, and in Chosŏn records his group is called Uriangkha. The Odori people, for their part, moved to the east and settled south of the Tumen River. The leader of the Odori was Möngke Temür, whom the Chosŏn called Tong Maengga Chŏmmoga or Kyaon Mŏngge t'emul.⁴³ He paid visits and tribute to the Chosŏn court in 1395, and in 1399 he was introduced as the head of the Odori in Omohoi (Hoeryŏng) in Hamgyŏng Province. In 1404, he was given the honorary military position of first deputy commander (K. *sanghogun*) by the Chosŏn court.⁴⁴

By the time Möngke Temür was receiving the Chosŏn court's titles, the Ming Yongle emperor, who also sought to subjugate the Jurchens in the northeast, began to approach the Odori leader to offer him Ming printed patents (*chishu*) and material rewards. Yongle's open ambition to extend Ming power to the Tumen River surprised the Chosŏn court, which implicitly advised Möngke Temür not to follow the Ming, because peace in the Chosŏn realm's north was impossible without the cooperation of powerful Jurchen leaders. The close relationship of the Chosŏn with the Jurchens, however, led Yongle to doubt Korean loyalty to the Ming emperor. After serving the Chosŏn court for two decades, in 1405, Möngke Temür finally paid tribute to the Ming court and was appointed the Ming commander of the Jianzhou Left Guard (*Jianzhou zuowei*).⁴⁵ However, as Chosŏn soldiers subsequently attacked his Odori people in revenge, Möngke Temür moved to Fengzhou and joined Li Manzhou in the Jianzhou Main Guard. In 1423 Möngke Temür managed to return to Omohoi (Hoeryŏng), but ended up being killed during internal fighting among Jurchen tribes in 1433. After Möngke Temür's death the Jianzhou Left Guard became weak and scattered, and in 1440 his brother Fanca likewise had to move to Li Manzhou of the Jianzhou Main Guard at the Tunggiya River, a place that later became the base of Nurhaci's grandfathers. Later eighteenth-century Qing court records refer to Möngke Temür as Mengtemu and describe him as the progenitor of the Manchu imperial family.⁴⁶

The Unified Gazetteer of the Great Ming (*Da Ming yitongzhi*), published in 1461, explains that "Jurchen [territory] reached the sea in the east, Uriangkha [territory] in the west, the Chosŏn in the south, and Nurgan in the north."⁴⁷ Some studies argue that the Ming lost the territory to the south of the Tumen River when Möngke Temür and his Jiangzhou Left Guard moved to the west, a retreat that made the

Yalu and Tumen Rivers the Ming-Chosŏn boundary.[48] However, it is doubtful whether the Jurchen residence could be claimed as an exclusive part of Ming territory. The Jurchens were dispersed across the Chosŏn northern provinces, an area that should be seen as an economic, political, cultural, and linguistic frontier between the Jurchens and the Koreans.[49] Various other Jurchen tribes, including the Morin Uriangkha and the Udike, were spread over the vast area between the Tumen River and the Possiat Bay and had more contacts with the Chosŏn than with the Ming. They made their living through fishing, hunting, and partial agriculture, as well as food donations that they requested from the Chosŏn.[50] The boundaries between the Ming, the Chosŏn, and the Jurchens were not clear-cut but rather unbounded and ambiguous; sovereignty over the Jurchen territories was overlapping and multilayered.

The Ming establishment of the Jianzhou Left Guard in 1405 did not stop Chosŏn efforts to expand northward in the area of the Yalu and Tumen Rivers. After the Morin Uriangkha and the Udike also paid visits to the Ming court in 1405–6, following the example of Möngke Temür, the Chosŏn decided to avenge their betrayal and ceased the practices of gift-giving and trading with the Jurchens. In 1410, when the Odori, the Udike, and Morin Uriangkha, feeling threatened, attacked Chosŏn territory, the Chosŏn raided their bases and killed their leaders.[51] King Sejong (r. 1419–50) took even more aggressive action by building military garrisons in the north, near Jurchen territory.[52] During the years 1416 to 1443, the Chosŏn established four counties (K. *sagun*) on the upper Yalu River: Yŏyŏn, Chasŏng, Much'ang, and Wuye. Additional garrisons on the Tumen River were founded between 1434 and 1449, including Hoeryŏng, Chongsŏng, Onsŏng, Kyŏngwŏn, Kyŏnghŭng, and Punyŏng. The six garrisons (K. *yukchin*) on the Tumen River were deemed successful, as the fortresses "are strong and affluent; soldiers' horses are fast and tough. They may not be enough to raise armies, but they are good enough for defense."[53] However, the counties on the Yalu River were not as successful as those on the Tumen because they were located very close to Jurchen bases; also, the land was barren and not suited to settlement and agriculture. By 1459, the Chosŏn court finally decided to close the counties on the upper part of the Yalu River, and this region came to be known as "the Four Closed Counties" (K. *P'yesagun*).[54] The Chosŏn expansion toward the north was, in fact, constantly opposed by the Ming, which was wary of the possibility of Korean-Jurchen collaboration and the potential threat to Ming control over Liaodong.[55] Ming-Chosŏn tensions over the Jurchens in Korea's northern region remerged in the mid-fifteenth century, when the Ming found many Jurchen tribal leaders in the Changbaishan region receiving Chosŏn court titles and paying visits to Korea. The Chosŏn king Sejo (r. 1455–68) was particularly eager to invite the Jurchens into his country, an action that inevitably attracted Ming attention. In 1458, when the Chosŏn court granted official titles to two of the Jianzhou Jurchen leaders, the

Ming Tianshun emperor (r. 1457–63) accused the Chosŏn king of violating the imperial order to refrain from making contact with the Jurchens. The following year, when the Ming court discovered that the Morin Uriangkha leader, Lang-bo-er-han, had received an official Chosŏn title, the Ming emperor criticized the Chosŏn king for being disobedient:

> The [Chosŏn] court has been a tributary [*fanguo*] in the east of China, being loyal and respectful since the previous court and never making contact with foreigners without permission. Then how did this happen in the current court? . . . Even though [the Jurchens] approached [the Chosŏn] on their own, [the Chosŏn] should refuse [their overtures] and admonish them to do their duty, keep their boundaries, and not create any trouble or cause of regret for the future.[56]

Sejo was apparently angry with the Ming intervention but had to order the Jurchens not to visit Korea, because "it is not necessary to violate what the Ming has prohibited."[57] Such Ming interventions in Chosŏn-Jurchen relations demonstrate that the geographical fact of the Chosŏn north's adjacency with Ming Liaodong—a crucial location for the security of China proper—played a decisive role in the formation of Ming-Chosŏn relations. In other words, the Chosŏn was able to maintain a peaceful relationship with the Ming court only by respecting the imperial authority and by keeping its distance from the Liaodong frontier.

As in their dealings with the Ming, the Jurchens expected to gain trade opportunities through their interactions with the Chosŏn. The Chosŏn policy toward the Jurchens in the north followed the Ming model, which entitled tribal rulers to visit the capital and frontier markets in exchange for the payment of tributes. The Northern Guest House (K. *Pukp'yŏnggwan*) was built in 1438 in the Chosŏn capital to receive Jurchen visitors, evidence that Chosŏn contact with the Jurchens had become more frequent despite the constant Ming warnings.[58] The number of visitors was, however, limited: in a good harvest year, 120 people could visit on seventeen occasions; otherwise, only ninety people were to come on twelve occasions. In order to avoid trouble with Beijing, the Jurchens were not allowed to enter Chosŏn territory at times when Ming emissaries were visiting Seoul.[59] The Jurchens presented the Chosŏn court with their local products, which included horses, leopard skins, bear and deer skins, and hawks; Chosŏn return gifts were mostly cotton fabrics.[60] Just as the Ming opened markets for tribespeople in Liaodong, the Chosŏn created markets for the Jurchens in the north. Markets for the Jurchens (K. *yain muyŏkso*) were opened in Chongsŏng and Kyŏngwŏn in 1406,[61] only a year after the Ming established its first market for the Jurchens.

The Chosŏn court deemed the Jurchens living near the Tumen River Korea's "subordinate barbarians" (K. *pŏnho*), a name for those who lived in Chosŏn territories, submitted to Chosŏn authority, volunteered to report about the movements of other tribal peoples, and protected local Koreans from threats posed by other tribes.[62] This name reveals the nature of the Chosŏn policy on the Jurchens, which aimed to foster peace in the north by embracing the Jurchens under Korean rule. By the early sixteenth century, the Chosŏn court praised its own benevolent practices, claiming that "the barbarians living near [Chosŏn] towns have lived in our territories for generations; they have been fed and clothed whenever they suffered from hunger and coldness, and they have received Chosŏn titles and rich rewards, thanks to our generosity."[63] As Kenneth Robinson puts it, "The Chosŏn court sought to restore peace and security to Korea's northern regions through a combination of diplomatic, naturalization, and trade policies."[64] It is important to note here that Chosŏn views on the Jurchens were largely based on the Ming model, which required foreign rulers to recognize Chinese superiority. As Chŏng Taham explains, the Chosŏn court attempted to apply its own version of a Sinocentric ideology to its inferior neighbors, namely, the Jurchens in the north, a practice that demonstrated "the construction of a multilayered hierarchy among the Ming, the Chosŏn, and the Jurchens."[65] In this tripartite relationship, the Jurchens and Koreans were both under Ming authority, while the Koreans claimed their own superiority to the Jurchens. This multilayered hierarchy provided the Jurchens with more opportunities to interact with Ming Chinese and Chosŏn Koreans and, in time, to grow to the extent that they could challenge these two neighbors.

THE RISE OF NURHACI

Compared with other tribal groups in Liaodong, the Jianzhou Jurchens enjoyed geographical advantages in waging war against their rivals. First, they had close access to profitable natural resources such as ginseng, sable, and pearls. And second, unlike the Haixi Jurchens and the Uriangkha Mongols, the Jianzhou Jurchens lived close to the Ming and the Chosŏn, which "gave them the leverage to demand and gain more concessions."[66] The great potential for profit at the frontier markets led Jurchen leaders to compete with one another for the privilege of access, until one of them succeeded in securing a monopoly on the entire profit from trade with China. In fact, the rivalries among the Jurchen tribes in Liaodong resulted from the Ming divide-and-rule policy, which sought to divide the frontier tribesmen and prevent any one of them from becoming too powerful. The rise of Nurhaci and the subsequent unification of the Jurchen tribes were a direct result of the failure of the Ming Liaodong policy.[67]

Before Nurhaci established his dominance, it was the Ming military commander of Liaodong, Li Chengliang (1526–1615), who controlled the rivalries among the frontier tribesmen.[68] While the Jianzhou Guard lived in the east of Liaodong, the Haixi Jurchens were forced by the Mongols to move to the area known as the four Hūlun confederations, which included the Ula, the Hoifa, the Yehe, and the Hada.[69] By 1548, the Hada chieftain Wang Tai had succeeded in subjugating all

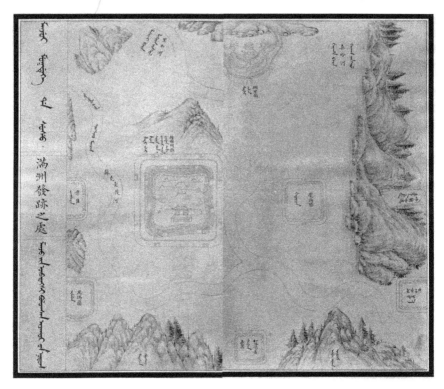

FIGURE 2. Hetu Ala and its surrounding area. From *Manzhou Shilu* (*Manchu Veritable Record*), 1779. Manuscript, 26.2 × 15.7 cm. Korea University Library. Used with permission.

four Hūlun confederations and had expanded his power over some of the Jianzhou Jurchens as well. When Wang Gao, a leader of the Jianzhou Guard, allied with the Mongols and attacked the Ming fort in Fushun in 1573, he was captured by his rival Wang Tai and executed by Li Chengliang. Wang Gao's son, Atai, succeeded his father as ruler of the Jianzhou Jurchens; among his followers were Giocangga and Taksi, descendants of Möngke Temür and the grandfather and the father, respectively, of Nurhaci. While serving Atai, Giocangga and Taksi are also believed to have made an alliance with Li Chengliang, but they were eventually killed in the battle between Atai and Li Chengliang.[70]

Just like his grandfather and father, Nurhaci is believed to have been very familiar with the Ming Liaodong commander. Giocangga and Taksi were official delegates of the Jianzhou Jurchen and also merchants who frequently visited the Ming market at Fushun. Nurhaci had visited Fushun often with his grandfather and father to trade horses and other products from Jurchen territories. After the deaths of Giocangga and Taksi, Nurhaci rebuked the Ming officials in Liaodong, calling them "the enemy who should not share the same heaven." At the same time, however, he demanded compensation from the Ming authorities, who eventually offered him thirty printed patents and thirty horses along with the title of assistant commander in chief (*dudu*).[71] Despite his constant criticism and condemnation of the Ming, Nurhaci continued to have access to Ming markets. In 1592, Nurhaci offered to send his Jurchen troops to join the Ming in their fight against the Japanese invasion of Korea.[72] The Ming did not accept his offer but praised his loyalty by granting him the title of dragon-tiger general (*longhu jiangjun*). Nurhaci continued to hold this title, which allowed him to send his people to Beijing and to access frontier markets, until he finally renounced the relationship with the Ming court in 1608.[73]

Close relations with the Ming authorities and frequent access to Ming markets gave Nurhaci wealth and power. Around the middle of the sixteenth century there were many Jurchen leaders who traded at Ming markets, but Nurhaci successfully competed with the others and established his base around Fushun and Qinghe. His desire to monopolize the huge profits available at the frontier markets led him to defeat other tribes and seize all trading rights with the Ming. The Hada were the first to be subjugated, between 1599 and 1601; the Hoifa followed in 1607, the Ula in 1613, and finally the Yehe in 1619. By defeating the Hada and the Ula, Nurhaci deprived them of their pearl and sable trade, closed the road to Kaiyuan, and instead opened a new market under his own control in Qinghe.[74] Even before he defeated the Ula tribe, Nurhaci tried to intervene in Chosŏn-Ula relations, suggesting that the Chosŏn should send Korean cotton fabrics to his Jianzhou Jurchens rather than to the Ula, who had been receiving this Chosŏn gift.[75] Nurhaci's trading activities are well described in a Ming record, the *Illustrated Writings on Kaiyuan* (*Kaiyuan tushuo*):

> The profits from ginseng, sable, and horse are all produced by the Jurchens. Some of the Jurchen merchants are coming far from the distant Sungari River and the Heilongjiang. . . . Ever since Huang-hu-tai and others constructed a fort at the mouth of the Sungari River, the profits have all fallen into the hands of Nurhaci. The cause of disputes among the Jurchens every year is that they are fighting over printed patents, that is, they are fighting over commercial profits.[76]

The primary customers for sable fur and pearls from Liaodong were a limited number of wealthy people in Beijing and Jiangnan, while ginseng was more widely circulated thanks to its light weight. There was strong demand for this expensive commodity in China proper; one *liang* of ginseng cost more than one *liang* of silver.[77] From the beginning of Nurhaci's career, the ginseng trade was very important for him. According to a folktale of his early days, Nurhaci had lost his birth mother and allegedly escaped his stepmother's abuse by fleeing to Changbaishan, where he learned about ginseng gathering and later made his living through the ginseng trade at the Ming markets.[78] Another story tells us that Nurhaci taught his men a new method of preserving ginseng. The Jurchens usually added water to ginseng in order to make it heavier to get a higher price for it at the market. However, when Chinese traders refused to buy the soaked ginseng, Nurhaci's men lost all of the profits for ten thousand *liang* of ginseng. Nurhaci is believed to have found a new way of preserving ginseng by steaming and drying it, and he thus taught his people to wait for a longer time to get a good price.[79] However, this story of ginseng preservation suggests that the practice of steaming and drying was already known to the locals and that Nurhaci may have merely introduced it to a broader audience among the Jurchens.[80]

These stories may have been created to highlight Nurhaci's enormous interest in and familiarity with the ginseng trade at the time when he became the ruler of the Jianzhou Jurchens. Nurhaci was well known for seeking exclusive profits in the trade with the Ming: "If any tribal leader was found to have traded a tiny amount of sable, pheasant, rabbit, pearls, or ginseng without Nurhaci's approval, he was executed. All the profits from trading were monopolized by Nurhaci."[81] The significance of the ginseng trade for the Jurchens is also described in Qing court records: "Our country produces pearls, ginseng, and sable, and all of them are so precious that [their value is high enough] to meet our demands. [We trade them] at the four markets of Fushun, Qinghe, Kuandian, and Aiyang, contributing to the development and affluence of our people in Manchuria."[82] With regard to the value of the ginseng trade, Nicola Di Cosmo has analyzed a sample of Ming records to estimate that the amount of ginseng Nurhaci traded in two years at the Ming markets was possibly as high as one hundred thousand *jin*, which "corresponded in value to approximately a quarter of the total foreign silver imported in China in a single year."[83] As Imamura Tomo puts it, Nurhaci's ability to amass power was based not only on his military superiority but also on commercial profits from the ginseng trade.[84]

Nurhaci's monopoly on the Ming markets caused fundamental changes in relations among local tribes as well as tensions with the Ming authorities. The frontier markets posed a severe financial burden to the Ming authorities, who had to give gifts to the tribal leaders and purchase Jurchen products at steep prices. In 1607, when Nurhaci brought several tens of thousands of *liang* of ginseng to the passes near Kuandian, Aiyang, Qinghe, and Fushun, the Ming had to push Chinese soldiers and merchants to buy the Jurchen ginseng by spending their salaries or even using up their property, out of fear that the Jurchens would otherwise make trouble.[85] Despite this huge burden, the Ming could not close the markets, because this would likely have triggered Jurchen raids on Ming cities. As Ming court officials lamented, "It is too much of a burden if we continue to bestow gifts on them, but it will possibly bring troubles if we [stop this practice and] fight with them. We have regretted this situation and endured it for such a long time."[86] The Ming managed the markets as a defensive method of pacifying the frontier people, not as an aggressive means of making profits. For Nurhaci, it was the other way around: the Ming markets were the primary source of his power in Liaodong. As Iwai Shigeki puts it, "The Ming-Qing transition could be regarded as an outcome of the growth of interregional trade and the mobilization of frontier society."[87]

Gertraude Roth Li finds the reason for Nurhaci's contentious behavior and attitudes in his political ambitions: "Aware that both the Ming and Chosŏn governments considered the Jurchens politically as well as culturally inferior, Nurhaci, an aspiring leader, rethought his goals and decided that being a Ming official in charge of the Jianzhou Guard was not good enough."[88] However, Jurchen economic concerns played an equally significant role in the formation of Nurhaci's political consciousness. As Di Cosmo points out, "From the very beginning Nurhaci's strategy aimed to control the flux of commercial products moving towards the market towns." Furthermore, "[Nurhaci's] tribute visits to the Ming court constituted important occasions to consolidate his power and retain trading privileges."[89] When the Ming court sought to tighten its grip on the Jurchens for the purpose of frontier control, Nurhaci found it impossible to continue to submit to Ming supremacy. In order to maintain both the economic profits and the political power that he had achieved, he now had to challenge the Ming in Liaodong.

JURCHEN BOUNDARY MAKING

By 1589, Nurhaci had completed the unification of the Jurchen tribes and further expanded his power westward of Liaodong. He began to seek to promote the status of the Jianzhou Jurchens in relation with their neighbors, among whom the Chosŏn were the most suitable for validating his newly elevated power. In 1595, Nurhaci attempted to make direct contact with the Chosŏn, despite the Ming court's warning not to do so. In a letter written to the Manp'o commander (K. chŏmsa), Nurhaci suggested that the Jurchens and the Koreans should not violate the boundary nor harm each other.[90] When a Korean interpreter, Ha Seguk, visited Fe Ala in the summer of that year, Nurhaci proposed an official letter exchange to the Chosŏn court.[91] Later, when the Manp'o commander, Sin Ch'ungil, visited Fe Ala, Nurhaci again expressed his desire to establish an official relationship with the Chosŏn. Sin Ch'ungil assumed that Nurhaci simply wanted to "demonstrate his close relations with the superior country [the Ming] and with us [the Chosŏn] in order to subjugate [his rival] barbarians [K. hoin]."[92] A decade later, however, Nurhaci began to indicate greater distance from the Ming by discarding his previous title as the head of the Jianzhou Jurchen guard.[93] In a letter to the Manp'o commander in 1605, he called himself "King of the Jianzhou region, Tong" (*Jianzhou dengchu difang guowang Tong*). In this letter, Nurhaci warned the Chosŏn king to adhere strictly to his boundaries:

> Since the Koryŏ [Chosŏn] is known for its richness in ginseng, people ride horses and go around the mountains looking for ginseng. . . . If you Koreans cross the river, I will arrest and kill you. If our people cross the river, you can arrest and kill them. This will make things even. If you arrest our people who cross the river and send them back to me, I will kill them. It will be my fault if I do not kill them.[94]

By 1607, Nurhaci's power reached further toward Chosŏn territory, as he had conquered the Weji tribe in the East Sea region (*Donghai woji*) north of the Tumen River. In 1609, Nurhaci's forces launched a major attack on the Ula in the battle of Munam near Chongsŏng, a move that positioned the Jianzhou Jurchens much closer to Chosŏn territory.[95] The same year, Nurhaci claimed that the Warka tribe, which lived in the northern part of Chosŏn territory, should be under his command, and he therefore asked the Ming emperor to force the Chosŏn court to send these people back to him. In the end, the Chosŏn had to send one thousand Warka households to Nurhaci.[96]

Nurhaci's efforts to expand his power led him to seek clear divisions between Jurchen territory and its neighbors. The agreement reached in 1608 between the Ming and Nurhaci was, in fact, a temporary consensus regarding the boundaries of the Jurchen tribes. After watching the Jianzhou Jurchens subjugate the Hada and the Hoifa, the Ming Liaodong officials were eager to confirm the boundaries of Nurhaci's power. The agreement, which entailed the erection of a stone marker and the sacrifice of a white horse, stipulated that the two groups should not violate each other's territories: "Whether they are Jurchens or Han Chinese, any trespassers caught should be killed without pardon. Local officials who do not kill trespassers should also be punished."[97] The inscription on the stone marker that Nurhaci and Ming Liaodong officials had built states, "You are China [*Zhongguo*], and we are a foreign country [*waiguo*]. The two big countries [*daguo*] are as close as one family."[98] This message shows that by the early seventeenth century Ming officials recognized that they now shared Liaodong with Nurhaci.

In 1616, Nurhaci finally announced the creation of the Jurchen state, the Aisin Gurun. When the Ming closed its markets as punishment for this challenge to the emperor, Nurhaci proclaimed a list of seven vexations with the Ming before launching a series of attacks on Ming fortresses in Liaodong.[99] He succeeded in capturing Tieling and Kaiyuan in 1619, Fushun in 1620, and Shenyang and Liaoyang in 1621. In the 1620s, Nurhaci announced that limits of his country "reach the sea in the east, the Liaodong boundaries with the Ming in the west, the Korchin Mongols near the Nonni River in the north, and Chosŏn boundaries in the south." Of people living within this area, "those who share the same language as the Jurchens are all subjugated [to us]."[100]

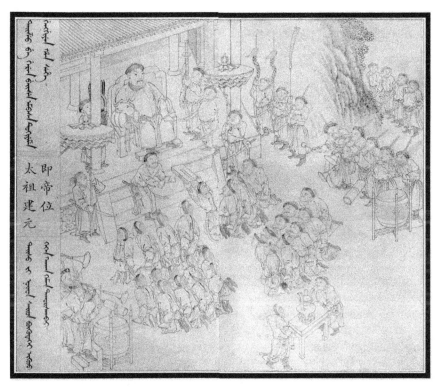

FIGURE 3. Nurhaci receiving the honorary title of *Genggiyen Han* of the Aisin Gurun in 1616. From *Manzhou Shilu* (*Manchu Veritable Record*), 1779. Manuscript, 26.2 × 15.7 cm. Korea University Library. Used with permission.

Being surrounded by the Ming, the Mongols, and the Chosŏn, the future of the Aisin Gurun relied on how well they built relationships with these neighboring powers. When Nurhaci died, this daunting task was left to his son, Hong Taiji (1592–1643). When the new khan took the throne in 1627, he immediately recognized that a serious crisis faced his country. The Manchu records describe the desperate conditions of the late 1620s: "The country had been starved . . . so that people were even pushed to eat human flesh. The country had much silver but few commodities, because there was nowhere to conduct business."[101] Hong Taiji himself had to confess in a letter to the Chosŏn king that his country was facing severe economic problems: "I have enough grain to feed my own people. But, as you may have heard, many Mongol princes, along with their people, are coming to follow me, fleeing from the misdeeds of [the Chakhar] Ligdan Han. There is not enough grain to feed all of these new subjects."[102] This economic shortage pushed Hong Taiji to contact the Ming Ningyuan commander, Yuan Chonghuan (1584–1630), and to send the latter a stream of letters proposing the exchange of gifts.¹⁰³ What he in fact needed was the resumption of the frontier markets, which he expected to follow from the gift-giving ceremony: "If Ming officials agree to make peace, we Jurchens, Han Chinese, and Mongols will collect ginseng and develop silver mines to trade with the Ming."¹⁰⁴

Trade with the Ming was surely important for Hong Taiji, but it was a lesser issue than securing the territory of the Jurchen state. In 1627, Hong Taiji sent a letter of complaint to Yuan Chonghuan enumerating seven annoyances, three of which were related to Jurchen boundaries with Ming China. He emphasized that the Ming court had repeatedly violated the agreement of 1608:

> We agreed that if Chinese violate the boundary they should be killed, just as Jurchens stealing into Ming land are to be killed. . . . However, in 1613, Chinese soldiers crossed the boundary to protect the Yehe and stationed themselves [in our Jurchen land]. . . . In 1608, we agreed that those who tolerate trespassing are to be punished in the same way as the trespassers. . . . However, when we punished Chinese trespassers, the Ming, blaming us for killing innocent people, arrested our envoy and killed ten Jurchen people in revenge. . . . Chinese soldiers burned the houses of Jurchen people and forced them to leave their land just before harvest. They also moved the stone marker standing at the boundary thirty *li* toward us, an action through which they could take that much land from us. They also plundered ginseng, furs, grain, and timber, all of which we Jurchens depend on for our lives. These are only the major grievances. How could I count all the minor problems?¹⁰⁵

When Yuan Chonghuan insisted in his reply that all of the Liaodong fortresses and Han captives held by the Aisin Gurun should first be returned to the Ming, the khan's response was firm:

> You [Yuan Chonghuan] say, "The khan should respect our Mighty Emperor to enhance his great grace and do his best to keep the peace at the boundaries." However, it is for you, not for other countries, to enhance the grace of your emperor. As for security at the boundaries, you control your territory, and we control ours. How could we control your territory?¹⁰⁶

Later in the same year Hong Taiji reiterated to Ming officials who visited him, "A peace agreement between two countries should discuss boundaries, settling where the limits of your territory are and where those of mine are. Only after the boundaries are set can peace come."¹⁰⁷ In his letters to Yuan Chonghuan, the khan emphasized that the Ming and the Jurchen state were physically divided and that each should respect and protect its own territory. As Pamela Crossley notes, Hong Taiji's emphasis on Jurchen territorial claims was related to his bid for "the credibility of the new khanate." He hoped that "the Later Jin and the Ming could divide the present Chinese territories, with the Ming presumably retreating from Liaodong and surrendering it to the jurisdiction of the Later Jin."¹⁰⁸ In fact, Hong Taiji was enraged that the Ming had repeatedly violated the boundary agreement of 1608 made between his father and Ming officials, seeing the violations as evidence that the Ming did not acknowledge the sovereignty of the Jurchen state. For the khan of the Aisin Gurun, territory and sovereignty were inseparable.

In his letter to the Chosŏn king Injo (r. 1623–49) in 1634, the khan sought endorsement of the Aisin Gurun as a power independent of the Ming and asked the Chosŏn to persuade the Ming to recognize Liaodong as Aisin Gurun territory:

> Recently I have several times tried to reconcile with the Ming, but they are now suddenly asking back the land of Liaodong [Liaoyang] and Guangning. Those people from Liaodong [Liaoyang] and Guangning whom heaven allowed us to rule and those Mongols who came to follow us are so numerous that our previous small territory cannot embrace all of them. . . . It is out of the question for so many people to live together in a house or to be fed [within our previous territory]. The old Liaodong [Liaoyang], which the Ming is now asking to have back, is not even as good as their current land. Beijing is not only safe and comfortable, but also spacious. This is not an overstatement; I would just try to follow the right path [*wangdao*]. If you, Chosŏn king, agree with me and mediate a peaceful negotiation between the two countries [the Aisin Gurun and the Ming], how wonderful it would be![109]

While negotiating the boundary with the Ming, Hong Taiji also sought to subjugate the Eastern Mongols. He finally acquired from the Chakhar the legitimate seal of the Mongol khan in 1636, when he ascended the throne of the emperor of the Great Qing (M. *Daicing gurun*), who ruled all of the Manchus, the Mongols, and the Han Chinese.[110] By 1642, Hong Taiji, as the Chongde emperor, succeeded in his military campaigns against the Chosŏn and the Eastern Mongols and subjugated all of Liaodong and the nearby Zhili Province to his rule. Once again, he proposed boundary making with the Ming. He demanded that the Ming exchange envoy visits, send gifts of ten thousand *liang* of gold and one hundred thousand *liang* of silver, and repatriate all Manchu, Han Chinese, Mongol, and Korean Qing subjects. He also proclaimed the specific location of the boundaries: "Your boundary is at Tuling between Ningyuan and Shuangshubao, and ours is at Tashan. Lianshan shall become a meeting place for trade between the two parties. If anyone from the two countries enters the area from the north of Tuling to the north of Ningyuan and Shanhaiguan, he should be executed."[111] By this time it was obvious that the Qing emperor intended to claim the mandate of heaven, but before launching into China proper, the Manchu ruler first needed to complete his boundary making with the Chosŏn.

THE CHOSŎN AND TRESPASSING

It is not surprising that people other than the Jurchens longed for the precious ginseng. The high value of ginseng attracted Koreans to the Yalu and Tumen Rivers and Changbaishan, where trespassing was not easily detected. The Ming Chinese, the Jurchens, and the Koreans often trespassed in one another's territory. As a Chosŏn official reported in 1446, "The place where the Jurchens hunt and fish is within only two to three hours' walking distance from Chosŏn territory."[112] There were occasional reports that Ming soldiers in Liaodong approached the Yalu River searching for ginseng and animals, but Chosŏn soldiers were instructed not to attack "Chinese [K. *Tangin*] ginseng collectors" or make any contact or communicate with them.[113] However, they were also aware that "those intruders, if they find that Korean soldiers do not attack Han Chinese, may pretend that they are Han."[114] The Chosŏn court's obvious discrimination against Jurchen intruders reflects the hierarchical order between the Ming, the Jurchens, and the Chosŏn in the fifteenth century. Han Chinese, Jurchen, and Koreans all violated one another's territories, but their actions were treated unequally depending on who they were. More importantly, at this time, ginseng gathering in others' territories was generally overlooked as long as the intruders did not commit crimes or cause trouble. The Chosŏn policy was therefore aimed primarily at controlling the "northern barbarians," not at enforcing a general restriction at the frontier. If the Jurchens did not cause serious problems in Korean territory, the Chosŏn preferred to ignore their trespassing for the sake of peace.

Jurchen violations of Chosŏn territory increased during the sixteenth century. Kanggye in P'yŏngan Province reportedly became a no-man's-land that attracted many Jurchens in search of ginseng. There was a report about some Jurchen ginseng poachers who fought back with swords when they encountered Korean soldiers.[115] Still, the Chosŏn court maintained the principle that Jurchen intruders should be treated carefully and not punished severely. In 1529 the court cautioned that "some Koreans on the frontier despise the Jurchen intruders and kill these ginseng poachers in the mountains. It is not an appropriate thing to do."[116] It is clear, however, that not all listened to royal commands to treat the Jurchens well, for in 1548, this demand had to be repeated: "Jurchens entering Chosŏn land for ginseng gathering should not be randomly killed unless they cause trouble. . . . If soldiers take lightly the killing of innocent people, it may cause problems at the frontier."[117]

It was not until the late sixteenth century, when Nurhaci unified all the Jurchen tribes and emerged as a contender for control of Liaodong, that he began to complain about the cruel behavior of Chosŏn soldiers. In 1592, when several Jurchens were arrested for ginseng poaching and killed in unusually brutal ways, such as by beheading and skinning, Nurhaci was upset with this abuse of Jurchens at the hands of Koreans and protested to the Chosŏn court, threatening to bring the matter to the Ming authorities. Three years later, when a Ming Liaodong official and a Chosŏn interpreter visited Fe Ala, Nurhaci promised his visitors that he would impose stricter regulations on his people in order to discourage them from entering Chosŏn territory. In return, he requested that the Chosŏn do the same: "In the future, if any Jurchen intruder into Chosŏn land is arrested and sent alive back to us, we will execute him. But when we arrest a Korean trespasser in our territory and send him back to the Chosŏn, you should do the same. Then there will be no resentment between us."[118]

As the Jurchens became more powerful, they began to raise their voice to the Chosŏn concerning trespassing. It was the ginseng that grew at their frontier that continued to strain the relations between the Aisin Gurun and the Chosŏn, especially once Hong Taiji took power. As the new khan put pressure on the Ming authorities in Liaodong, it became more difficult for Ming Chinese to steal into Jurchen territory to gather the precious root. In contrast, Koreans continued to cross the Yalu River in search of ginseng, which caused incessant trouble with the Aisin Gurun. The issue of illegal ginseng poaching was, in fact, not related solely to territorial violation. At this time, Hong Taiji was desperate to open trade with the Chosŏn, because the Jurchens were blockaded from accessing Ming markets as punishment for their offensives against Ming fortresses in Liaodong. The Jurchens needed the Korean market, where they could exchange various products, including ginseng, for products from China as well as from Korea. Therefore, Hong Taiji's efforts to stop Koreans from poaching ginseng in his territory were aimed at both the establishment of Aisin Gurun boundaries and the protection of the Jurchen ginseng trade.

Jurchen-Chosŏn relations were aggravated by the Ming general Mao Wenlong, who was stationed with his army on an island belonging to the Chosŏn. Mao's soldiers enticed Ming Chinese farmers in Liaodong to escape from the Jurchens, which posed a serious threat to Hong Taiji, who planned to build an agrarian state in Liaodong. Mao's presence in Korea also indicated the perpetual respect of the Chosŏn for the Ming court and, simultaneously, its hostility toward the Aisin Gurun.[119] Only a war could solve these problems. On February 23, 1627, in the first year of his reign, Hong Taiji ordered his cousin, Amin, and other princes (M. *beile*) to lead armies to Korea to defeat Mao Wenlong.[120] Two months later, the Chosŏn court surrendered to Amin and promised a treaty of brotherhood with the Aisin Gurun. By establishing an official relationship with the Chosŏn, Hong Taiji could expect to receive an annual tribute and gifts, as well as the opportunity to finally open regular trading markets (K. *hosi*) with the Koreans.

More importantly, the first military campaign of 1627 empowered Hong Taiji to make further complaints about Korean trespassing. In 1628 he issued a warning to the Chosŏn king: "It should be thoroughly prohibited for people from the two countries to cross the boundary at will."[121] Under such pressure from the Aisin Gurun, the Chosŏn court had to punish Koreans stealing into Jurchen territory. In 1631, two Koreans collecting ginseng on Jurchen land were executed in Seoul in the presence of Hong Taiji's envoy.[122] Korean trespassing provided the khan with a good excuse to accuse the Chosŏn on other contentious issues, such as the poor conditions at the trading markets and the maintenance of Chosŏn relations with the Ming. Markets at Zhongjiang (K. *Chunggang*) were not producing as much profit as Hong Taiji had anticipated because Korean traders, afraid of being bullied by Jurchen visitors, were not willing to come to them. The Chosŏn court also continued to acknowledge and serve the Ming as the superior court, with no apparent intention of changing their long-established relationship. In addition, Hong Taiji was not satisfied with the amount and quality of Chosŏn tribute and gifts for his court.[123] As his relations with the Chosŏn court were generally not progressing as he had expected, Hong Taiji made Korean trespassing into a bigger issue in order to impose more pressure on the Chosŏn court. Korean ginseng collecting in Jurchen territory could certainly have been treated as minor trespassing, but the khan wanted to discipline the Chosŏn and therefore turned these infractions into serious crimes.

In the 1630s, discussions between the Aisin Gurun and the Chosŏn were all about Korean trespassing for hunting and poaching, low ginseng prices, and slow trading. In 1633, Hong Taiji sent Inggūldai and Daisongga with two hundred *jin* of ginseng to trade in Korea. Bringing eighty people with them, Hong Taiji's envoys asked to open a market "in order to borrow grain from Korea."[124] In the same year, Hong Taiji blamed the Chosŏn for lowering the ginseng price from sixteen to nine *liang* per *jin*, adding complaints about the constant intrusion of Koreans into Aisin Gurun territory:

> [All of these intruders] escaped your country and entered our territory. Only some of the cases have been reported to me. Who knows how many Koreans are trespassing on our land? You have broken your promise to us and let your people come into our land to collect ginseng and hunt animals. Your country is also full of animals, but were any of our people stealing into your land to get them?[125]

To prevent further Korean intrusions, Hong Taiji decided to push the Chosŏn court to punish not only intruders but also local officials administering the area in which the trespassing had occurred. In 1635, when thirty-six Koreans in Wiwŏn were arrested for poaching ginseng on Jurchen land across the Yalu River, Hong Taiji insisted that the Korean prefect and other local officials should also be jailed. While the Chosŏn court officials were anxiously defensive, arguing that local officials had never been disciplined for trespassing before, the Chosŏn king, who wanted to avoid the Jurchen khan's reprimands, agreed to punish the local administrators for negligence of their duties.[126] Gradually, the Chosŏn lost its power to argue its case regarding trespassing. The Chosŏn king Injo could only ask for pardon when Hong Taiji blamed Koreans for constantly stealing into his country: "It is a pity that our [Chosŏn] people have sought ginseng profits and violated boundaries. From now on I will surely impose strict regulation to eradicate such crimes." While asking for Hong Taiji's forgiveness, Injo also bribed the khan's envoy to repatriate the Korean trespassers who were held.[127] In Injo's language, there was no longer any trace of dismissing Jurchens as "wild people" or as uncivilized barbarians who Koreans once believed deserved to be killed or skinned.

GINSENG FOR QING MANCHUS

As the Jurchens asserted their right to rule Liaodong, the significance of ginseng evolved. In addition to being a valuable commodity and a physical indicator of Jurchen territorial boundaries, ginseng also became a unique symbol of Jurchen identity.[128] Ginseng, along with pearls and furs and as a gift equivalent to gold, silver, and silk, was often sent as an official gift of the Aisin Gurun to foreign rulers and envoys. In 1627 Hong Taiji suggested in his letters to Yuan Chonghuan that "we [the Aisin Gurun] would send ten *tana* pearls, one thousand sable pelts, and a thousand *jin* of ginseng to the Ming; the Ming would return ten thousand *liang* of gold, one million *liang* of silver, a million bolts of silk, and ten million bolts of cotton linen."[129] Ginseng was also sent to the Chosŏn court as a gift from the khan. Even while blaming Koreans for poaching ginseng in his country, Hong Taiji presented the coveted root to the Chosŏn envoy who was visiting his court to discuss Korean trespassing.[130] These actions show that Hong Taiji considered ginseng not only a special resource growing in Jurchen territory but also a symbol of the Jurchens themselves. This view reinforced the idea that non-Jurchens should not be allowed access to it. As the Aisin Gurun continued to expand its territory, its neighbors, especially the Koreans, were further restricted from collecting ginseng and trespassing was even more severely punished. The Jurchen monopoly on ginseng, Hong Taiji believed, would be firmly ensured only when the Jurchens succeeded in establishing the superiority of their status vis-à-vis the Chosŏn and in preventing Koreans from approaching their ginseng and their territory at all.

Ascending the Qing imperial throne and renaming his people the Manchus, Hong Taiji, now the Chongde emperor, formally announced his intention to challenge Ming supremacy. He first sought to enhance his status by transforming his relationship with the Chosŏn, the neighbor with whom he had had so many disputes over trespassing, captive repatriation, annual tribute, and trade. Above all, the Chosŏn court's official recognition of his imperial authority would constitute important political capital for the Qing in waging war against the Ming. To attain such recognition, military action was inevitable.[131] On December 29, 1636, the Chongde emperor himself led armies to attack Korea, and in less than two months the Chosŏn court surrendered to him without condition.[132] Following the military success, the Qing was able to impose an onerous and humiliating peace treaty upon the Chosŏn. The Chosŏn had to end its relationship with the Ming and instead use the Qing title in its official documents and receive the calendar issued by the Qing court. Chosŏn royal princes and high officials' sons were also to be sent to Shenyang as hostages. In the event of future Qing attacks on the Ming, the

Chosŏn was required to provide soldiers and weapons for the Qing. The Chosŏn must send tribute embassies to the Qing court for the emperor's birthday, the New Year, and the winter solstice, among other occasions. These embassies were to follow the same regulations as those observed when visiting the Ming court. Runaway captives were to be sent back to their Manchu owners. The Chosŏn could no longer trade with the Uriangkha Mongols in Liaodong but were allowed to continue to trade with Japan. In addition, the Qing made a long list of specific items—gold, silver, furs, tea, dye, paper, cotton fabrics, and grain, among others—that the Chosŏn court was to present to the Manchu emperor.[133]

There was one significant omission in the Chongde emperor's list of required gifts: it did not include Korean ginseng, which had been the most important item in Chosŏn tributes to the Ming emperors. Among the various rulers in China, the Ming court was the most eager to receive Korean ginseng; the court even listed ginseng as one of the Korean tributes in the *Statutes of the Great Ming Dynasty* (*Da Ming huidian*). Given that the Jurchens occupied most of the ginseng-producing area, Korea was the most reliable provider of ginseng for the Ming court. Indeed, throughout the Ming period, the best-quality Korean ginseng was carefully selected and sent to Beijing.[134] The omission of ginseng from the Chosŏn tribute to the Qing court did not mean that Chongde had no interest in this precious root. On the contrary, not requesting Korean ginseng emphasized that the Manchus did not consider ginseng a local Korean product, a specialty of a vassal's domain (*fangwu*). As James Hevia explains, a local product paid as tribute, as regulated in the Qing imperial guest ritual, was in fact "a means for differentiating one domain from another."[135] Unlike the Ming court, which had considered ginseng a unique local product of Korea, the Manchus saw it as a product of Manchu lands and a symbol of the Manchu people. In addition, as a *fangwu* symbolizing the division of distinct domains, ginseng, the Manchu product, indicated Qing separateness from the Chosŏn. Ginseng was defined as a local product of the Manchus, and therefore, the Chosŏn presentation of ginseng in tribute was no longer accepted.

After the second military campaign of 1637, Korean transgressions and ginseng poaching evoked even harsher criticism from the Qing court. The Chosŏn prince Sohyŏn (1612–1645), who was held hostage in Shenyang, received frequent complaints from Manchu officials about Korean trespassing and the poor control of the Chosŏn over their boundaries.[136] In 1645, when local people from Kanggye in P'yŏngan Province were arrested for crossing the Yalu River into Qing territory to poach ginseng, the Qing envoy went to Pyŏngyang and took a local Korean official there into custody, putting him in a cangue.[137] It became a regular rule that Korean intruders, arrested for trespassing and poaching ginseng in Qing territory, would be beheaded on the shore of the Yalu River and, in addition, that local officials in the responsible Korean district would be dismissed or banished.[138]

In 1642, the Chongde emperor may not have anticipated that within two years his son would enter Beijing to rule China proper, but he was well aware of the territorial limits of his country:

> I have succeeded to the great enterprise of Taizu and ascended the throne with heaven's help. All the people living from the eastern sea to the northwestern sea have been subjugated, including the tribes of Dog Keeper [*Shiquan*] and Reindeer Herder [*Shilu*], and those who make their living by fishing and hunting, not through agriculture, in the region where black foxes and black sables live; the Oirats [*E-lu-te*] and others who live far away near the origin of the Onon River. The Mongols and the Chosŏn have also been incorporated [*ru bantu*].[139]

After the war of 1637, the two countries continued to deal with trespassers, most of whom now came from the Qing side into Chosŏn territory. Facing the aggressive Qing expansion, the Chosŏn king insisted that Chosŏn territory should be respected. Injo pleaded with the Qing to do something about disturbances caused by Qing soldiers and civilians within Chosŏn territory that Chosŏn authorities were finding difficult to control. Injo's conciliatory 1641 request to the Chongde emperor was markedly different in tone from Sŏnjo's condescending letter in 1592 asking Nurhaci to stay within his limits:

> Even though this small country [the Chosŏn] is deemed by the great court [the Qing] to be as close as a family, it is also true that each has its own territory. These days it is necessary to check people coming and going, whether or not they possess written or spoken permission, because otherwise arbitrary crossings and trade get out of control. If [trespassers] are not firmly curbed now, territories [K. *kangyŏk*] will not be clearly fixed and the towns within them will not be stable. If crossing [the rivers] were prohibited except for those having an official document and proof, we believe that local people will be relieved and future problems prevented.[140]

In the same way that Nurhaci had underlined the significance of territorial limits in order to protect his fragile Jurchen state from the neighboring Ming and Chosŏn, the Chosŏn king Injo stressed the boundaries that divided his kingdom from Qing lands in order to protect Chosŏn territory and authority. Just as the emerging Jurchen power had wanted to defend its land from the great Ming, the tributary Chosŏn court now sought to distinguish its territory from the suzerain Qing empire. All of these calls for respecting boundaries and sovereignty were efforts to survive the severe competition around Liaodong in the late sixteenth to early seventeenth centuries.

. . .

Ginseng carried high economic, political, and cultural value during the period of transition from the Aisin Gurun to the Qing empire. During the Jurchens' initial rise, ginseng was one of the most valuable commodities from which Nurhaci made the huge profits that enabled him to consolidate his power. In the second stage, when Nurhaci had succeeded in unifying the Jurchens and began to challenge Ming power, ginseng gradually came to be used for the purpose of indicating the territorial boundaries between the Ming and the Aisin Gurun. In the third phase, once Hong Taiji ascended the throne, ginseng came to bear a more political significance in foreign relations. Hong Taiji attacked Korea in order to achieve two goals: the economic goal of protecting ginseng profits from Korean intruders, and the political goal of enhancing the position of the Qing state as a contender for control of Liaodong. However, the tributary relationship, established as the result of the military campaign of 1637, failed to resolve permanently the perennial challenges of sharing natural resources near the Yalu and Tumen Rivers. Despite two devastating wars, Koreans soon resumed the practice of crossing the rivers to collect ginseng. Throughout the Qing period, the Manchu rulers had to renegotiate their tributary relationship with the Chosŏn, which required them to maintain the borderland with the Chosŏn, as discussed in chapter 2.

2

Making the Borderland

In the fall of 1685, acting upon the Kangxi emperor's (r. 1662–1722) orders, a garrison officer (*zhufang xieling*), Le-chu, and his men began to survey Changbaishan and to map the topography of the region near the Yalu River.[1] Their field investigation was part of an ambitious project to create *The Unified Gazetteer of the Great Qing* (*Da Qing yitongzhi*). When they approached a place named Sandaogou on the western bank of the Yalu River, they encountered a group of Koreans who had illegally crossed the river and were searching for ginseng. This illicit expedition had been organized by a local Korean official who had assembled a group of thirty-one "vagabonds and wanderers," all natives of Hamgyŏng Province. The Qing officials began to shoot arrows at the illegal intruders to drive them away. This frightened the Koreans, who fired back with their rifles, killing a Qing official and twelve horses and injuring two other people. The Korean intruders managed to escape from the area, but because the Shengjing military governor reported the incident to the Board of Rites in Beijing, the incident soon escalated into a serious diplomatic issue between Beijing and Seoul.[2]

The respective responses of the Qing and Chosŏn courts to this incident dramatically illustrate the complexities of the relationship between the two states. Shortly after the incident, the Kangxi emperor's emissary went to Seoul to investigate the case and forced the Chosŏn court to execute all of the offenders and the local officials involved. The Chosŏn king Sukchong (r. 1675–1720) was also asked to write a long and apologetic memorial to the Kangxi emperor and to pay a fine of twenty thousand *liang* of silver. As a short-term measure to prevent further trespassing for illegal ginseng gathering, the Chosŏn court forbade the Korean tribute embassy from engaging in private ginseng trading during its missions to Beijing and banned the ginseng trade with Japan via Pusan. But this was not the end of the matter. The Kangxi emperor's second response came in 1711 in the form of an investigation into the Changbaishan area, a place that traversed the Qing-Chosŏn boundary. The emperor announced:

> The Huntong [Sungari] River flows north from Changbaishan, goes northeast alongside Jilin [*Chuanchang*] and Dasheng Wula, and then meets with the Heilongjiang flowing into [the sea]. All of this is Chinese territory [*Zhongguo difang*]. The Yalu River flows southeast from Changbaishan, then to the southwest between Fenghuangcheng and Ŭiju and on to the sea. Northwest of the Yalu River is all Chinese territory, and to its southeast is Korean territory [*Chaoxian difang*]. The Tumen River flows east along the perimeter of Changbaishan, then southeast to the ocean. Southwest of the Tumen is Korean territory; northeast of it is Chinese territory. All of these [boundaries] are already known, but the area between the Yalu and the Tumen is still unclear. . . . Now I am sending the Butha Ula superintendent [*Wula zongguan*] Mu-ke-deng to survey [the area]. . . . You must take this chance to examine the area thoroughly in order to investigate the boundaries and report what you find [*wu jiang bianjie chaming laizou*].[3]

The last sentence in the emperor's order suggests that China and Korea were about to start the project of examining their mutual boundary for the first time in their long shared history.

This chapter analyzes the 1712 investigation of Changbaishan from three different perspectives. First, it points out that this survey project initiated by Kangxi was closely related to Qing empire building. After successfully defeating the rebellion of the "Three Feudatories" (*Sanfan*) in South China and the Zheng family in Taiwan, Kangxi was able to turn his attention north toward Russia, which had been a source of worry to the Qing in Manchuria. Alongside military defense, the emperor also launched a series of projects to research the geographical contours of the empire and lay out its boundaries on maps. The survey of Changbaishan was just one part of this larger plan. Second, this investigation of the northeastern region was also necessary and useful for the purpose of promoting the status of the Manchus in the empire. As the birthplace of the Manchu ancestors, Changbaishan would receive special attention and respect. In addition to political considerations, the natural resources growing in the region's mountains—most notably ginseng—needed to be protected for the imperial court. The emperor had, therefore, every reason to desire more information about this area.

Finally, the process and outcome of the imperial investigation provide excellent evidence of how the Qing and Chosŏn courts understood one another, especially with regard to territories and sovereignty, and how the asymmetrical relationship between them actually worked when they discussed important issues such as boundaries. The Qing court—representing the "great country"—supposed that it controlled the mountains at the boundary with the Chosŏn, whereas the Koreans believed that they enjoyed at least partial sovereignty over these same mountains. The area was Golmin šanggiyan alin or Changbaishan for the Manchu emperor, but it was also Paektusan for the Chosŏn royal family. Despite its symbolic signifi- cance, both the Qing and Chosŏn courts had only limited geographic knowledge about Changbaishan, largely because of the area's deep forests and tough terrain. When the Qing rulers attempted to clarify the empire's boundaries, especially the area between the Yalu and Tumen Rivers, however, the Chosŏn court fell back on the rhetoric of the age-old tributary relationship to fend them off. As this chapter shows, this rhetoric did not favor the Qing efforts; instead, it allowed the unclear limits of the two neighbors' territories on the upper reaches of the Tumen River to stand, thus creating the Qing-Chosŏn borderland.

QING EMPIRE BUILDING

Hong Taiji died in 1643, before the Qing armies crossed Shanhaiguan. It was thus his son, the Shunzhi emperor (r. 1644–61), who entered the Ming capital to an- nounce that the mandate of heaven had transferred to the Qing. But although the imperial court settled in Beijing, China was not actually quite conquered. Li Zicheng and other rebels were still alive, and important cities and towns in the north remained in the hands of former Ming commanders or local elites. In the 1640s, the ultimate success of the Qing empire could not have been predicted. However, Prince Regent Dorgon (1612–1650) and a group of commanders and banner officials survived the political intrigues during the early years of the con- quest and eventually succeeded in consolidating Manchu power by incorporating Han Chinese officials into the Qing empire.[4]

Domestic consolidation and military stability at the empire's margins were largely achieved during Kangxi's reign, a period that has been considered "not only the longest but also one of the most vibrant and complex in the history of im- perial China."[5] Holding onto Qing rule, however, required Kangxi to wage a series of wars against domestic rebels and external rivals. The first and the most serious disruption to his rule was caused by the Three Feudatories, who had been given extraordinary powers and enormous domains in southern China as rewards for serving the conquering Qing court in the 1640s and 1650s. In Yunnan, Guizhou, Guangdong, Guangxi, and Fujian, these former Ming soldiers were granted civil and military authority to police, tax, and trade largely outside of Beijing's control. By 1672, the Kangxi emperor determined that the main threat to the survival of the Qing was the independent military power of these Three Feudatories and decided to curtail their power. The most powerful of the three, Wu Sangui, responded to Beijing by revolting, but Kangxi eventually succeeded in defeating the rebels and establishing centralized rule in the south. In addition to the Three Feudatories, Zheng Chenggong, who captured Taiwan in 1661 and supported the Ming cause, posed another threat to the shaky foundations of the Qing. The presence of the Zheng family in Taiwan also hampered trade along the Fujian coast as well as in Zhejiang and Guangdong. However, the last members of the Zheng family surrendered to Qing forces in 1683, and Taiwan was finally incorporated into the Qing empire.[6]

Even before defeating these domestic rebellions in South China, the Kangxi emperor had to deal with the northeastern region, where Russian settlers clashed increasingly with Mongol and Manchu residents. He was agitated in particular by the growing number of Russian settlers who promoted agriculture along the Heilongjiang and had won the local tribes around Nerchinsk and Albazin over to their side. Qing armies were dispatched to destroy the Russian settlements at Albazin, but Russia and the Qing court eventually reached a diplomatic solution, resulting in the signing of the Treaty of Nerchinsk in 1689. This important agreement between the Qing emperor and the Russian tsar granted Russians access to Chinese markets but, more importantly, helped the Qing prevent the Zunghar Mongols from making an alliance with Russia. The Zunghar leader, Galdan, had been trained as a lama under the Fifth Dalai Lama and therefore possessed great spiritual authority among the Zunghars and other Mongol tribes. With an ambition for another Mongol empire in the steppe, Galdan began to get involved in rivalries among the Khalkas, thereby posing a serious challenge to Qing rule in Mongolia. Solidifying his position with Russia with the Treaty of Nerchinsk, Kangxi was determined to put an end to Galdan's ambitions. From 1690 to 1697, Kangxi led personal expeditions to defeat Galdan, who died hopelessly surrounded by Qing forces. By the time Kangxi died in 1722, the Qing empire had not yet reached its greatest size, but its boundaries were generally secure, and Manchu rule was firmly established in China.[7]

Qing empire building was envisioned through cartographic investigations that were rigorously promoted by the Qing rulers.[8] These mapping projects were, in fact, closely linked to the broader context of the rise of powerful and expansionist empires in Eurasia during the seventeenth and eighteenth centuries, when sovereignty was gradually becoming tied to territorial integrity. Before the seventeenth century, the rulers of European and Asian states did not have clearly delimited conceptions of the boundaries of their domains. During the seventeenth century, however, the major states of Eurasia negotiated fixed linear boundaries in order to stake out their territories against competitors. Multiple sovereignties, which allowed small states to pay tribute to more than one neighboring country, became impossible as maps gradually came to demarcate fixed boundaries between states. The Qing emperors shared with the rulers of European empires such as France and Russia a common awareness of the need to establish their territorial boundaries, and like their European counterparts, they used maps as a vehicle to this end.[9]

The Kangxi era was a crucial moment in the Qing cartographic and boundary-making project. As the Jesuits at the Kangxi court recorded in their memoirs, the emperor clearly recognized the potential threat from his neighbors, in particular the future threat posed by the Russians to the Qing empire.[10] The prospect of a formidable Russian challenge from the north and the repeated defection of nomadic tribes into Manchuria indicated to the Kangxi emperor that there was an urgent need to clarify the empire's territorial limits. It was the lack of a clear boundary in the Heilongjiang region that had led to the conflict with Russia, so resolving the ambiguity of the boundary in that area was an essential precondition of the Treaty of Nerchinsk. This agreement helped the two parties eliminate cross-boundary mobility and fix loyalties along the boundary, forcing local tribes to submit to clearly defined states occupying demarcated territories.[11]

The Kangxi emperor's desire to map the boundaries of his expanding territory was satisfied thanks to the timely arrival of cartographic techniques developed in Europe. When he began to promote his mapping project, he found that some of the Jesuits visiting his country possessed the necessary measurement technology, and he allowed them to accompany him on his northern campaigns against Galdan. Most of the foreign surveyors who participated in map making for Kangxi were from France, Europe's leader in cartography. The first commission for the Jesuit cartographic project was to survey and map the environs of Beijing in 1707. Kangxi was pleased with the results and requested a second survey of portions of the Great Wall in 1708.[12] Later, when the survey of the whole of the northern Zhili region was completed in 1710, the emperor finally commissioned the production of an atlas of the entire empire, later known as the *Jesuit Atlas* or *Map with a Complete View of the Imperial Territories* (*Huangyu quanlan tu*). The map was produced in woodblock twice, in 1717 and 1721, and in copperplate in 1719. As Peter Perdue explains, the name of the atlas indicated Kangxi's desire to encompass the entire realm in his gaze: "The compilation of the atlas was just one component of a broader project to systematize and rationalize the ruler's knowledge of space and time."[13] The Jesuits surveyed the homeland of the Manchus around Mukden, Jehol, and the Ussuri and Heilongjiang Rivers. In fact, many Qing officials, including those who had participated in surveys of the boundaries with the Chosŏn, developed technologies for cartographic investigation while working with the Jesuits.[14]

These mapping projects helped the Qing emperors both promote their power within the empire and clarify the territorial limits of the imperial domains. Maps provided better knowledge of the realm and offered concomitant military advantages for conquests as well as for subduing revolts. Since "representing territory cartographically was one way to lay claim to it," the *Huangyu quanlan tu* defined what China was territorially to the rest of the world.[15] Furthermore, the Kangxi emperor's mapping of the Manchu homeland was clearly linked to his desire to distinguish Manchu identity from Han Chinese culture. It was intended "to enhance

Manchu identity by inscribing Manchu place [and] to define the extent of Qing imperial space."[16] Later, in the mid-eighteenth century, the mapping of the northwestern region helped to systematize and clarify the Qianlong emperor's knowledge of his empire's territory. Therefore, military conquests alone did not complete the process of incorporating new territory into the Qing empire (*ru bantu*). As James Millward notes, "Mapping and research into the geography were instrumental in making this area [the northwest] part of a new, expanded conception of China."[17] In other words, it was the map that completed the process of Qing empire building, in both the northeast and the northwest.

THE QING NORTHEAST AND GINSENG

The northeastern region carried special meanings for the Qing imperial court. First, the area was the sacred birthplace of the Manchu court. Called the "land from whence the dragon arose" (*longxing zhi di*), the "cradle of the Manchus" (*faxiang zhi di*), and the "place of Manchu origins" (*genben zhi di*), this vital region was considered a reserve for the conservation of Manchu identity, which included martial prowess and nomadic resilience. These were important traits for securing Qing political power and distinguishing the Manchus from other ethnic groups in China. Even after settling in Beijing, the Qing court built an auxiliary capital (*peidu*) in Shengjing, the old capital of Nurhaci and Hong Taiji—evidence that the Qing rulers gave the northeast significant attention.[18] Second, it was a geopolitically crucial location for stabilizing the boundary with Russia, pacifying the Mongols in eastern Mongolia, and controlling the Chosŏn in the south. The northeast was also the gateway for entry into China proper and Beijing. The Kangxi emperor's efforts to negotiate the boundary with Russia clearly show this strategic significance of the northeast in the Qing empire. It was also considered the last refuge to which the Qing imperial court could retreat and from which it could defend itself against the Han Chinese.[19]

The Qing court's special concern with the northeast was well expressed in "imperial eastern tours" (*dongxun*) to the region. Inspecting the realm is an ancient feature of leadership in China, but the practice reached full fruition during the Qing period.[20] Imperial touring was emphasized, especially by Kangxi, as a useful opportunity to strengthen Qing rule over the domain. Kangxi visited the northeast three times, in 1671, 1682, and 1698.[21] Despite their official stated purpose of "visiting ancestral tombs and fulfilling filial duty," such tours to the Shengjing area had more important motivations. For the Qing emperors, the sight of a ruler on horseback was a sign of vitality and strength as well as a demonstration of powerful affinity to Inner Asian precedents—evidence of "Qing ethno-dynastic rule," as Michael Chang puts it.[22] Accompanied by Manchu and Mongol princes, nobles, and bannermen, the emperors often participated in hunting expeditions during

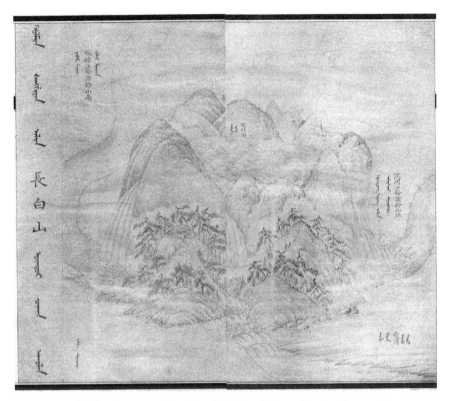

FIGURE 4. Changbaishan. From *Manzhou Shilu* (*Manchu Veritable Record*), 1779. Manuscript, 26.2 × 15.7 cm. Korea University Library. Used with permission.

these journeys. The necessity of coordinating great numbers of people into an entourage and organizing the logistics of encampment made the tours very similar to military campaigns, thereby also providing a good opportunity to check military preparations and improve the martial skills of the bannermen.[23] The eastern tours were also intended to serve the political interests of the emperor. Kangxi made his first visit to Shengjing right after he took charge of his court in person. For the young emperor, who needed to verify his imperial status to Manchu aristocrats and Han officials, the eastern tours provided a proper occasion to perform the role of the emperor, such as by making sacrifices at the tombs of Nurhaci and Hong Taiji. Conducting this ceremony in the old capital helped connect Kangxi with the ancestors of the dynasty and confirm his political status as the legitimate ruler of the Qing empire.[24]

In addition to their political and military value, the lands of the Qing northeast provided the ruling house with important sources of the imperial court's privy revenue. As explained in chapter 1, the rich natural resources of the northeast were a crucial factor in the initial development of the Jurchen state and the formation of Manchu political identity. Once Qing rule was consolidated in China proper, greater emphasis was put on Manchuria, the cultural reservoir of the old and pure Manchu traditions. The Qing policy on Manchuria after the 1644 conquest was not aimed merely at immediate material sustenance, but rather at the purpose of "imperial foraging." As David Bello explains, the Qing court sought to develop a strategy to preserve and promote Manchu cultural identity and military skills in their sacred birthplace. Both hunting and gathering were considered integral elements of a distinct Manchu identity. This Manchu tradition required the Qing court to preserve a separate space isolated from the Han Chinese population, and the northeast provided a perfect location for this project. A great number of imperial estates were built in eastern Fengtian and southwestern Jilin. These enclaved spaces and the practice of imperial foraging in Manchuria are evidence of the Qing strategy to maintain the spatial and cultural conditions for the preservation of the dynasty's pre-conquest ethnic identity endangered by Han acculturation pressures.[25]

Once Qing rule was consolidated in China proper, the court developed a more complicated system of ginseng monopoly. The Imperial Household Department (*Neiwufu*) took responsibility for providing various natural resources, including ginseng, for imperial demands. The Imperial Household Department was separate from the regular bureaucracy and solely managed the extraction of wealth for the imperial court. It was exclusively staffed by bannermen from the Three Upper Banners (*Shangsanqi*), namely the Plain Yellow, the Bordered Yellow, and the Plain White, which were directly controlled by the emperor.[26] Among a number of its subsections, the Office of the Imperial Hunt (*Duyusi*) was in charge of hunting and gathering of ginseng, pearls, honey, and furs, and provided these tributes to the imperial court. In Manchuria, the Imperial Household Department built two institutions to manage ginseng monopoly: the Shengjing branch of the Imperial Household Department (*Shengjing Neiwufu*) and the Butha Ula superintendent (*Dasheng Wula zongguan*).[27] The Shengjing branch, previously called the bondservant captains of the Three Upper Banners in Shengjing (*Shengjing Shangsanqi baoyi zuoling*), managed imperial estates and ginseng mountains scattered around in the region.[28] By 1667, the Shengjing branch took over responsibility of the ginseng monopoly and dispatched fifty people from each banner to collect ginseng on specified mountains every year, along with officers and soldiers who watched the movements of these collectors.[29] The Butha Ula superintendent was directly supervised by the Imperial Household Department, even though it was physically located within the jurisdiction of the Jilin military governor. During the mid-seventeenth century, the Butha Ula superintendent was at first a lower official of the sixth rank, but by 1698 it was promoted to the

third rank, a position being selected by the emperor and inherited for generations.[30] During the Kangxi era, when the management of imperial foraging in
Manchuria became more important for the Qing court, the roles of the Butha Ula
superintendent continued to increase. Ginseng mountains (*shenshan*) as well as
battue hunting grounds (*weichang*), scattered all around from the Sungari and
Mudan Rivers to Changbaishan, were under jurisdiction of the Butha Ula superintendent.[31] Ginseng tribute from Butha Ula was sent to the Imperial Household
Department in Beijing, where it was carefully reviewed and divided by quality
for imperial usage.[32] Ginseng management was removed from the responsibility
of the Butha Ula only in 1745, when the Qing court established a special office
for ginseng management in Shengjing, Jilin, and Ningguta in order to further
strengthen the state monopoly of ginseng.[33]

Besides the ginseng management of the Imperial Household Department,
the Eight Banners (*baqi*) had long participated in ginseng gathering. Prior to the
1644 conquest of China proper, the right to hunt and gather pearls, sable pelts,
and ginseng was reserved for the Manchu imperial families and their banners.
The court announced an equal division of the right to collect ginseng among the
eight banners and enforced a prohibition on violations of other banners' allocated
ginseng mountains. This practice of dividing ginseng collection among the banners showed that Hong Taiji continued to acknowledge the principle of the equal
privileges of the eight banner houses (*bajia junfen*).[34] After moving to Beijing, the
Shunzhi emperor continued to allocate specific ginseng-producing mountains
to each banner and allowed only those with imperial princely rank to dispatch a
given number of men to harvest a given amount of ginseng within a designated
area. Unauthorized bannermen and civilians were punished if found gathering
ginseng.[35] Cong Peiyuan explains that the ginseng gathering of the Eight Banners
differed in some ways from that of the Butha Ula superintendent. While the Eight
Banners dispatched a large number of soldiers irregularly, the Butha Ula had a
set number of butha soldiers (*dasheng zhuangding*), who were obliged to pay a
given amount of ginseng for the imperial court on a regular basis. The number of
soldiers that the Eight Banners and the Butha Ula superintendent dispatched for
ginseng gathering was constantly changing depending on their demands.[36]

Systematic ginseng management became particularly pronounced during the
Kangxi period. In 1684, the emperor reduced banner privileges for exclusive ginseng gathering by ending the allocation of specific ginseng mountains to each banner. He also limited the number of gatherers and the amount of ginseng permitted
for each of the princes and aristocrats, who had to pay taxes at Shanhaiguan for the
surplus ginseng that they collected beyond the set amount.[37] In 1709 the practice of
allocating ginseng-producing mountains to the Eight Banners finally ended. This
decision shows that by this time the Qing efforts to manage the ginseng monopoly
within the framework of the traditional banner organization were failing, because

TABLE 1   The ginseng-gathering privileges of princes and aristocrats by rank.

Rank	Number of men dispatched to gather ginseng	Amount of ginseng permitted to be gathered (*jin*)
qinwang	140	70
shizi	120	60
junwang	100	50
zhangzi	90	45
beile	80	40
beise	60	30
zhenguogong	45	22
fuguogong	35	17
huguo jiangjun	25	12
fuguo jiangjun	20	10
fengguo jiangjun	18	9
feng'en jiangjun	15	7

SOURCES: *Shengjing shenwu dang'an shiliao*, 26 (Kangxi 23/1/24; Kangxi 23/3/17); Imamura, *Ninjinshi*, 2:224.

wild ginseng was overharvested and rapidly declining, while state regulations to tackle widespread illegal poaching were ineffective.[38] The court temporarily closed overexploited ginseng-producing areas at the boundaries of Liaoning and Jilin, while seeking to develop new ginseng mountains in northern Jilin and to the east of the Ussuri River. However, the Elmin and Halmin areas in Shengjing were still open every year for ginseng gathering.[39] Importantly, even after the abolition of banner privileges for ginseng gathering, the Qing court did not ease the prohibition on Han Chinese entering and gathering ginseng in these protected locations. In 1709, the Kangxi emperor warned: "Ginseng has an important use at the court and thus should not be in shortage. Ginseng gathering is allowed for Manchu soldiers but not for Han Chinese. [Illegal Han Chinese ginseng pickers] should be arrested."[40] Kangxi considered ginseng in Manchuria to belong exclusively to the Manchus, just as his grandfather Hong Taiji had done.

CHANGBAISHAN AND PAEKTUSAN

Changbaishan, located at the boundary with the Chosŏn, was respected as the birthplace of the Manchu imperial family. The mountain was called by different names, including Golmin šanggiyan alin ("long and white") by the Manchus, Changbaishan ("long and white" or "ever-white") by the Chinese, and Paektusan ("white head") by the Koreans. These names stemmed from the fact that the mountain looks white throughout the year because of the snow on its peaks. This phenomenon inspired many folk explanations, such as "The Bodhisattva wears white clothes and lives in the mountain"; "The animals living on the mountain are all white"; and "Only white flowers grow on the mountain." It was during the Liao (907–1125) and Jin (1115–1234) dynasties that the name Changbaishan first appeared in Chinese records. The name Paektusan appears in Korean documents from the early Koryŏ dynasty (918–1392).[41]

Soon after the Manchu rulers rose to power in Liaodong, their strong interest in Changbaishan became apparent. Their respect for the mountain is evident in the following account, which appears on the first page of the *Qing Veritable Records* of the reign of Nurhaci (*Qing Taizu shilu*):

> Qing Taizu Aisin Gioro [Nurhaci's] ancestors emerged from Changbaishan. It is two hundred *li* in height and one thousand *li* around. Trees are extremely dense there. On the top of the mountain is a small lake called the Tamun, which is eighty *li* in circumference. It is both deep and wide. Three rivers, the Yalu, the Huntong [Sungari], and the Aihu [Tumen],[42] originate from it. The Yalu River begins on the south side of the mountain and flows west to the sea south of Liaodong. The Huntong River comes from the north side of the mountain and flows northward to the North Sea. The Aihu River flows eastward and enters the East Sea. The three rivers have marvelous spirits, and the pearls produced in this region are highly valuable for generations to come. . . . The mountain named Bukūri in the east of Changbaishan had the lake of Bulhūri, where three daughters from Heaven had come to take a bath. . . . The youngest daughter, Fekulen, took a red fruit delivered by a divinely magpie and then became pregnant. Later she gave a birth to a child, whose surname was Aisin Gioro and given name was Bukūri Yongšon.[43]

This passage states clearly that Changbaishan was associated with the origin of the Manchus. The legend of the sacred mountain and its role in the Manchu rise to power thus predated the Qing conquest of China proper.[44] To Qing rulers, Changbaishan was undoubtedly Manchu territory.

The Kangxi emperor paid special attention to this sacred mountain. In 1677 he sent imperial emissaries led by Umene (?–1690) to investigate Changbaishan and make sacrifices to the mountain.[45] Such sacrifices became a regular occurrence during the reigns of his descendants. Kangxi even dedicated a poem to the sacred mountain. Along with these rituals, he also elevated the status of the mountain in the geographical hierarchy of sacred mountains to the extent that China's premier mountain, Taishan, was imagined to come from Changbaishan. The Kangxi emperor argued that since Changbaishan was the birthplace of the Manchu imperial court, it should have the highest position among all the mountains in China. Kangxi's interest in this sacred place led him to seek to know more about its environs as well. Surveys of Changbaishan provided an excellent opportunity to promote the eminence of the imperial court; at the same time, geographic information gathered in the northeast could also be used for security purposes.[46]

However, mapping the empire's margins required the Qing court to recast its relationships with its neighbors. The problem in regard to Changbaishan was that the Koreans did not think that this mountain belonged to their neighbor. In their vision of a hierarchical order encompassing all Korean mountain chains, Paektusan was quite literally conceived as the summit of the system. The Koreans believed that this mountain accumulated its energy (K. *ki*) from Manchuria and dispensed it throughout the peninsula.[47] The high status of Paektusan in Korean geomantic conceptions also contributed to the mystification of the mountain in Korean history, and it has been routinely associated with the rise of the old Korean kingdoms. In his book *Lost History of the Three Kingdoms* (K. *Samguk yusa*), Koryŏ's famous Buddhist monk, Iryŏn (1206–1289), noted that all the founders of Korean kingdoms, including Ko Chosŏn, Parhae, and Koguryŏ, had been born in the Paektusan area.[48]

The northern region surrounding Paektusan had even more significance for the Chosŏn than it had for previous dynasties, as discussed in chapter 1, because the founders of the Chosŏn originated in the region of the Tumen River. *Songs of Flying Dragons* (K. *Yongbi ŏch'ŏnga*), which celebrates the founding of the Chosŏn dynasty, mentions this area as the birthplace of Yi Sŏnggye's great-grandfather. Hamgyŏng Province, where Paektusan and the Tumen River are located, was the very place in which Yi Sŏnggye built his power through a series of expeditions against the Jurchens. Thus, it was considered "the northern gate of the country" (K. *pungmun*) and "the place where the king arose" (K. *hŭngwang ŭi chi*). Like the Qing rulers who treasured their northeastern region, the Chosŏn kings believed that Hamgyŏng Province was their sacred birthplace.

Interestingly, despite the mountain's close connections with the royal family, sacrifices to Paektusan were not included in the Chosŏn court's official list of national rituals until the middle of the eighteenth century. In 1414, when the Chosŏn Board of Rites selected major mountains and rivers in the territory, Paektusan was merely one of the minor mountains to which local officials, not the king, offered sacrifices.[49] In 1437, the Board of Rites even proposed an end to the practice of making sacrifices to Paektusan, because "it is not within our country's territory" (K. *Paektusan pi pon'guk kyŏngnae*).[50] The exclusion of Paektusan from the Chosŏn territory is also described in the section on geography in the *Veritable Records of the Chosŏn Dynasty* (K. *Sejong sillok chiri chi*) during the Sejong reign (1419–50), which does not list Paektusan as a renowned mountain in Hamgil (Hamgyŏng) Province. Yet this section on geography also mentions that "mountains originating from Paektusan reach to the south up to Chŏllyŏng," suggesting that Paektusan was the summit and origin of all the mountains on the peninsula. Such ambiguity in the early Chosŏn understanding of Paektusan is also evident in a discussion between the Chosŏn king Hyŏnjong (r. 1660–74) and his court officials. When the king asked whether the mountain was located on Chosŏn land, his officials answered, "It is in the foreign land [K. *hoji*]," but added that "it is also the very summit of our mountains and rivers."[51] These records demonstrate that during the early Chosŏn period, the northern provinces—Changbaishan and the Tumen River area, in particular—were largely considered to be a place where the Jurchens lived, quite beyond the reach of Chosŏn control.[52] It was only in the middle of the eighteenth century that the assumption that all of mountains in Chosŏn territory originated from Paektusan was extended to claim that the mountain itself was actually within Chosŏn territory.

During the early Chosŏn period, in fact, neither Paektusan nor Hamgyŏng Province was fully under Chosŏn control. As chapter 1 explained, the early Chosŏn rulers all sought to bring this northern province under Chosŏn rule; nevertheless, this expansionist movement was largely an independent action by the Chosŏn, not the result of an agreement with the Ming. The two neighbors had established a stone marker near the Yalu River in 1605, but it served to demarcate only a small portion of their boundary. The exact northern limits remained rather unclear.[53] In addition, access to the region of the six garrisons near the Tumen River, surrounded as it was by mountain ranges, was very limited for both the local population and the central administration. And the region projected northward toward Jurchen territory, making Chosŏn military control nearly impossible. Given the harsh environment and limited access, only a few groups of people settled in Hamgyŏng Province, a situation that led the Chosŏn court to virtually abandon its northern region.[54] Another reason for the isolation of Hamgyŏng Province from the central politics of the Chosŏn kingdom lay in its cultural affinity with the Jurchens, who had intermingled and intermarried with their Korean neighbors. In the eyes of Seoul, Hamgyŏng Province was beyond the reach of civilization. It was not only geographically remote but culturally foreign as well.[55]

From the sixteenth century onward, the stability of the Chosŏn northern region was more closely dependent on the actions of the Jurchens and, later, the Manchus. During the Japanese invasions of 1592–98 and the subsequent struggles for restoration, the Chosŏn court could not afford to pay attention to the north. The northern region, especially P'yŏngan Province, was devastated by Hong Taiji's campaigns against the Chosŏn in 1627 and 1637, when Manchu forces passed through and pillaged the area. Hamgyŏng Province was also insecure and vulnerable; a number of Warka, Hūrha, and other Jurchen descendants who had lived around the Tumen River area for generations, often called the subordinate barbarians of the Chosŏn, had been relocated to Liaodong and mobilized into the eight banner forces. During the years of Nurhaci and Hong Taiji, Manchu troops continued to attack the local tribes near the Tumen River and moved many of these populations to the Manchu center, an action that made the Chosŏn northeastern margins even less populated.[56] However, the Chosŏn court was not yet given a chance to begin the national project of rebuilding the northern region. What was required first was removing any Qing doubts about the Chosŏn court's loyalty and normalizing its relationship with the suzerain power. With the relationship with the Qing still tense, the Chosŏn court could not risk allowing the growth of permanent settlement in the Hamgyŏng Province.

In fact, by the late seventeenth century, when the Three Feudatories revolted in South China and the Mongol prince Buruni attacked Mukden, Qing power in China still seemed precarious to Chosŏn Koreans. News of civil wars in China led the Koreans to anticipate the fall of the Qing court. The Chosŏn court had been concerned about the possibility of political disorder in China and the subsequent threat posed by the retreating Manchus. The Koreans commonly believed that foreign conquerors could not control China proper for more than one hundred years. These expectations, based on historical observations, were confirmed by the breakout of the Three Feudatories' rebellion, which convinced the Koreans that the Qing was in danger of imminent collapse. Koreans believed that in the event of a dynastic collapse, the Manchus would retreat to their homeland in the northeast and eventually invade Chosŏn territory again.[57]

News of the rebellion of the Three Feudatories strengthened the Chosŏn court's hostility toward the Manchus. Some court officials were empowered to call for aggressive action against the Qing, and they welcomed the revolt in South China as an opportunity to take revenge on the Manchus: "The uprising of Wu Sangui is so righteous that we should take advantage of it to clear the disgraceful experience of the invasion [of 1637]. Therefore, how could we dare to dispatch forces to help [the Qing] repress [the Three Feudatories]!"[58] Tribute emissaries who had visited Beijing and Shengjing also delivered news of the Qing domestic crisis to Seoul. In 1682, Yun Ije, returning from his emissary service in Beijing, reported to King Sukchong:

> In Shengjing, there were well-prepared city walls and a numerous population. However, the city gates in Beijing and the main hall [*Taihedian*] of the palace have crumbled and have not been repaired. It seemed to me that [the Manchus] are planning to retreat, so they do not care about the regions inside [Shanhaiguan] and instead pay attention to the areas around Shengjing and Ningguta as their base. Therefore, their claim to pacify the south is not trustworthy. . . . I was also told that the [Kangxi] emperor is going on a massive hunting expedition in Xifengkou, despite his brother's dissuasion. This hunting trip is apparently aimed at displaying Qing military power to the Mongols.[59]

He further quoted the Qing interpreter Li Yishan: "A very difficult situation is coming soon." Yun's report worried Sukchong: "If the Mongols become powerful, the world will be in chaos. How can we be sure that the Chosŏn will be safe?"[60]

Amid such uncertainty about the future of Qing authority in Beijing, the Chosŏn court could not consider its northern region. Until Manchu rule in China was stabilized and the relationship with the Qing secured, discussions about population resettlement or economic development in P'yŏngan and Hamgyŏng Provinces would be difficult.[61] In fact, only the lonely voice of Nam Kuman (1629–1711) claimed the importance of defending the Yalu and Tumen Rivers. Based on his experience as governor of Hamgyŏng, Nam argued that an effort to protect the northern margin (K. *pyŏnji*) would be a better strategy for the state's security than would building more defense facilities near Seoul. He also rejected the idea that the Manchus would retreat to the northeast via the Chosŏn north in the event that they had to leave China proper; he found it more reasonable to expect the Manchus to take familiar routes from Shengjing to Ningguta instead of using unknown roads in a foreign country. Thus, he argued that the Chosŏn should develop the northern region:

> We have not planned to build garrisons even on lands that our records indicate belong to the Chosŏn; we have simply abandoned them to grow rich forests where no one lives. There are only vicious people who come and go illegally to poach ginseng, but nobody can control them. It is to be regretted that court officials, who worry only about trespassing, do not understand that deserting the land is a more serious problem.[62]

In response to Nam's strong arguments for the development of the northern region, the Chosŏn court made a short-lived effort to reopen garrisons near the Yalu River and to encourage people to settle there in the 1670s. However, this reopening was soon canceled. The majority of Chosŏn officials were worried that any development of the northern region would cause more trouble. Specifically, they feared that road building in the north would help enemies invade the country, and population settlement along the Yalu and Tumen Rivers would loosen security and cause more people to trespass. In 1685, when reports that local Koreans were illegally crossing the Yalu River reached the Chosŏn court, the court immediately closed the roads and garrisons in the area. Chosŏn access to its northern margins had to wait until its relations with the Qing were settled.

THE INVESTIGATION OF THE MOUNTAIN

In addition to his political and historical interest in Changbaishan, Kangxi had another urgent motive for launching an investigation of the Qing-Chosŏn boundary: Koreans continued to cross the rivers and illegally enter Qing territory. Chosŏn court records include numerous cases of Korean trespassing and subsequent discussions with the Qing authorities about the repatriation of the offenders. The Qing emperor frequently sent emissaries to Korea to research the situation and to deliver letters ordering the Chosŏn to control its boundaries more effectively. Once in Seoul, the Qing officials joined the Chosŏn king and court officials in examining the criminals, deciding their sentences, and reporting the cases to the Qing emperor, who finally authorized the punishment.[63] As Qing-Chosŏn relations gradually settled by the 1660s, Beijing sent imperial emissaries to Seoul less frequently than before. If the number of trespassers was small, the Qing allowed the Chosŏn to investigate the cases on its own and to report back to the Qing afterward. Punishments of local officials in charge of the regions in question were also lightened. Harsh sentences, such as that meted out in the 1647 case in which a Qing emissary pressured the Chosŏn court to decapitate a local official for overlooking trespassing in his jurisdiction,[64] were generally replaced with demotion or dismissal. Sentences for trespassers were often reduced through imperial amnesty.[65]

Not surprisingly, the Chosŏn court sought to avoid conflict with Beijing caused by Koreans crossing illegally into Qing territory. Regardless of how lenient the Qing became toward the Chosŏn, trespassing cases involving Korean subjects always brought trouble for Seoul. The Chosŏn court was especially keen to avoid the presence of Qing officials in Korean territory, since military facilities and strategic locations could be easily exposed during the latter's investigatory visits. All the court could do was to impose heavy sentences on trespassers and hope to avoid incurring Qing criticism. In 1672, the Chosŏn court decided that individuals convicted three times of trespassing should be decapitated, but in 1686 it strengthened the regulation so that all first convictions would lead to beheading on the shore of the Yalu River. A complete prohibition of any ginseng gathering was imposed to stop people from trespassing; this law was included in *The Supplement to the National Code* (K. *Sok taejŏn*) published in 1746.[66]

Among the numerous trespassing cases, the Sandaogou incident of 1685, in particular, demonstrates how the Kangxi emperor understood Qing-Chosŏn relations. The emperor was already quite suspicious of Chosŏn loyalty to the Qing, as shown in his decision to impose a heavy fine of twenty thousand *liang* of silver on the Chosŏn king for neglecting his duty to prevent his people from crossing the Yalu River. In fact, the Ming court had had the same system of fines in place but had applied it only to domestic subjects, never to the Chosŏn king.[67] The Kangxi emperor's unusually rigorous attitude toward the Chosŏn was closely linked with his awareness of the fact that the Chosŏn court was informed of the rebellion of Three Feudatories and that anti-Qing sentiment consequently resounded in Korea. The Kangxi emperor and his Manchu officials believed that the Chosŏn was disrespectfully anticipating the decline of the Qing dynasty and even considering the possibility of cooperating with anti-Qing forces, such as the Zheng family in Taiwan. Qing suspicion and distrust of the Chosŏn was apparent in 1679, when Korean emissaries were criticized for disregarding the appropriate formalities in writing letters to the emperor.[68] The Chosŏn king was eventually fined ten thousand *liang* of silver for the errors in his letter, a decision announced soon after the final defeat of the Three Feudatories in order to send a strong warning to the Chosŏn court.[69] Later, in 1683 and 1685, Kangxi refused to accept the petition of the Chosŏn for temporary closure of the regular trading markets in Chunggang (C. *Zhongjiang*), Hoeryŏng, and Kyŏngwŏn, expressing his suspicions of the Chosŏn: "In controlling foreign countries, there should be a balance between rigorousness and coaxing. The Koreans are naturally cunning and often lie. If we accept their petition now, they will nag endlessly in the future."[70]

After the Sandaogou incident, Kangxi decided to launch his investigation of Changbaishan and the surrounding territories. He first asked the Chosŏn court to participate in a joint survey in 1691, because he knew that an investigation of the mountain could not possibly proceed without the cooperation of local Koreans. In his letter to the Chosŏn king, the emperor explained that he wanted to compile a comprehensive gazetteer (*Da Qing yitongzhi*), but that the records held in Shengjing and Ningguta were all inaccurate. He wrote, "Since the areas south of Ŭiju and the Tumen River all fall within Chosŏn territory, there must be local people familiar with the boundaries [*jierang difang*]. . . . [The Chosŏn court] should find such locals and prepare postal stations to receive the Qing imperial emissaries."[71] When he was told that all Chosŏn roads from Ŭiju to Changbaishan were closed and inaccessible to both people and horses, the emperor reprimanded the Chosŏn king for his reluctance to participate in the investigation: "Our officials used to see your patrols in the Changbaishan region while they were surveying the land. How is it possible that the Chosŏn has no local people familiar with the boundaries?"[72]

The Qing opportunity to press the Chosŏn court into cooperating with the investigation finally came in 1710, when Yi Manji, a Korean from Wiwŏn, P'yŏngan Province, illegally crossed the Yalu River, killing and injuring Qing merchants and stealing their ginseng. The Kangxi emperor immediately asked the Chosŏn embassy in Beijing about the area where the incident took place and about the distance of Wiwŏn from Qing territory. In 1711, the emperor announced the dispatch of an imperial emissary to the Chosŏn to investigate Changbaishan and its surrounding areas:

> You have my order to survey the area with Chosŏn officials, following the river to reach [the mountain]. You can go by way of Chinese territory [*Zhongguo suoshu difang*]. If Chosŏn officials are accompanying you in Chinese territory, they, too, can go. If Chinese territory is too rough to traverse, you can enter Chosŏn territory. You must take this chance to examine the area thoroughly in order to investigate the boundaries and report what you find.[73]

However, the Kangxi emperor's proposal for a joint survey of Changbaishan was not welcomed at the Chosŏn court. For the Koreans, repeated visits to Changbaishan by Manchu officials, and their survey of the boundaries, seemed

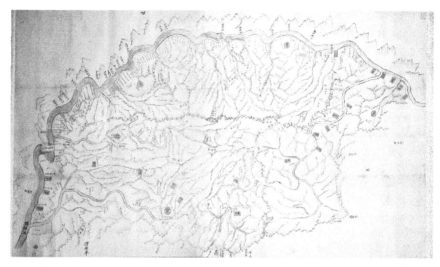

FIGURE 5. *P'yesagundo* (map of the Four Closed Counties), early nineteenth century. Manuscript, 115 × 194.5 cm. Kyujanggak Institute for Korean Studies of Seoul National University, no. ko-pok-ch'uk 4709–94. Used with permission.

to presage the possibility of an impending Qing retreat. Korean suspicions of the Qing interest in the boundary had been expressed already in 1680:

> King Hyojong (r. 1649–59) once remarked that the Manchus would surely be attacked by the Mongols along the route to Shenyang, so they will try to find their way via Korean territory, crossing through Ŭiju, Yangdŏk, Maengsan, and Hamgyŏng Province to enter their old bases. . . . [The Manchus] will seek their path of retreat through our territory to return to their original place. This is why they inspect the area under the excuse of sacrificing to the mountain, ask us to build roads, and claim the land south of Changbaishan as their territory. If they are defeated, they will, by necessity, return to their homeland via our territory.[74]

Given such suspicions at the Chosŏn court, it is understandable that the Kangxi emperor's request for a joint survey in 1691 was not well received. While the Chosŏn court refused to help the Qing investigate the boundary, it was also very careful not to leak any domestic information to its neighbor. In 1698, when a Qing official from Ningguta tried to investigate the area near Kyŏngwŏn and Hoeryŏng and succeeded in mapping the locations of cities and towns, the Chosŏn court decapitated the two interpreters who had cooperated with the Qing official on the project. This practice later became law: anyone who informed foreigners about the condition of roads in Korea would be sentenced to death.[75]

The Chosŏn officials were suspicious of the Kangxi emperor's motives for proposing the joint investigation. As one of them angrily complained, "If they just needed geographical information for compilation of a comprehensive gazetteer, it would have been much easier to ask us to investigate the area and draft a map. Why would they bother to send so many officials and to travel inside another country's territories by themselves? . . . They are cheating us with some excuses."[76] In fact, the Qing court clearly stated that the investigation would not violate Chosŏn territory. The Kangxi emperor's letter to the Chosŏn court in 1712 stated that the proposed survey aimed to examine the boundaries from the Qing side and would not bother the Chosŏn. Only in cases when the roads in Qing territory were too arduous to travel would the Qing officials ask for help from the Chosŏn court.[77] However, these assurances did not relieve Korean anxiety about the Manchu court's intentions. While waiting for the imperial emissary charged with undertaking the investigation, the Chosŏn court decided to refuse all requests for information about the Chosŏn northern region. Instead, it sought to convince the Manchu official, as well as the Qing emperor, that the Yalu and Tumen Rivers served as the boundary between the Qing and the Chosŏn and that "all the territory south of the rivers is ours."[78]

MU-KE-DENG'S MISSION

Although Jesuit missionaries had been involved in other mapping projects carried out by the Qing court, they could not participate in the Changbaishan survey. The Kangxi emperor, who had an understanding of Korean sensitivities, knew that as Westerners they would never have been allowed into Korea. Therefore, the map of the boundary with the Chosŏn had to be filled in by Butha Ula superintendent Mu-ke-deng, a Manchu official who was accompanied by a Chinese mathematician and a surveying team trained by the Jesuits.[79] Mu-ke-deng's first attempt to investigate Changbaishan, which took place in 1711, faced carefully designed obstruction by the Chosŏn court and local officials. All the Koreans with whom Mu-ke-deng dealt endeavored to discourage the Manchu official from undertaking the dangerous journey to the mountains and refused to cooperate with the survey: they misguided him to more difficult paths and declined to provide proper information about their country. On his first visit, Mu-ke-deng thus failed to achieve his mission, succeeding only in having his front teeth broken.[80]

In 1712, Mu-ke-deng made a second visit to Ŭiju, telling the Koreans that his visit was authorized by an imperial edict and that he had been sent to demarcate the Qing-Chosŏn boundary. This mission was, he declared, designed to "prevent vicious people from disturbing the boundaries."[81] He also asked the local Korean official, Pak Kwŏn, whether the latter's office had any documents or information related to the location of the boundary and whether military guards were stationed to the south of Changbaishan. The official answer to all of these questions was no.[82] When Mu-ke-deng began his survey, Pak Kwŏn, his Korean counterpart, could not keep pace with him and eventually abandoned the project. Pak suggested to Mu-ke-deng that marching up the steep side of the mountain through the heavy underbrush and forest was too arduous and that they should engage interpreters and locals instead of doing the work themselves. However, Mu-ke-deng insisted on taking this route.[83] Assisted only by his Korean interpreter, Mu-ke-deng was able to map the course of the Yalu River quickly, because he traveled against the current of the river. The mouth of the Yalu was wide, and the river narrowed toward its source at the top of the mountain, making it easier to follow the river from the mouth to its source. Traveling the other way was substantially more difficult, because the river disappeared underground or divided from time to time. Because he started his investigation of the Tumen River from the top of Changbaishan, Mu-ke-deng found it difficult to identify the river's actual source. He eventually selected a spot and ordered a stone marker to be erected to mark the watershed from which the Tumen flowed east. The stone marker reads as follows:

> The Great Qing Ula superintendent, Mu-ke-deng, received imperial orders to survey the boundary. From this marker to the west is the Yalu River, and to the east is the Tumen River. Therefore, here at this watershed is a stone marker, which was erected and inscribed on June 18, 1712 [Kangxi 51/5/15].[84]

Besides erecting the stone stele, Mu-ke-deng asked Chosŏn officials to build fences to make the boundary visible. In fact, the Tumen River flowed underground for several dozen *li* from its watershed, eventually becoming a wide, easily crossable stream for a distance of about one hundred *li*. In order to prevent confusion and trespassing, Mu-ke-deng emphasized that the Koreans should decide how to guard their side of the boundary.[85] Before leaving for Jilin the following month, Mu-ke-deng sent a copy of his map of Changbaishan to the Chosŏn king Sukchong. Later, Sukchong praised the Kangxi emperor for his efforts to demarcate the boundary: "Last summer, the imperial emissary demarcated the boundary without asking for any help from foreigners [the Chosŏn]. Imperial virtue prevented dishonest people from disturbing the boundary. Our small country's king and people altogether appreciate your great kindness. . . . [You] made the river the boundary, marking the north and the south of the mountain."[86]

The following year, in 1713, Mu-ke-deng visited Seoul. He asked Sukchong for maps of Changbaishan as well as a general map of Chosŏn.[87] The king and court officials obviously did not want to share detailed information on the geography of their country with the Manchu official, but they nonetheless had to find a way to

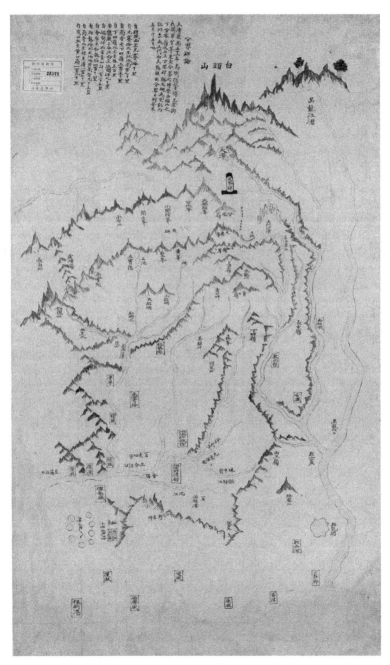

FIGURE 6. *Paektusan chŏnggyebi chido* (map of the stele of Changbaishan), date
unknown. Manuscript, 97.6 × 56.9 cm. Kyujanggak Institute for Korean Studies of
Seoul National University, no. kyu 26676. Used with permission.

convince the Qing emissary that the Chosŏn was willing to comply with the imperial order. The Chosŏn supreme councilor (K. *yŏngŭijŏng*), Yi Yu, informed the king: "Although the nation's defense maps are too detailed, we have just acquired a map that is neither too precise nor too general, with many mistakes on the Paektu rivers. Let us show him this."[88] Mu-ke-deng made copies of this map, saying, "We are taking one copy with us, and leaving one with you, so that our name and fame can spread to this place."[89] With this third visit to the Chosŏn, Mu-ke-deng's official mission was complete.

Mu-ke-deng's long, strenuous mission did not, however, resolve all of the boundary issues between the Qing and the Chosŏn. To the contrary, it opened up a new dimension in their ongoing debate. The primary question concerned the location of the Tumen riverhead. After Mu-ke-deng's departure, the Chosŏn officials charged with building wooden fences along the Tumen River found that the spot Mu-ke-deng had identified as the river's origin was, in fact, to northeast of the river and thus incorrect. The Chosŏn court faced a dilemma: if it followed Mu-ke-deng's guidelines, fences would be built in the wrong place, in Qing territory. However, if it ignored the Manchu official's findings and erected the fences at its own discretion, this would create problems in its relationship with the Qing court. If the Qing emperor received word that Mu-ke-deng had made a mistake in identifying the Tumen riverhead, the Manchu official could be in trouble. If the Qing court decided to dispatch another official for reexamination, the Chosŏn could face another round of investigation and eventually lose its territory.[90] After much discussion, the Chosŏn court decided to explain the difficulty of building and maintaining the fences along the boundary to Mu-ke-deng, not to the Qing emperor.[91] The Chosŏn court thus sought to protect its territory by convincing the Manchu official of its perspective, without agitating the Qing emperor.

The Qing court's attitude was very different from that of the Chosŏn. There is no evidence that the Kangxi emperor or his successors ever verified the location of the stone marker, a fact that was revealed during boundary surveys in the late nineteenth century and eventually undermined the legitimacy of it as a verification of demarcating the two territorial realms. Instead, Mu-ke-deng was seemingly untroubled about his designation of the Tumen riverhead and its subsequent effect on Qing territory. When Korean interpreter Kim Chinam asked for a copy of the map of Changbaishan, Mu-ke-deng generously answered, "It would be impossible [to give a copy of the map to you] if [the mountain were in] the great country's territory, but because it is in yours, it is not difficult [to give you a copy]."[92] In addition, after choosing the location for the Tumen riverhead, Mu-ke-deng stated, "The spot was located ten *li* further north than you Koreans thought, so the Chosŏn actually gained more territory." The Koreans accompanying Mu-ke-deng were delighted to hear this and no longer doubted his decision about the site of the stone marker.[93]

Later on, Mu-ke-deng reassured the Chosŏn that it need not worry about the location of the marker and noted that he would not survey the mountain again. He added that local Koreans should not bother to build the fences during the busy harvest season.[94] In fact, when Mu-ke-deng visited Korea the following year, he did not mention the location of the Tumen riverhead at all. The Chosŏn court soon realized that the Qing did not care about the location of the stone marker as much as the Chosŏn did. A year after Mu-ke-deng's survey, a Chosŏn official, Hong Ch'ijung, found that Mu-ke-deng's stone marker was very small and not firmly positioned. Even the characters inscribed on it were wrong. Hong observed that this "shows that even though he was an imperial emissary, Mu-ke-deng did not do his best."[95] Because of the apparent indifference of the Qing, the Chosŏn side had no reason to bring up the issue of the Tumen riverhead again. After all of the investigations and discussions, the origin of the Tumen River—the actual location of the Qing-Chosŏn boundary—still remained unclear.

We can find more than "Mu-ke-deng's ignorance and Kangxi's negligence"[96] in the investigation of Changbaishan and in the ambiguity regarding the Tumen riverhead. The events and circumstances surrounding this survey reveal the uniqueness of the tributary relationship between the Qing and the Chosŏn. Contravening conventional assumptions about the submissive attitude of an inferior tributary state, the Chosŏn court did not passively welcome the Kangxi emperor's proposed joint survey of the mountain. The Koreans were suspicious that the Qing court intended to force them to yield territory to China. Significantly, their concerns about Qing encroachment into Korean territory were closely related to anti-Manchu sentiment. Since the "Manchu barbarians" had conquered China proper, the Koreans believed that civilization had been lost or greatly compromised in China. They further believed that civilization should be protected from the barbarians and transferred to the Chosŏn. The Koreans did not completely accept Manchu supremacy, even though they fulfilled all of their obligations as a tributary state to the Qing empire.[97] Therefore, instead of following the norms of a tributary state during the Changbaishan investigation, the Chosŏn officials deliberately hampered Mu-ke-deng's mission and declined to help him. As Andre Schmid says, "The Chosŏn court displayed a subdued defiance of the wishes of the Kangxi emperor," which gives us good evidence to challenge "the Sinocentric image of [the Chosŏn as] a dependent and loyal vassal state."[98]

By contrast, the Qing court adopted a different approach toward its territorial boundary and political relationship with the Chosŏn. For the Kangxi emperor and his emissaries to the Chosŏn, the exact location of the Tumen's source or, indeed, the exact limits of the empire's territory were not as crucial as they were for their

Korean counterparts. The Qing seems to have felt that the surveys of Changbaishan signified Qing suzerainty over the Chosŏn. As the dominant power, the Qing believed that the imposition of imperial authority was sufficient to maintain the proper relationship and clarify the boundaries between the empire and its tributary state. The presentation of imperial virtue and power, rather than the demarcation of clear territorial boundaries, was the important issue. The great country did not need to quibble with a small neighboring state over a few dozen *li* of land. The location of the boundary on the upper Tumen River remained unclear, but the imperial authority was not compromised at all. The Chosŏn court joined the Qing-initiated survey, but the Koreans managed to protect their territory by not clarifying the boundary at the Tumen River. The tributary state succeeded in interpreting the idea of Qing superiority for its own purposes and in misleading the Qing officials during the survey process. Mu-ke-deng's investigation of Changbaishan was aimed at achieving a seamless and clearly demarcated line between the Qing and Chosŏn territories, but what it ended up creating between them was a borderland. The two countries were willing to tolerate this borderland as long as the tributary relationship was not challenged.

SHARED SYMBOL, SEPARATE BOUNDARIES

The investigation of 1712 served to promote further the connection of the Qing imperial court to Changbaishan. The Kangxi emperor's grandson, Qianlong, followed in his grandfather's footsteps by making homage to Shengjing (M. Mukden) a part of the imperial eastern tours. In 1743, after his first visit to the northeast, Qianlong wrote the "Ode to Mukden" (*Shengjing fu*), a panegyric on the magnificence of Mukden. The emperor glorified the mountains: "Our Great Qing dynasty arose from origins in Changbaishan. Marvelous humors there gathered—it was a most resplendent and auspicious place."[99] By drawing a direct connection between Mukden and Changbaishan, Qianlong sought to "rekindle Manchu ethnic pride and encourage the preservation of traditional customs" in the eighteenth century, a time when rapid acculturation, exemplified by the loss of the Manchu language and a decline in martial skills among the bannermen, threatened the basis of Manchu power.[100] During the late years of his reign, Qianlong further stressed the inseparable link between his ancestors and the mountain in his *Researches on Manchu Origins* (*Manzhou yuanliu kao*), a 1783 imperial publication that reveals Qianlong's understanding of the history and culture of the Manchu people. In the very first chapter of *Manzhou yuanliu kao*, the emperor states that "the ancestors of the Jin imperial clan lived in the Wanyan territory, where the White Mountain and the Black River were located." He further explains that the Qing dynasty received the mandate of heaven and his ancestors were born with the blessing of the red fruit when the heavenly maiden Fekulen went to the Bulhūri Lake at Changbaishan.[101] As Pamela Crossley points out, it is not very likely that the Aisin Gioro family originated in Changbaishan, but Qianlong surely wanted to incorporate his ancestors into the myths of the sacred mountain, since it had long been respected by many northeastern peoples.[102] As such, throughout the eighteenth century Changbaishan was seen as the source and symbol of Qing imperial power.

The investigation of the mountain in 1712 became the genesis of significant cultural shifts in the Chosŏn that the Qing court would not necessarily have predicted or desired. First, it encouraged Koreans to take a greater interest in Paektusan. As noted earlier, prior to the eighteenth century, Koreans did not really think of Paektusan as part of Chosŏn territory, although they believed that it constituted the peak of the geomantic hierarchy of mountain chains on the peninsula. This ambiguous understanding of Paektusan was transformed after the investigation of 1712 into a conviction that the mountain was actually situated on Chosŏn land. The joint survey of the mountain and the erection of the stone marker led the Koreans to believe that the Qing court recognized the land south of the Yalu and Tumen Rivers as Chosŏn territory and therefore that they should lay stronger claim to their territorial sovereignty. Not surprisingly, the Koreans' confidence in their territoriality was most obviously expressed in their increasing interest in Paektusan and the northern region.

In 1761, when the Chosŏn court sought to identify the major mountains in the country, the minister of the Board of Rites, Han Ingmo, proposed that Paektusan should be named the Northern Peak (K. *Pugak*), stating, "Our northern land was the birthplace of the dynasty. . . . There are no rivers or mountains that do not originate from Paektusan. This mountain is surely the origin of our country."[103] Han's claim corresponded to the intentions of King Yŏngjo (r. 1724–76), who sought to promote his kingly power against bureaucracy by elevating the status of Paektusan and the royal homeland. In the same way that the Kangxi emperor took advantage of the eastern tours and sacrifices to Changbaishan to demonstrate his imperial power, Yŏngjo wanted to strengthen his royal authority through rites for Paektusan and his ancestral homeland. Unlike Qing court officials, however, the Chosŏn officials disagreed with their king. They argued that it was very difficult to offer sacrifice to such rough mountaintops near foreign territory (K. *hogye*), and in addition that it was inappropriate for the Chosŏn king, who was enfeoffed by the emperor, to perform rituals for a place outside his territory.[104] This debate lasted four months without yielding a conclusion, and Yŏngjo had to wait another six years to raise the issue of making ritual offerings again.

In 1767, the subject of offerings at Paektusan reemerged. This time, Yŏngjo insisted more firmly on offering sacrifices to the mountain. He even ordered senior court officials to read the *Yongbi ŏch'ŏn'ga*, the mythical account of the Chosŏn dynasty's origins in the Paektusan area—an order that emphasized his determination to uphold his power against the bureaucracy. However, his opponents were also persistent. The minister of the Board of Punishment, Hong Chunghyo, for one, disagreed with the idea of making offerings at Paektusan:

> There has been a discussion that Paektusan is the summit of all the mountains in our country, and therefore it should be offered sacrifices. However, the Book of Rites [*Liji*] says that feudal lords should offer sacrifices to mountains and rivers within their territory. I do not know whether this mountain is within our territory. Mu-ke-deng had previously built a stone marker at the watershed and demarcated the boundary. The watershed is located a day trip's distance from Paektusan. Therefore, it is hard to say that [the mountain] is on our land.[105]

Hong's remarks show that, as late as the 1760s, Chosŏn officials still believed that Paektusan did not lie in Korean territory. But this time Yŏngjo did not give in to the pressure of the bureaucrats:

> The first chapter of the *Yongbi ŏch'ŏn'ga*, which I had ordered you to read, says, "Our ancestors had their homeland in Kyŏnghŭng." This passage is obvious evidence that Paektusan is in our territory. Therefore, even if the mountain were not on our land, it should still be offered sacrifices in order to venerate [the origin of the royal family]. It goes without saying, then, that if it is in fact on our land, [it should certainly be offered sacrifices].[106]

He then ordered his officials to perform sacrifices to Paektusan and to write a ritual address to it. The first official rite of the Chosŏn court for the mountain was finally offered in 1768, when the mountain was formally named the Northern Peak.[107]

The Chosŏn court's demonstrated interest in Paektusan extended to the northern region—a second change that the 1712 investigation inspired among the Koreans. The Chosŏn court had long believed that the upper region of the Yalu River, where four counties had been established and later closed, should remain uninhabited and closed off for the purpose of preventing trespassing. By the time of Yŏngjo's reign, however, discussions about developing the upstream areas of the Yalu River had resumed. Yŏngjo sympathized with the suggestion that people should be settled in the northern region, which would also help strengthen security, but the majority of the court officials shared the traditional assumption that the more people gather at the boundary, the more illegal crossings will happen. Therefore, the dominant position at the Chosŏn court was that the land near the Yalu and Tumen Rivers should remain empty in order to prevent trespassing and subsequent trouble with the Qing.[108] This belief that an uninhabited buffer zone at the boundary would protect Korean territory from the Qing continued to prevail at the Chosŏn court until the very late nineteenth century, as seen in later chapters.

The idea of developing the land at the upper reaches of the Yalu River was brought up again during the reign of King Chŏngjo (r. 1777–1800). Nam Chaehŭng, a member of the local elite living in the northern region, argued in a lengthy proposal that it had been a terrible mistake to abandon the four counties near the Yalu River and the fertile land in the north:

> In the Four Closed Counties . . . the land is vast and fertile. The fields are even, the weather is moderate, and grain grows well, so that it is truly a paradise for a pleasant life. However, the land was occupied by Jurchen barbarians [K. *Yŏjin yain*] from the late Koryŏ to the early [Chosŏn] period, and therefore the four counties were abandoned and undeveloped. After the Qing arose, the barbarians [K. *hoin*] who had lived near the [Yalu] River all left. Afterward, for 140 to 150 years, the land north of the Yalu, as wide as one thousand *li*, has been empty, with no trace of barbarians living there. It is such a pity that all our fertile land south of the river has been simply discarded.[109]

Interests in the northern region at this time were not, of course, the exclusive sphere of the monarch and the court, but became prevalent more broadly among the Korean literati. It was the Korean literati in the late eighteenth century, rather than the Chosŏn kings, who were most interested in the northern region, as well as the territorial limits of their country. Some of the scholars of the "practical studies" movement (K. *Sirhak*), including Yi Ik (1681–1763), Sin Kyŏngjun (1712–1781), and Hong Yangho (1724–1802), believed that the 1712 investigation and the established stone marker had set the boundary between the Qing and the Chosŏn, resulting in a substantial loss of territory for the Chosŏn. Their sense of territorial loss developed into a kind of irredentism based on the assumption that the Qing-Chosŏn boundary was in reality located not on the Tumen River but in a place farther to the north. Some argued that the boundary was the Heilongjiang; others insisted it lay seven hundred *li* north of the Tumen River. Even those who accepted the Tumen as the boundary still believed that the Chosŏn had lost several hundred *li* of land in the upper region of the Tumen through the investigation. In order to recover this lost territory, these scholars argued, the Chosŏn should strengthen its military defenses in the north, especially by reopening the Four Closed Counties near the upper Yalu and the Six Garrisons near the Tumen.[110]

Chŏng Yagyong (1762–1836) was one of the most notable figures among the Chosŏn scholars who argued for Korean territorial sovereignty in the north. In his *An Investigation of Our Nation's Territory* (K. *Abang kangyŏkko*), Chŏng claimed that the Chosŏn dynasty had ruled over its territory, which was distinct from that of China, since the late fourteenth century. For Chŏng, who believed that territoriality was the essence of a state, there was no more urgent matter than reclaiming the northern land. Neglecting the Yalu River and abandoning the Four Closed Counties, he argued, were terrible mistakes from a security standpoint. Chŏng hoped that the eighteenth-century Chosŏn kings would endeavor to protect their territory in the north just as their great fifteenth-century ancestors, who launched military expeditions to conquer the Jurchens and secure the Tumen River, had done.[111]

The Chosŏn court finally made the decision to develop the land near the Yalu River in 1793, when part of the Four Closed Counties was opened for settlement. Local officials in P'yŏngan Province recognized that population settlement and land reclamation were more efficient ways to achieve security than the stationing of military guards would have been. As new settlers were granted a three-year tax exemption and permission to collect ginseng, a growing number of people moved to the north.[112] This population growth led the Chosŏn court to assign officials to govern local affairs, but not until 1823.[113] Only in the early nineteenth century, then, did Paektusan and the Yalu and Tumen Rivers, having long been considered part of foreign territory outside of the Chosŏn realm, come to be fully incorporated into Korean administrative control. It thus took a century after the investigation of 1712 for the Chosŏn to begin to demand full sovereignty over its northern region.

· · ·

Triggered by Korean trespassing and ginseng poaching, the 1712 investigation of Changbaishan demonstrates that the Qing court continuously sought to achieve two goals—the imposition of Qing superiority and the demarcation of the territorial boundary—in its relationship with the Chosŏn court. The nature of their conceptions and practice of territoriality and sovereignty, together with the tributary relationship, played a crucial role during the investigation. It was the Qing court, not the Chosŏn, who initiated the investigation of the mountain sitting between them. The Manchus gathered geographic information about their sacred birthplace, but the wish of the Qing emperor to establish a clear boundary with the Chosŏn was not fulfilled. Instead, he bequeathed to his successor a borderland, characterized by uncertainty regarding the location of the Tumen riverhead and the exact limits of Qing territory, both authorized and sanctioned by the tributary relationship. Unexpectedly, it was the Chosŏn court and the Korean people whose understanding of their territorial realm was profoundly inspired and transformed by the information generated by the survey. Whether this outcome was planned or unexpected, the joint mapping project helped to confirm to the Koreans that the areas south of the Yalu and Tumen Rivers lay within the Korean realm and to increase Korean interest in its previously neglected, or abandoned, northern region. The lengthy debates regarding the offering of sacrifices to Paektusan and the reopening of the Four Closed Counties demonstrate the transformation of the

Chosŏn court's perception of the northern region from a foreign land to Korean territory. Ironically, the investigation of Changbaishan, which was begun as part of a Qing empire-building strategy and completed under the terms of the tributary relationship, eventually helped foster a sense of Korean territory distinct from the Qing empire. These two seemingly contradictory ideas—Chosŏn territorial sovereignty and Qing rulership over a tributary state—coexisted without much trouble until the late nineteenth century, as discussed in chapter 3.

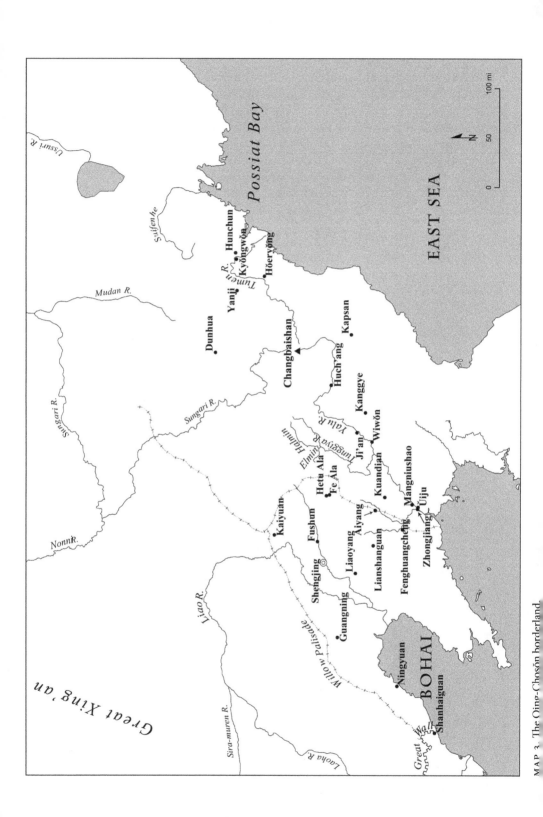

MAP 3. The Qing-Chosŏn borderland.

3

Managing the Borderland

On June 10, 1727, the Chosŏn Ŭiju magistrate (K. *puyun*), Yi Sŏngyong, sent an express letter to Seoul, reporting that Qing subjects had trespassed in Chosŏn territory.[1] The letter said that several hundred people from Qing territory had appeared aboard boats on the Yalu River and tried to trade goods on the shore. Yi Sŏngyong sent his soldiers to investigate the situation and also dispatched people across the river to inform the senior commandant (*chengshouwei*) of Fenghuangcheng about this intrusion:

> That night, I witnessed that the passengers of numerous ships came on shore and made a fire; I realized that these intruders would not be defeated by words. The Fenghuangcheng office sent sixty Qing soldiers to arrest the criminals. When we approached the intruders, who were well aware of the seriousness of their crime, they fiercely resisted and tried to find a way to escape. They attacked our soldiers, five of whom were hurt and drowned to death. We arrested only twenty-nine people; the rest of them ran away. . . . The discarded ships and other things turned out to belong to illegal traders and ginseng poachers from Shandong and Shanxi Provinces.[2]

The Chosŏn court immediately reported the incident to Beijing, highlighting the serious implications of the case: "Our small country [K. *sobang*] has been worried about the possibility of trespassing, since it is adjacent to the great country. The previously imposed regulation was certainly rigorous, but illegal crossings have recently increased, finally reaching the present extent." The Chosŏn court demanded a clear response from the Qing government: "Illegal crossings have happened before, but there has never been a case such as this, with several hundred people arriving on several dozen ships, injuring soldiers of the superior country [K. *sangguk*], and killing those of our small country. Had the situation not been corrected immediately, it is not even necessary to mention what might have happened in the future."[3]

This trespassing case concluded with the strangulation and decapitation of nine criminals, one of whom was Guo Lianjin, a Qing bannerman. But Guo Lianjin and his men were hardly the last Qing subjects to enter Chosŏn territory illegally. Trespassing incidents, involving both bannermen and civilians, continued after the Guo Lianjin group was punished. In an effort to stop trespassing, the Yongzheng emperor dispatched a special envoy to the Shengjing area and maintained regular communication with him. Numerous palace memorials and imperial responses were exchanged between the emperor in Beijing and the special inspector in Shengjing, demonstrating that the emperor and local officials alike recognized that Qing policy toward the Chosŏn was closely linked to security at the empire's northeastern margin—Manchuria.

This chapter discusses the Qing court's management of Manchuria and the boundary with Chosŏn in three aspects. First, it examines the Qing restriction on entry into Manchuria, later known as the "quarantine policy" (fengjin). After moving to China proper, the Qing court divided Manchuria into several regions, assigning different groups to each, and restricted people's movements in order to confine the Han Chinese to Shengjing, the Manchus to the northeast, and the Mongols to the northwest. This restriction policy was intended to protect local tribes from the majority Han Chinese population and to preserve untainted Manchu ethnic traits and practices in Manchuria. The Qing strategy for restricting access to Manchuria was to build physical barriers to separate this region from the outside world. Right after moving the capital to Beijing, the Qing emperor began to rebuild the Willow Palisade (liutiaobian), along which gates (bianmen) were built at given intervals to prevent people from coming in and going out freely. Second, it was expected that this restriction of Manchuria would help the Qing court monopolize the natural resources—especially ginseng—in Manchuria. In 1745, the court established the Ginseng Office (Guanshenju) in Manchuria as a new institution for more effective and comprehensive management of the state ginseng monopoly. Through this exclusive office for ginseng monopoly, the court sought to ensure the ginseng quota and curb illegal ginseng poachers in Manchuria.

Finally, this chapter further explores the ways in which the Qing restrictions on entry into Manchuria contributed to the peculiar nature of the boundary with the Chosŏn, and how the rhetoric of the asymmetrical relationship worked to the small country's benefit with regard to its boundary management. When Qing emperors and officials sought to tighten security along the boundary with the Chosŏn, Koreans felt their territory threatened and resisted the Qing approach. In seeking to deter Qing movements, the Chosŏn court relied on the norms of the tributary relationship. By highlighting the inferior status of the Chosŏn vis-à-vis the great Qing, the Koreans succeeded in preventing the construction of a Qing military facility on the Yalu River; as the benevolent ruler of the suzerain court, the Qing emperor accepted the Chosŏn request to maintain the vacuum at the boundary by force. Qing and Chosŏn conceptions and practices of territory, which were based on asymmetrical tributary relations, differed from those governing borders between modern states. The Qing-Chosŏn boundary was rather "a thick line with a broad horizontal context."[4] However, as long as the Chosŏn remained submissive to Qing imperial authority, the key features of the Qing-Chosŏn borderland—the empty zone on the Yalu River side and the unclear territorial limits on the Tumen River side—caused few troubles between the two neighbors.

THE WILLOW PALISADE

The conquest of China in 1644 provided the Manchus with a new capital in China proper. Soon after the move to Beijing, the situation in the northeast became very unstable. The long war against the Ming army had destroyed both the land and the population.[5] In 1653, in response to the severe depopulation of Liaodong, the Shunzhi emperor made a proposal on recruitment and cultivation in Liaodong (*Liaodong zhaomin kaiken ling*): an imperial edict that encouraged Han Chinese immigration and offered compensation in order to repopulate the northeast. Immigrants were granted titles and ranks, provided with land and farming tools, and exempted from paying taxes. The Liaodong resettlement policy continued into the Kangxi reign, and even political and criminal exiles were sent to Liaodong to supplement the meager population.[6] By the end of the seventeenth century this immigration effort had proved successful, and the Han population in Liaodong continued to increase. One result of the booming immigration was that many people, most notably illegal ginseng gatherers, were able to pass unnoticed through Shanhaiguan. The recovery and stabilization of the northeast eventually alarmed the Kangxi emperor, who worried that Han immigration would undermine Manchu privileges in this region. He finally ended the promotion policy in the northeast in 1668.[7]

The Qing policy of stabilization in the northeast was accompanied by administrative reorganization. The region was divided into three jurisdictions headed by military governors. The Shengjing military governor ruled the populous area of Shengjing, while the headquarters of the military governors of Ningguta and Heilongjiang were established in Jilin Wula and Qiqihar, respectively. Throughout the Qing period, the area under these three military governors was known as the "three eastern provinces" (*Dong sansheng*).[8] Within the three eastern provinces, the Shengjing military governor had a particularly wide range of responsibilities, including the prevention of illegal immigration and control of the boundary with the Chosŏn. A map in *The Unified Gazetteer of Shengjing* (*Shengjing tongzhi*) shows that his domain covered an area demarcated by Hetu Ala in the east,

FIGURE 7. Willow Palisade. From *Shengjing tongzhi* (*Gazetteers of Shengjing*), 1784 (Shenyang: Liaohai chubanshe, 1997), *Shengjing quantu*: 1.

Shanhaiguan in the west, Ninghai in the south, Kaiyuan in the north, Zhenjiang in the southeast, the Bohai (K. *Parhae*) Sea in the southwest, Weiyuanbao in the northeast, and Jiuguantai in the northwest near the Mongol areas. Pastures and hunting fields near the Yalu River were also under his command.[9] Two administrative divisions within the Shengjing office were closely related to Chosŏn affairs: the post of the Xiongyue garrison lieutenant general (*fudutong*), who directed the Yalu River region, and that of the Fenghuangcheng senior commandant, who supervised the boundary with the Chosŏn.[10]

In addition to the military governorship, another distinctive feature of Qing rule in the northeast was the Willow Palisade, a physical defense facility that was designed to control access to this vital region. The Qing Willow Palisade was in fact based on the Liaodong Frontier Wall that the Ming had built. After its conquest of China, the Qing court began to rebuild the palisade, which was composed of the eastern line, the western line, and the northern line. In 1661, the Shunzhi emperor relocated the residents along the western line and separated the pastoral Mongols in the west from the sedentary Manchus and Han Chinese in the east.[11] Later, the Kangxi emperor continued to expand the fences until 1697, when the Willow Palisade reached its final form. The expansion of the eastern line allowed old cities such as Fushun, Qingyuan, Fe Ala, and Hetu Ala as well as the tombs of the early rulers to be safely enclosed within the palisade. The western line reached from Weiyuanbao to Shanhaiguan, and the eastern line from Weiyuanbao to Fenghuangcheng. The two lines together stretched across 1,950 *li*. The northern line, also called the New Palisade, was built north of Weiyuanbao during the period from 1670 to 1681. The lines connecting the four points of the palisade, namely Shanhaiguan, Weiyuanbao, Fenghuangcheng, and Fatha, formed the shape of the Chinese character *ren*.[12]

According to Richard Edmonds's research, the Willow Palisade had a total of thirty-four gates, whose locations underwent considerable change over the Qing period.[13] *The Complete Gazetteer of Shengjing*, compiled in 1748, lists six gates on the eastern line and ten on the western line.[14] Each gate had a tower staffed with a certain number of officers and soldiers. The management of the palisade was the responsibility of the banner soldiers stationed at the gates and outposts (M. *karun*). While the gates were located along the palisade, the outposts were built inside and outside of it. They were added after the Willow Palisade was completed, providing a strong indication that the palisade itself was not adequate to prevent illegal intruders from entering the prohibited land. Outpost personnel were primarily charged with arresting illegal hunters, ginseng poachers, and unlawful settlers outside the palisade.[15]

All of the major functions of the palisade, the gates, and the outposts were about restriction of people's movements. The Qing court sought to contain its Han Chinese subjects within China proper and Shengjing, and by doing so to protect other ethnic groups. The first function of the Willow Palisade was to distinguish the administrative districts of the three military governors, enabling the separation of the Han Chinese from the Manchus, the Mongols, and other tribal people in Jilin and Heilongjiang. The central Shengjing area was settled by the Han Chinese, the land outside of the western line was reserved for the Mongols, and the territory north of it was designated for hunting peoples such as the Solon, Dagur, and Orochon tribes.[16] The second function of these installations was to protect the rich natural resources in the region. The Qing rulers established numerous graveyards, pastures, hunting fields, and ginseng mountains outside of the Willow Palisade, all of which were reserved for the exclusive use of the imperial household: "Along the road from Fenghuangcheng to Shanhaiguan and from Kaiyuan to Sa-lin-wo-li, the Willow Palisade is to be built and commoners are to be prohibited from entering."[17]

In the area north of the Yalu and Tumen Rivers and near Changbaishan, especially rigorous restrictions were enforced soon after the Qing conquest of 1644. The Kangxi emperor announced that "Changbaishan is the sacred birthplace [*faxiang zhongdi*]" and prohibited any settlement or cultivation.[18] The restriction on entry into the area beyond the eastern line of the Willow Palisade was also designed as a deterrent to exploiters of ginseng, furs, and pearls, who came from Shengjing and China proper as well as from Korea. The gates on the eastern line were opened for such special occasions as imperial eastern tours, hunts, and ginseng gathering outings, as well as a Chosŏn tributary embassy's journey.[19] When he followed the Kangxi emperor's eastern tour in 1682, Gao Shiqi described the eastern line thus: "The Willow Palisade divides [the inner land] from the Mongols. It reaches the Chosŏn in the south and Shanhaiguan in the west. Illegal intruders beyond [the palisade] are severely punished. . . . Within the preserve, barren mountains bar the passages, so that the roads are decayed and closed."[20]

GINSENG IN THE SACRED BIRTHPLACE

Soon after acceding to the imperial throne in Beijing in 1723, the Yongzheng emperor realized that good management of the gates and outposts was key to the security of the northeastern region as well as to the imperial monopoly of ginseng. In the early eighteenth century, Qing ginseng policy oscillated between the two directions of banner allocation and merchant licensing. The court entrusted merchants with ginseng collection in 1714, then transferred the task to the banners in 1724, and again hired merchants to run the business in 1730. These changes indicate that as the ginseng harvest declined and the bannermen had difficulty recruiting and provisioning ginseng gatherers, the state had to devise various alternative plans to secure the ginseng quota. Whether through bannermen or through merchants, the purpose of the Qing ginseng monopoly was to collect the amount of ginseng specified by the court. It is also likely that the changes in ginseng policy were part of the overall administrative and financial reforms that the Yongzheng emperor implemented throughout his reign.[21]

It was very clear that the ginseng quota reflected the needs of the state, not the natural conditions of ginseng production. As the Shengjing military governor Tang-boo-ju said, "Ginseng production is of huge importance for state revenue, and therefore the quota [of ginseng] should be predetermined [before collection]."[22] In 1730 the state printed ten thousand ginseng licenses and commissioned wealthy merchants to recruit gatherers and to collect sixteen *liang* of ginseng per license; in exchange for recruiting and provisioning their gatherers, the merchants received six out of every sixteen *liang* of ginseng in their quota.[23] This new arrangement was designed to guarantee the set ginseng quota for the court, while merchants and gathers were able to sell their surplus ginseng and make a profit. According to Wang Peihuan's analysis, in 1740 the Qing court issued 4,562 licenses and collected 45,620 *liang* of ginseng; the licensed merchants received 20,138 *liang* of ginseng, which was equivalent to 402,760 *liang* of silver at the market price in Beijing.[24]

Soon, however, the licensed merchants became unable to secure the high ginseng quota predetermined by the government, and in 1736, the Shengjing Board of Revenue proposed that the state, not merchants, should manage the ginseng monopoly: "Illegal ginseng poachers continue to increase, not because they do not know of the strict state regulations, but because they are not afraid of punishment in exchange for huge ginseng profits. Instead of relying on merchants, the government should issue ginseng licenses, recruit gatherers, and control their collection."[25] In 1745, after years of discussion, the Qianlong emperor implemented a major reform of the ginseng monopoly, which established Ginseng Offices in three places: Shengjing, Jilin, and Ningguta. The Ginseng Offices held exclusive responsibility for the state ginseng monopoly, taking charge of collecting and inspecting ginseng and sending it to the Imperial Household Department in Beijing.[26] Despite its physical location in Manchuria, it was under the direct control of the Board of Revenue, not under the supervision of the military governors. However, the military governors of Shengjing and Jilin were involved in the ginseng monopoly, because the authorized routes for ginseng gatherers passed through all three districts.[27] All ginseng gatherers and the soldiers escorting them were required to possess standard permits for entering the ginseng mountains (M. *temgetu bithe*; C. *jinshan zhaopiao*).[28] When merchants passed through Shanhaiguan into Manchuria to trade surplus ginseng, they had to possess permits stating the quality, grade, and quantity of their ginseng. They were allowed to trade ginseng in China proper only after returning these permits to the Board of Revenue in Beijing.[29]

Despite such efforts to regulate the ginseng monopoly, a variety of illegal activities persisted. Some gatherers entered areas not authorized by their specific permits or places where any access was entirely prohibited, such as Changbaishan or Chosŏn territory. Others ran away with the ginseng they had harvested or bypassed the designated location for submission in order to avoid inspection. Some gatherers stayed in the mountains to cultivate land or to grow ginseng. All of these illegal actions were punished, while officials and soldiers who addressed smuggling successfully were rewarded.[30] As part of his efforts to secure the ginseng monopoly in the northeast, in 1723 the Yongzheng emperor sent a Manchu official, Yong-fu, to Shengjing as a special inspector of six gates on the eastern line of the Willow Palisade (*bianmen zhangjing*). Yong-fu reported to his emperor about the conditions in Shengjing:

> The gate of Weiyuanbao leads to Jilin, Ningguta, and Heilongjiang. The gate of Fenghuangcheng is adjacent to the Chosŏn. Outside the gates of Ying'e, Wangqing, Jianchang, and Aiyang are imperial hunting fields and ginseng-producing areas. These gates are thus extremely important; [however,] there are a great number of workers, bannermen, civilians, and huntsmen living near the gates, so that it is nearly impossible to prevent people from passing through and poaching ginseng.[31]

The Shengjing military governor Tang-boo-ju likewise reported that ginseng poaching continued to take place in his jurisdiction:

> Illegal ginseng poachers travel in groups to go deep into the mountains but often end up getting lost and dying of hunger, being attacked and wounded by wild beasts, or hurting each other fighting over ginseng profits. As these situations affect human lives, [the court] has already prohibited entering the mountains. But in spite of the soldiers' patrolling, illegal ginseng poaching never disappears. . . . No matter how thoroughly patrolling and prohibitions are imposed, people still seek the huge profits of ginseng. Those from Tianjin and Shandong come by boat; others pass through Shanhaiguan and enter Shengjing and Jilin Wula. It is extremely difficult to track down every smuggler.[32]

The emperor had a bigger concern than illegal entrance and poaching by Han Chinese: bannermen, who supposedly embodied the "Manchu Way" and represented the dignity of the ruling elite, were increasingly involved in ginseng poaching outside the palisade. In the very first year of his reign, Yongzheng was informed about several dozen bannermen suspected of ginseng poaching. The vice minister of the Shengjing Board of War, Majintai, reported that among those arrested for ginseng poaching were thirty-two bannermen (M. *gūsai niyalma*) and sixty-two civilians from China proper (M. *dorgi ba i irgen*). Punishments for infractions in the prohibited area were harsh: whether civilians or bannermen, criminal leaders had both of their Achilles tendons cut and their accomplices had one; bannermen were sent back to their banners and civilians to their original registers.[33] Later, the punishment became even more severe. In 1771, Han Chinese poachers were beaten one hundred times with a heavy flogging stick (*zhang*) and sentenced to penal servitude (*tu*) for three years. The punishment for bannermen was reduced by a degree to wearing a cangue for two months and receiving one hundred lashes by a flogging leather (*bian*).[34]

Reports about banner soldiers engaged in ginseng poaching continued to reach Beijing. Yong-fu sent reports to his emperor about various cases, including that of a company captain (*zuoling*) and a corporal (*lingcui*) who confiscated ginseng from illegal intruders and traded it privately; a corporal who engaged in ginseng poaching himself; and huntsmen who stealthily delivered illegal ginseng and sable skins through the gates in collusion with merchants.[35] Yongzheng's response to the disturbances in the Willow Palisade was, not surprisingly, firm and resolute: "We Manchus should do our best in everything, work twice as hard as Chinese-martial bannermen [*hanjun baqi*] and Han Chinese do, and not expect silver in reward. [Such a crime as trespassing] is a truly corrupt practice."[36] Yongzheng's concern was not limited to the fact that these bannermen had abandoned their duties in favor of illegal activities. Many of the cases of unauthorized crossing for ginseng collection also related to the neighboring Chosŏn—an issue that made the Qing government's management of the northeast even more complicated.

MULTIPLE BOUNDARIES WITHIN THE EMPIRE

Of the numerous trespassing cases involving bannermen in the northeast, it was the incident of Guo Lianjin in 1727 that received the greatest attention at Yong-zheng's court. The news that several hundred ginseng poachers had intruded into Chosŏn territory and killed Korean soldiers reached the current Shengjing military governor, Yen-tai, through a report from the Fenghuangcheng military commander, Bo-xi-tun. Yen-tai's report to the emperor explained that Sun Guangzong, one of Guo Lianjin's accomplices and also a local civilian living in Fenghuangcheng, had attracted several hundred people with his plan, bribed the patrolling soldiers to allow him and his followers to cross the Yalu River, entered Chosŏn territory to poach ginseng, and ended up killing people. The patrolling soldiers were supposed to check illegal traffic but instead accepted bribes for several years and helped criminals pass through the gate and make trouble in Chosŏn territory.

Upon receiving the report, Qing court officials agreed that "this case involves foreign people being held and killed" and that such violations could be not tolerated: "The Chosŏn is close to China [Zhongguo] and it has long been loyal, because our [Qing] court has taught them with benevolence, treating them equally with the domestic [Qing] subjects [neidi chenmin]." Then Qing officials suggested that officers should be dispatched to the scene to arrest the criminals and that soldiers who took bribes should be investigated. It was also deemed necessary for the emperor to empower the Chosŏn king to arrest Qing intruders in Chosŏn territory whenever they injured people or poached ginseng; Chosŏn soldiers should also be authorized to kill Qing intruders if they resisted arrest. These were considered inevitable decisions, required to "prevent Qing subjects from trespassing and embrace the Chosŏn with imperial benevolence."[37]

The Yongzheng emperor ordered all trespassing suspects to be brought to Shengjing for investigation. During the investigations at Shengjing, it was revealed that the first reporter of the case, the Fenghuangcheng military commander Bo-xi-tun, was also involved in corruption and bribery. Despite his position as an "important official to protect the boundary" (fengjiang yaoyuan), Bo-xi-tun had accepted about a thousand liang of silver in bribes to help ginseng poachers pass the inspection at the gates. The military commander did not admit his wrongdoings, but others—including those who were involved in giving and delivering the bribe to Bo-xi-tun—all confessed their crimes.[38] Sun Guangzong also admitted that he had bribed the military commander.[39] The Qing court was full of criticism for these corrupt officers and soldiers: "The trespassers formed a group to carry out evil activities and break the law. All this happened because soldiers were negligent in watching the gates and instead accepted bribes, while their officers did not recognize their misconduct. These soldiers and officers should be dismissed and investigated thoroughly by the Shengjing military governor."[40]

The new Shengjing military governor, Gioro I-li-bu, discovered that Guo Lianjin had originally lived in Shanhaiwei and moved in 1726 to Fenghuangcheng. When Guo was planning the ginseng poaching with his neighbors, Sun Guangzong had provided money to support the plot. Subsequently, Guo and his accomplices gathered ginseng illegally in Yanghe outside of the gate, and Guo used part of the haul to repay Sun. The following year, Guo and as many as two hundred men returned to Yanghe to poach ginseng again. At the gate, they were approached by two of the patrolling soldiers, who demanded one hundred *liang* of silver as a "fee" for illegal entry. Guo's group paid the silver and passed through the gate to Mangniushao, where they were caught by Chosŏn soldiers.[41] Besides the sheer number of people participating in the conspiracy, what was stunning about this case was the extent of rampant corruption among the banner soldiers stationed at the gates. Wang Tingzuo, a corporal, received four hundred *liang* of silver as a bribe from Sun Guangzong and promised to procure a ginseng-gathering permit for him. When he failed to obtain such a permit, Wang agreed instead to let Sun's people pass through the gate in order to poach ginseng. Upon hearing of Wang's actions, his senior officer, a company captain, demanded that Wang share the bribe with him.[42] Outside the gate, Sun and his people were discovered by another corporal, who did not arrest them but instead demanded a bribe to let them go. Sun gave him five hundred *liang* of silver, which the corporal shared with nine other soldiers at the gate.[43] This veritable chain of corruption was common at many gates along the Willow Palisade.

In 1728, Yongzheng issued the final sentences in the Guo Lianjin case: Guo Lianjin was decapitated and eight other people were strangled, while additional accomplices were exiled or beaten according to their crimes. Although he was a bannerman, Wang Tingzuo was not spared given the seriousness of his crime and the amount of the bribe he had accepted. However, other bannermen involved in the Guo Lianjin case benefited from their privileged bannerman status: the sentences of most of the soldiers who received bribes from Guo were reduced because "they were bannermen [*qiren*]."[44] Despite his firm treatment of those involved in this and similar case, Yongzheng did not believe that Qing subjects were the only ones to be blamed for trespassing and the resulting Korean casualties. The emperor criticized the Chosŏn king for his failure to fulfill the duties of a tributary state:

> Previously, Shengzu Ren Huangdi [Kangxi] had written an edict to the Chosŏn king saying, "If bandits enter your country to plunder it, the king should arrest and kill them and return the rest [to the Qing]." After succeeding to the throne, I also explained to the king several times that if any wanderer without a legitimate pass should cause trouble [in Chosŏn territory], the king should punish him according to his law. As prohibitions and regulations are now strongly imposed, outlaws in China proper [*neidi*] can find nowhere to hide and therefore flee to a foreign country

[*waiguo*] to save their lives. The Chosŏn king has already been included among the tributaries [*fanfeng*], so he is obliged to serve the [Qing] court by arresting bandits and pacifying the population. Despite the issuance of several edicts by Shengzu Ren Huangdi and myself, the king has a weak character and has failed to follow these decrees. Therefore, the outlaws of China proper have come to consider Chosŏn territory a hiding place to avoid punishment. Such an evil practice is not to be endured. Hereafter, if the Chosŏn soldiers and officials fail to arrest trespassers and troublemakers, the king should punish them, and the [Qing] Board of Rites should discipline the Chosŏn king for failing in his duty as a tributary king to follow the imperial edicts to arrest bandits and pacify the people.[45]

Interestingly, this edict refers to the Chosŏn simultaneously as "a foreign country" and as "a tributary state." The use of these two different labels for the Chosŏn indicates that people within the Qing empire held different conceptions of the boundary with the Chosŏn, depending on their location and status. On the one hand, "bandits" in Shengjing, like Guo Lianjin and his fellow troublemakers, regarded the Chosŏn state as a foreign country where they could avoid Qing regulations; on the other hand, the Qing emperor in Beijing considered the Chosŏn a tributary state that had an obligation to serve the Qing court. Seen from the northeastern periphery, the Chosŏn was a foreign country, but from the perspective of the center the same neighbor was regarded as a tributary state.

Yongzheng's edict also reveals the ways in which the emperor understood the territoriality of the empire. He recognized that the Willow Palisade served to divide the inside from the outside, but he simultaneously thought that areas both inside and outside the palisade fell within the empire's territory. This view corresponds with his conception of the Chosŏn state. The Chosŏn king governed his people by his own law; nevertheless, he was, above all, a tributary ruler whom the emperor had enfeoffed. The Willow Palisade was deemed a boundary, and so was the Yalu River. In other words, the Qing empire had multiple boundaries within it. Further, each boundary carried a different meaning according to its location in the empire and represented the imperial power in a different way and to a varying extent. The imperial authority gradually extended over these boundaries from the center to the periphery and then farther beyond to the tributary state.

Yong-fu seemed to share Yongzheng's conception of the Qing empire's territoriality and the status of the Chosŏn state. After the Guo Lianjin case closed, Yong-fu reported to the emperor that Qing subjects continued to trespass in Chosŏn territory. He asserted that those who intruded into Chosŏn lands violated the law more seriously than did those who simply poached ginseng outside the Willow Palisade:

Guo Lianjin and his fellow criminals received serious punishments for violating Chosŏn territory. This time, [the trespassers] were also involved in intruding into [Chosŏn] land and poaching ginseng. Their crime is so serious that it should not be treated as a simple case of ginseng poaching. These people should be sent to Shengjing for investigation and heavy punishment. They should serve as an example to warn people who try to trespass and break the law.[46]

The Yongzheng emperor and his official Yong-fu thus believed that the division between the inner and outer territories was not fixed but rather changeable according to context.[47] From one perspective, what lay west of the pass at Shanhaiguan corresponded to the inner land—China proper—while the territory to the east of the pass was the outer land. However, this outer land was divided again by the Willow Palisade, which created a different set of "inner" and "outer" lands. In turn, the remote territory outside the palisade was divided by the Yalu and Tumen Rivers. If the area north of these rivers was the inner land of the empire, the southern areas were outside of the empire—they comprised the lands of the Chosŏn, a tributary of the Qing empire.

Qing imperial authority reached everywhere under heaven, beyond Shanhaiguan, the Willow Palisade, and the Yalu and Tumen Rivers. However, each of these multiple boundaries had different functions and meanings for the empire. Shanhaiguan and the Willow Palisade served to create boundaries between ethnic groups, including the Manchus, the Han Chinese, and the Mongols, while the Yalu and Tumen Rivers separated the empire from the tributary state. Unauthorized entrance into Shanhaiguan and beyond the Willow Palisade meant violating state laws meant to segregate ethnic groups and protect imperial property. In comparison, crossing the Yalu and Tumen Rivers was deemed to disturb the tributary state under the protection of the imperial court. What, then, did the territorial boundary between the empire and the tributary state mean to the Qing emperor and the Chosŏn king? Did the two share similar ideas about the Yalu and Tumen Rivers? The ways in which these rulers viewed the territory and sovereignty of the Qing empire and the Chosŏn kingdom are revealed in their debates over the issue of the potential outpost at the Yalu River, a discussion that continued through the Yongzheng and Qianlong periods.

TRESPASSING CONTINUED

Until the late seventeenth century, one of the most vexing issues between the Qing and the Chosŏn had been Korean trespassing on Qing land. At the turn of the eighteenth century, however, cases of Qing subjects encroaching on Chosŏn territory and, for the most part, poaching ginseng there also began to be reported. In 1707, a group of Qing ginseng hunters were reported to have entered P'yŏngan Province and to have taken away a Korean soldier and food supplies.[48] The following year, the Hamgyŏng governor (K. *kwanch'alsa*), Yi Sŏnbu, disclosed that at least ten Qing ginseng poachers had built tents near the Kapsan area and had made several attempts to rob Korean residents. When arrested and interrogated by Chosŏn soldiers, these Qing intruders stated that they had legitimate ginseng permits issued by the Shengjing authority and claimed, "We simply got lost while searching for ginseng and ended up coming here after wandering around the Changbaishan area for some time."⁴⁹ Although it was evident that a growing number of Qing people were approaching Chosŏn territory at this time, it was difficult for Chosŏn officials to confirm their status as legitimate ginseng gatherers. In 1711, Seoul received another report of trespassing in the Kapsan area; again, ten people from Qing territory had been arrested for ginseng poaching and for making contact with local Koreans. After some discussion, the Chosŏn court decided to report this particular event to the Qing as a mere accident rather than as an intentional intrusion.⁵⁰

In 1714, when Qing hunters entered the Yisan area in P'yŏngan Province, the Chosŏn court finally took the step of complaining to Beijing about the ever-increasing intrusions by Qing subjects and officially requested the Qing to take action to prevent such violations:

> People of the superior country come and go [across the boundary], forming groups of several dozen or hundreds to hunt animals and gather ginseng. While hunting in the winter and digging for ginseng in the summer, they set up tents and stay for extended periods of time. Their secret contacts with local people in our small country caused the previous trespassing incidents. . . . Now they have violated the rule again by crossing the boundary to abduct a patrolling soldier. If this kind of crime is not stopped now, we cannot anticipate what will happen in the future. . . . Trespassing by the people of the superior country is not something in which this small country can intervene, but I dare to bother Your Highness by reporting this incident. . . . I beg Your Highness to curb illegal trespassers and to stop them from plundering the food supplies and frightening the people of our small country.⁵¹

Upon receiving the Chosŏn court's report, the Kangxi emperor ordered the imposition of strict regulations for trespassers and local officials. He went further and gave the Chosŏn government his permission to arrest Qing intruders: "If Chosŏn soldiers arrest trespassers and send them back [to the Qing], these criminals should be thoroughly questioned and punished. The Chosŏn should also be informed in writing to strengthen patrolling at the boundary and, in the event of discovering such trespassers, arrest them and send them back to the Qing."⁵²

In fact, the Kangxi emperor had already given permission for the Chosŏn to arrest Qing intruders two years before this incident, in 1712, explaining, "If [such criminals] enter [Chosŏn territory] and plunder there, the Chosŏn people will think helplessly, 'We cannot do anything to the people of the Heavenly Court.' This is something I cannot endure." The emperor then ordered the Shengjing military governor to stop illegal seafaring near Chosŏn territory and also instructed the Chosŏn court to arrest and punish Qing trespassers, not to pardon them on the basis of their being "imperial subjects."⁵³ Thus, if Chosŏn soldiers arrested a Qing subject for seafaring without an authorized pass or for causing a disturbance in Chosŏn territory, they were allowed to punish the Qing criminal under Chosŏn law. However, the emperor also made it clear that this permission did not mean that the Chosŏn court had been given free rein to punish Qing subjects: "[This power] is given to the Chosŏn only as a means of serving the emperor."[54]

The fact that the Kangxi emperor allowed the Chosŏn to arrest and punish Qing trespassers reflects a profound change in Qing-Chosŏn relations at the turn of the eighteenth century. In the early years of the Kangxi reign, the Chosŏn king had had to pay an excessive fine as a punishment for Korean trespassing, but now, in the last decade of his rule, the emperor granted the Chosŏn court imperial permission to punish Qing subjects for boundary violations. There is no doubt that this change reflected the growing strength of Qing rule in China in the early eighteenth century. The Qing emperor harbored no serious concerns regarding the relationship with the Chosŏn, and this confidence allowed for greater leniency in his Chosŏn policy. In short, the consolidation of the Qing empire opened up opportunities for the Chosŏn court to assert its power at the boundary.

In 1714, the Chosŏn court expressed grave concern over the discovery of Qing seafarers who had built houses and begun to cultivate land around the Kyŏngwŏn area in Hamgyŏng Province. A statement made by these Qing intruders is indicative of the situation: "We were told that people from Ningguta were going to move here, so we wanted to take this fertile land before they came."[55] The subsequent investigation by the Chosŏn court revealed a plan proposed by the Ningguta military governor according to which Qing soldiers would be stationed in Hunchun, across from Kyŏngwŏn, and the surrounding area would be declared a military post.[56] The Chosŏn court's response to the Qing plan to develop the land on the Tumen River reveals Korean conceptions about the Qing and their mutual boundary:

> In Ming times, Jiuliancheng and several other garrisons near the boundary were so close to us that even crowing cockerels and barking dogs could be heard. If people from Liaodong came to our land to till it, we reported [the intrusion] to the [Ming] Liaodong commander so he would stop it and erected a stone marker to demarcate the boundary. The world was then like one family, and our people and the Chinese people [*hua*] were close neighbors; but we were still worried about not having a defense line. It is not even necessary to mention [the importance of the boundary] now. We cannot understand the real intention of the Qing, but it is truly worrisome, since frequent contacts across a narrow river will cause trouble.[57]

This comment implies that drawing clear boundaries had been an important issue during the Ming period and that it became even more critical when the Chosŏn faced the Qing. It assumes that the Qing Manchus could be more threatening to Chosŏn security than the Ming Han Chinese had been.

The Chosŏn court sent a letter to Beijing requesting that the Qing court halt the Ningguta military governor's plan. Contrary to its tacit belief that the Qing represented a greater threat to the Chosŏn than the Ming had been, the Koreans politely explained to the Kangxi emperor that they did not agree with the development of the land near the Tumen River because such development conflicted with previous policy: "[The emperor] built a gate at Fenghuangcheng and checked the entrance, leaving the land outside the gate uninhabited and preventing people from living there. This made a clear distinction between [the great country] and our small country, avoiding their mixing. It was due to imperial thoughtfulness that the boundary has been safe thus far."[58] Apparently convinced by the argument that trespassing could be prevented only by keeping the area near the river empty of people, the Kangxi emperor accepted the Chosŏn appeal and ordered all Qing subjects residing near the Tumen River to evacuate. In 1715, the Qing Board of Rites sent a letter of confirmation to the Chosŏn, stating that houses and shelters near Kyŏngwŏn had been cleared and that the Ningguta soldiers had also been repositioned. The letter further promised a strict prohibition on Qing people crossing the Tumen River or building houses on or tilling the land near the river; in essence, if illegal residents were discovered near the river, Qing soldiers and officials would be punished for negligence.[59]

Despite Chosŏn oppositions and protests, the Qing had, in fact, established a military garrison in Hunchun, across the Tumen River from Kyŏngwŏn, in 1714. Under the jurisdiction of the Ningguta military governor, the Hunchun regiment colonel (*xieling*) was newly appointed to supervise 150 Kūyara soldiers, who were organized into three companies (M. *niru*), and forty Manchu banner soldiers.[60] That same year the Chosŏn court dispatched interpreters to deliver a letter expressing its concerns to the Qing,[61] but there is no further record of how the Qing court explained to the Koreans its decision to build the banner garrison in Hunchun, from where Kyŏngwŏn could be visited in a single day's round trip. In the end, the Chosŏn court did not succeed altogether in stopping the Kangxi emperor from stationing Qing soldiers near the Tumen River. But it was at least able to prevent the Qing from developing the land at the Tumen River, because the Ningguta military governor decided to open land in a different location, far away from the river, for his soldiers being stationed in Hunchun.

Li Huazi points out that Kangxi's decision to cease Tumen River development can be deemed a diplomatic victory for the Chosŏn court. She argues that it had a negative effect on Qing boundary management, because the Qing military presence at the Tumen River became insecure and was thus unable to prevent Koreans from crossing the river in the late nineteenth century.[62] It is true that the Chosŏn court applied the rhetoric of the benevolent emperor who had great trust in his loyal tributary state and that it succeeded in persuading Kangxi to retract his plans for development of the Tumen River area. However, there is more to the decision than the Chosŏn manipulation of the tributary relationship and its taking advantage of the diplomatic language of loyalty to attain certain objectives. Kangxi's decision not to develop the area was also related to the conception of the boundary as a buffer zone that should be empty of people to prevent troubles with one's neighbor. The empty space at the boundary near the Tumen River did not cause serious problems during the eighteenth century, when the Qing authorities were still strong enough to control traffic across the rivers. It was only in the late nineteenth century that the two states were no longer able to stop people's movements and the uninhabited buffer zone invited a growing number of immigrants and settlers hungry for land.

THE MANGNIUSHAO POST

The Kangxi emperor's authorization of the active involvement of the Chosŏn in patrolling the boundary was confirmed by his son, who in 1728 issued the Yongzheng Imperial Decree (*Yongzheng huangzhi*) to give Chosŏn soldiers permission to arrest Qing intruders in Korean territory and even to kill them in the case of resistance.[63] Beyond the imperial efforts in Beijing to curtail trespassing, the Shengjing military governor at the time, Nasutu, identified additional effective methods for achieving security at the boundary, one of which was to build a military post at the mouth of the Yalu River. He paid special attention to a small sandbank called Mangniushao, located where two streams—the Caohe and the Aihe—converged and flowed into the Yalu. This sandbank was used as a foothold by criminals and as a port for delivering provisions to ginseng poachers and trespassers. Nasutu's problem was that although the west side of the sandbank was under the jurisdiction of Fenghuangcheng, the east side fell within Chosŏn territory. Nasutu explained to his emperor that the sandbank enabled criminals to easily evade Qing soldiers because it was located along the boundary with the Chosŏn.[64] In order to prevent further transgressions, the military governor suggested, ships and soldiers should be stationed at a new military post on Mangniushao. The Yongzheng emperor's first response to Nasutu's proposal was to discuss the matter with the Chosŏn. Despite being the ruler of the superior country, matters pertaining to a boundary with a foreign country could not be decided unilaterally by the Qing emperor.

Upon receiving the Qing court's letter concerning the possible establishment of a military post on Mangniushao, the Chosŏn court assumed that the Qing intention was to "open the land along the Yalu River for settlement." Second State Councilor (K. *chwaŭijŏng*) Cho Munmyŏng said:

> Since the Shunzhi reign, the land outside the [Fenghuangcheng] gate has remained empty and no one has been allowed to approach it from either side, a decision that was made after careful consideration. It is very worrisome that recent criminal

activities by our subjects have repeatedly violated the boundary and caused trouble for the superior country. We should stop any attempt at building a military post near the boundary.[65]

Cho's argument against a military post near the Yalu River was the same as the one that had been used in 1714, when the Chosŏn court had opposed development of the land near the Tumen River during the Kangxi reign: if the area is opened for settlement, people will immigrate, and illegal crossings will increase. In 1731, the Chosŏn king Yŏngjo sent a letter to the Qing court, drawing on familiar rhetoric to remind the emperor of the precedents of the Shunzhi and Kangxi emperors, who had displayed consistent benevolence and care on matters relating to the Chosŏn:

In the past, Taizong Wen Huangdi [Hong Taiji] . . . built the Willow Palisade, enforced regular patrols in the region, and kept the land empty; people were not allowed to settle there. It was a truly considerate and extraordinary decision. During the rule of Shengzu Ren Huangdi [Kangxi], the Ningguta military governor stationed soldiers opposite Kyŏngwŏn to the north of this small country. When he further tried to build camps and develop the land, however, the emperor disapproved of the proposal after reading the letter from this small country and showed that imperial benevolence is always deep and eternal. Thanks to his decision, this small country was able to reduce temporarily the burden of patrolling at the boundary.[66]

In the face of Chosŏn complaints, the Yongzheng emperor finally bestowed his favor on the Chosŏn king rather than on his Shengjing military governor. In the same year, 1731, the Qing Board of Rites informed the Chosŏn court of the emperor's objection to the proposed military post on Mangniushao:

[The emperor] understands that the two streams of Caohe and Aihe run along the boundary with the Chosŏn and therefore asks the Chosŏn whether there is any problem [with the proposal]. Since the Chosŏn king begs to follow past precedent, the plan to build a military post will be stopped. It is not necessary for the Board of War to discuss it again.[67]

As an effective way of preventing trespassing, the emperor favored the Chosŏn idea of maintaining an empty buffer zone at the boundary over his own local official's proposal to station soldiers on Mangniushao. Yongzheng's decision was not simply the result of successful Chosŏn diplomacy; rather, the emperor recognized that the Qing empire and the Chosŏn state shared a zone between their territories and he decided to maintain the area uninhabited by force instead of pursuing maximum strategic efficacy in controlling the boundary.

The decision not to build an outpost on the waterway limited Qing efforts to open up new mountains for ginseng collection. In 1738, Yong-fu, now vice minister of the Shengjing Board of War, proposed that more ginseng-producing mountains be opened up and gatherers be allowed to enter via the waterway into Bendou

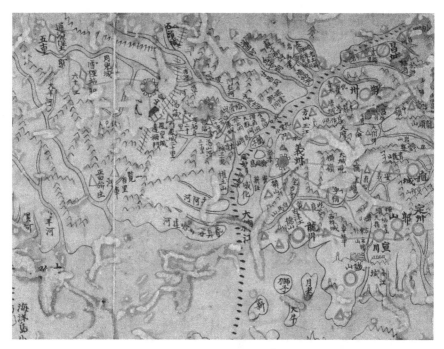

FIGURE 8. The Fenghuangcheng gate, the Yalu River, and Ŭiju. Details from *Sŏbuk kyedo* (map of the northwestern boundary), 1777–91. Manuscript, 140 × 135 cm. Kyujanggak Institute for Korean Studies of Seoul National University, no. ko 4709–89, vol. 5. Used with permission.

and Huanggou outside the eastern line of the palisade. This region was located to the southeast of Elmin and Halmin, the old ginseng preserve in Shengjing. When Yong-fu's proposal was delivered to Beijing, however, the primary concern of the Qing court was not the probable ginseng yield of Bendou and Huanggou but rather the likely reaction of the Chosŏn court, which had been very displeased with the idea of Qing soldiers or ginseng gatherers approaching its territory. In the end, the Qing court rejected the proposal, reasoning,

> If we open a waterway to Bendou and Huanggou, which is separated only by a river from Chosŏn territory, some unlawful people may trouble the Chosŏn people and mar the imperial benevolence to embrace the small country. Therefore, ginseng gatherers going to Bendou and Huanggou are not allowed to take the waterways; instead, they should enter through the nearest gates of Jianchang and Aiyang.[68]

The fervent appeal of the Chosŏn for Qing magnanimity evidently pressured the Qing court to take extra precautions at the boundary and to limit voluntarily its efforts to improve ginseng collection in its own territory.

After the proposal for a military post was rejected, Mangniushao continued to serve as a foothold for illegal ginseng poachers. By the time the Qianlong emperor took the throne in 1736, it was clear that the Willow Palisade had failed to check the constant flow of Han Chinese immigrants and ginseng poachers into Manchuria. It was also at this time that the acculturation of the bannermen became a serious concern at the Qing court: signs were omnipresent that the bannermen were losing their traditional means of securing their livelihood, the military skills of horsemanship and archery, and their command of the Manchu language.[69] As a part of efforts to halt the deterioration of the "Manchu Way," in 1740 the Qianlong emperor decided to prohibit further immigration to Shengjing and to send illegal residents back to China proper. The same regulations were enforced in Jilin and Heilongjiang in the following years.[70] Later history tells us that this restriction could not stop tens of thousands of hungry peasants looking for a living in the northeastern region, and the Qing court failed to protect its homeland from Han Chinese immigrants. However, the court did not officially abandon the restriction on entry into the northeast until the end of the nineteenth century, because it was directly linked to the Manchu identity and the basis of the Qing empire. Even in the face of the reality of an increasing Han population in Manchuria, the Qing court doubled down on its efforts to promote the symbolic status of the northeast as the Manchu homeland. From the Qianlong period onward, the Shengjing region in particular began to be called "the place of our Manchu origin" (*Shengjing xi wo Manzhou genben zhi di*), indicating that the Qing court connected the physical locality of Manchuria directly with the ethnicity of the Manchus.[71]

Ginseng in Manchuria was still a matter of importance when Qianlong and his officials were discussing places appropriate for the relocation of Beijing bannermen to Manchuria as a way of resolving the "Eight Banners livelihood problem" (*baqi shengji wenti*). Poverty had been increasing among banner soldiers since the eighteenth century for various reasons, including loss of banner lands and the growth of the banner population, and thus the Qing court was confronted with the challenge of finding solutions to the growing economic problems of the bannermen.[72] In 1741 the court considered the possibility of relocating the bannermen stationed in Beijing and their families to the northeast, where arable land was available. In the course of the discussion regarding appropriate destinations for the bannermen, Grand Secretary Liang Shizheng pointed out that the areas around Hunchun and the Burhatung and Hailan Rivers—two tributaries of the Tumen River—were not to be included among possible resettlement locations, because "these are ginseng-producing areas." He warned that since the bannermen were not familiar with cultivation, they would have to hire Han Chinese peasants to till the land, and these Han people would certainly try to poach ginseng. Therefore, Liang explained, ginseng-producing areas should not be made available for the bannermen's relocation.[73] Every aspect of Qing policy in Manchuria, even concerning the benefits of the bannermen, thus had to give way to the imperatives of the state's ginseng monopoly.

It was for the same purpose of strengthening security in Shengjing and Jilin in general and of checking ginseng poachers at the boundary with the Chosŏn in particular that the idea of a post at Mangniushao was raised again. As briefly discussed in the introduction, in 1745, fifteen years after Nasutu's initial proposal, the newly appointed Shengjing military governor Daldangga wrote a memorial to the Qianlong emperor about the significance of security in Shengjing. Before mentioning the Mangniushao post, Daldangga argued that the Willow Palisade should be repaired and the area between Fenghuangcheng and Weiyuanbao opened for cultivation.[74] For him, a guard post at Mangniushao was not only a matter of securing the boundary with the Chosŏn; it was part of an overall plan to reinforce security in Shengjing. Well aware that his predecessor, Nasutu, had failed to persuade the Yongzheng emperor of the merits of the plan, Daldangga first provided the new emperor with a detailed explanation of the geographic features around Mangniushao. In particular he emphasized that the two streams that converged at Mangniushao, the Caohe and the Aihe, both originated from Changbaishan—the sacred homeland of the Manchu court—and that the region was rich in ginseng, the imperial family's precious asset. Even though a number of outposts had been built and soldiers patrolled regularly to protect the ginseng mountains in the imperial preserves, Daldangga cautioned that "vicious people are still illegally building ships to transport food; they pass through Mangniushao and enter the ginseng preserves in secret."[75] In order to stop them, he argued, one hundred well-trained banner soldiers with nautical experience should be dispatched to Mangniushao. These soldiers should also be allowed to cultivate the land and build houses near the guard post.[76]

Daldangga knew very well that the previous proposal had been rejected mostly because of the Chosŏn court's appeal against it. He thus made a point of refuting Chosŏn arguments, which he believed were absurd and irrational, arguing that security at the boundary would be beneficial for the Chosŏn as well:

> If we miss this opportunity to station soldiers and defend key posts, there will be more people looking to make a profit [at the boundary] as time goes on. There will also be incessant cases of [Qing subjects] coming into contact with Chosŏn people, violating the boundary, and causing trouble. . . . [This military post] will not only prevent unruly people from stealing ginseng but also pacify the boundary with the Chosŏn.[77]

Based on a report from the Xiongyue commander, Daldangga made it clear that the proposed location was outside of Chosŏn territory. All Qing soldiers and ships would be stationed on Qing land, thus precluding any violations of Chosŏn territory. If an illegal Qing ginseng poacher were to be discovered within Chosŏn territory, the military governor's men would be dispatched and would cooperate with Chosŏn soldiers to arrest the perpetrator.[78]

In addition to local officials in Shengjing, court officials on the Board of Rites in Beijing also supported Daldangga's proposal. Even though the previous emperor had accepted the Chosŏn appeal, they emphasized, "strategic locations at the boundary must be thoroughly secured," and the proposed location lay clearly within Qing territory. Court officials further argued that the "decision to construct a military post within Qing territory [*neidi*] should be made by the presiding local official, not necessarily in consultation with the Chosŏn king."[79] In essence, they believed it wrong to compromise the country's security out of fear of disturbing a relationship with a neighboring country. Unlike the Yongzheng emperor, who gave priority to diplomatic relations with the Chosŏn, the emperor's officials in Beijing and Shengjing all emphasized the urgency of the local situation.

IMPERIAL AUTHORITY AT THE MARGINS

News of resumed discussions in Beijing regarding the Mangniushao post soon reached the Chosŏn court. Through several channels, including the tributary envoy in Beijing and local interpreters in Fenghuangcheng, the Chosŏn court managed to gather fragments of information and came to the conclusion that the Qing court was making an attempt to relocate the gate of the Willow Palisade closer to the Chosŏn side.[80] This led to further speculation that by moving the gate, the Shengjing military governor and Qing people would first try to occupy the land at the Yalu River and eventually demand control of Ŭiju and other cities in the Chosŏn northern region. Hence, King Yŏngjo claimed that the Chosŏn would "lose five to ten *li* of its territory every day." Describing the Qing action as analogous to "someone else building a fence outside my gate," Yŏngjo insisted that any relocation of the Qing gate should be prevented.[81]

Anxious to uncover the Qing court's true intentions, especially after receiving news that the Xiongyue commander had already visited the Yalu River, the Chosŏn court decided to ask the Qianlong emperor directly.[82] Given that the Chosŏn letters were usually delivered to the Qing Board of Rites either in Beijing or in Shengjing, any direct form of contact with the emperor was deemed to be "a violation of the heavenly dignity." This unusually direct channel of communication demonstrates how seriously the Chosŏn court took the Qing state's movements at the Yalu River:

> Ever since the imperial court has ruled the world, Your Highness has firmly set the boundary between inside and outside. Concerned with the possibility of vicious

people crossing the boundary in secret, Your Highness built gates and instituted checks at the entrances. The land from the [Qing] gate to the Yalu River, as wide as a hundred *li*, has remained empty, with no one allowed to live on it or till it, and thus people [on either side of the boundary] have not seen or heard each other. It was a considerate plan that permanently secured people's welfare.[83]

Yǒngjo then reminded the Qianlong emperor that the Kangxi and Yongzheng emperors had not approved of land development or the stationing of soldiers at the boundary with the Chosǒn. He also talked about the special relationship between the Qing and Chosǒn courts: "This small country, despite being an outer dependency [K. *oebǒn*] of the imperial court, has considered itself to be within the empire [K. *naebok*]. We have voiced all our concerns, and [the imperial court] has listened to our requests. From these sincere reactions, we have felt [that the imperial court] has expressed unparalleled devotion to us."[84] Yǒngjo described the relationship between the two countries as amicable; it was a relationship in which the Chosǒn had served the Qing with sincerity for generations and, in return, the Qing had treated the Chosǒn generously. Yǒngjo implied that he now expected the Qianlong emperor to listen to the Chosǒn court's request to stop plans to build the Mangniushao post.

The language in the Chosǒn king's letter, which reflected the hierarchical role of a submissive inferior court to "serve the great [court]" (K. *sadae*) and that of a benevolent imperial court to "care for its tributaries" (K. *chaso*), was typical of the tributary relationship. But the same rhetoric could carry very different meanings depending on the context. Hong Taiji had applied this rhetoric in the early seventeenth century when he demanded that the Chosǒn king Injo punish Korean trespassers and emphasized the obligation of the Chosǒn to "serve the great." The mid-eighteenth-century letter from the Chosǒn king Yǒngjo used the same expression but purposely put more weight on the imperial duty to "care for its tributaries." Hong Taiji had used this language to coerce the Chosǒn to accept his authority, whereas Qianlong heard the same words when being asked to accept the Chosǒn court's demands. Another interesting point is that the Chosǒn letter tried to portray the Qing rulers as typical Chinese emperors upholding Confucian virtues, a depiction that supported the Chosǒn demand that Qianlong follow past precedent. In spite of their contempt for the Manchus as non–Han Chinese, the Koreans were willing to bestow the epithet of the Confucian sage king on the Qing emperor in order to bolster their claim against the military post. In this sense, the Koreans were exceptionally adept at manipulating the traditional rhetoric of the tributary relationship for their own purposes.

It is not surprising that Qianlong was displeased with the persistent complaints of the Chosǒn about the plans for the empire's northeastern margins. Daldangga explained repeatedly that a military post at the boundary would benefit the Chosŏn as well, and all the officials in the Boards of Rites, Work, and War concurred with him. Beyond that, the emperor had already approved the plan. Qianlong said to his officials: "The Chosŏn king's memorial admits that some people in his country have taken advantage of the opportunities for trespassing and illegal ginseng gathering. If we station soldiers and patrol [the boundary], these [Koreans] will not be able to cross in secret. The memorial is surely contemptible. People in the small country do not understand what is important; they merely pursue profits and neglect security at the boundary."[85] However, it was equally inappropriate for Qianlong to simply ignore the repeated Chosŏn protests in order to follow Daldangga's proposal. The Chosŏn was one of the oldest tributaries of the Qing empire, a neighbor long favored by the imperial court. If Qianlong desired to live up to the model of a benevolent Confucian king, as Yŏngjo portrayed him, the emperor needed to acknowledge and duly consider the Chosŏn court's petition.

In addition to the Chosŏn court's strong resistance, there were internal voices against the plan. The Grand Councilor, Bandi, after inspecting conditions at the proposed location, secretly reported to the Qianlong emperor that building a military post at Mangniushao would not have a great effect on security, since it was not the only place where illegal trespassers could come and go. He further pointed out that the plan would impose on the court the huge expense of provisioning the soldiers and create a diplomatic problem in its relations with the Chosŏn court.[86] In 1746, Qianlong decided to discontinue the Yalu River development, thereby rejecting one part of Daldangga's plan and at the same time assuaging the biggest concern of the Chosŏn:

> With regard to Daldangga's memorial about the [Yalu River] development, the Chosŏn king mentioned that the land outside the gate has remained off-limits and empty and the inside and the outside have been separated, so that people have been prevented from coming and causing trouble. This rule must be enforced. As for the relocation of the gate, let this plan be stopped, since the Chosŏn king has appealed against it. Let the Board [of Rites] forward this decision to the Chosŏn king.[87]

As this imperial decree called for the cessation of development at the Yalu River, Daldangga's master plan for managing the Shengjing region, which included the renovation of the Willow Palisade from Fenghuangcheng to Weiyuanbao and the relocation of soldiers to military posts at the Yalu River, could not move forward. To maintain military forces at the boundary, Daldangga needed housing and land, which he sought to secure in the empty areas near the Yalu River. When the emperor announced his decision to cease further development near the river, officials on the Board of War attempted to change his mind by reiterating the importance of building a post at Mangniushao. The officials, who described themselves as being "concerned about boundary control," emphasized the good intentions of Daldangga, who "tried to track down vicious thieves and to secure the boundary for eternity." They argued that the Mangniushao post would "terminate any trouble at the boundary forever and be beneficial to the outer dependency [the Chosŏn] as well." They stressed that the Chosŏn complaints were not necessarily serious concerns and that Daldangga's proposed plan should be put into action.[88]

Between his own court officials, who insisted on erecting a guard post at the Yalu River, and the Chosŏn king, who petitioned to stop it, Qianlong favored the Chosŏn, following his father's precedent:

> The proposed location for the new post is within Qing territory, and it is thus irrelevant to the Chosŏn. However, the Chosŏn king, who has been loyal and submissive to our court for generations, is now worried about being held responsible if his people violate the proposed regulation, and he is therefore pleading with us not to build such a post. . . . I could not bear to see the Chosŏn king being blamed for his people's wrongdoings. In accordance with his petition, let the building of the Mangniushao post be stopped; [the Board of Rites should] teach the Chosŏn king to control his people better.[89]

Regardless of the urgency of the need for a military post at the boundary, the Qing emperor could not pursue the proposed plan in the face of the Chosŏn court's persistent appeals against it. The Yongzheng and Qianlong emperors, who sought to uphold the virtues of a Confucian ruler and to embrace the Chosŏn tributary state, decided to sacrifice the potential benefits of a military post at the Yalu River in order to pursue these higher goals. The failed proposal for the Mangniushao post shows that the Qing-Chosŏn relationship had changed significantly over the previous century. The relationship between the two countries was still premised on the asymmetrical hierarchy of a superior and an inferior partner, but it now also allowed space for negotiation and discussion. In addition to this flexible, if not wide open, relationship they also shared an empty zone between their territories, in which the superior court could display its imperial honor while allowing the inferior tributary to keep its benefits. Daldangga's proposal was unsuccessful not simply because the small Chosŏn kingdom succeeded in protecting its territory against the military might of the Qing empire. The emperor's desire to embody the role of the universal ruler, the increasingly negotiable relationship between the imperial center and its tributary state, and a shared conception of territory and sovereignty all combined to obviate the necessity of a clearly drawn line between the two neighbors. Instead, they agreed to perpetuate the borderland by maintaining the existing buffer zone and using force, if necessary, to keep it empty and uninhabited.

The gate and the outposts between the eastern line of the Willow Palisade and the Yalu River remained under the jurisdiction of the Shengjing military governor throughout the Qing period. By the 1770s, there were a total of thirty-seven outposts both inside and outside the eastern line, with each of the outposts being staffed with one officer and ten soldiers. Soldiers were stationed at the outposts located inside the eastern line from winter to next spring and then moved to those outside the line from summer to autumn of each year. This schedule for the patrolling soldiers was surely related to the routine of ginseng gathering, which usually took place during the summer outside the eastern line of the palisade. By the end of the Qianlong reign, the number of outposts around the eastern line had changed, to twelve outside the eastern line and twenty-two inside the line.[90] However, the Qing military presence was not fully visible at this margin of the empire; as Richard Edmonds explains, the Willow Palisade functioned as "an internal boundary rather than the demarcation of the Chinese-Korean border." Even though Qing soldiers supposedly continued their regular patrols and inspections to prevent ginseng poaching and illegal logging, the empty buffer zone demonstrated "the lack of strategic or political concern at the Qing court for a clearly defined boundary with Korea."[91]

Qianlong might have had little interest in a clearly drawn boundary line with Chosŏn territory because he was full of confidence in the superiority of his status vis-à-vis his Chosŏn tributary. His ideas about the territorial limits of the Qing empire can perhaps be glimpsed in his famous poem about the Willow Palisade, which he wrote in 1754, less than a decade after the debates over the Mangniushao post, when he went on a hunting trip from Jehol through Inner Mongolia to Jilin. The physical barrier in the northeast, the emperor announced, had now become insignificant:

> Building it is the same as not having built it
> In so far as the idea exists and the framework is there, there is no
>   need to elaborate
> The methods of predecessors are preserved by descendants
> When there are secure fortifications it is peaceful for ten thousand
>   years
> How can this be dependent upon these insignificant willows?[92]

When he wrote this poem, Qianlong seemed "to believe that the deterioration of the Willow Palisade was a sign of the virtue of his rule, for no barrier was necessary to regulate the movement of people when the ruler was a true sage."[93] It is surely questionable whether Qianlong's confidence was based on the reality of Qing supremacy or merely expressed an ungrounded wish. However, it is clear that his confidence in his rulership was not limited to Qing territory but also reached the boundary with the Chosŏn. In his view, the imperial power of the Qing extended beyond such trivial barriers as the Willow Palisade; the emperor's prominence was not circumscribed by the narrow rivers dividing the great country and the tributary state. Just as his grandfather Kangxi had done in the case of the 1712 Changbaishan investigation, the Qianlong emperor believed the presentation of imperial power was more important than securing a clear boundary with the Chosŏn.

. . .

The debates around the Mangniushao post at the Yalu River demonstrate that the Qing-Chosŏn borderland was managed and practiced in accordance with the dual principles of the Qing policy on Manchuria and its relationship with the Chosŏn. The Qing economic interest in ginseng production in Manchuria was one of the main reasons why the Qing authorities paid special attention to preventing access by Han civilians to the region. This restrictive policy was also aimed at keeping Koreans away from the Yalu and Tumen Rivers and Changbaishan. The desire of the Qing to protect Manchuria, together with the Chosŏn court's wish to avoid trouble with the great country, led the two states to ban settlement at the boundary and eventually to create the borderland through the imposition of an empty buffer zone between the two countries. This incident also helps us understand the changeability of Qing-Chosŏn relations. Korean trespassing in Qing territory was a constant occurrence from the Nurhaci era to the Qianlong reign, but the Qing court's responses changed over time. The early Manchu rulers imposed harsh punishments on Korean criminals—a policy aimed at forcing the Chosŏn court to accept their power. Unlike their seventeenth-century predecessors, however, the Qing emperors in the eighteenth century ruled over a vast territory populated by diverse groups of people, and they sought to represent themselves as the universal rulers of all subjects of the empire, including the Manchus, the Han, the Mongols, the Uighurs, and the Tibetans.[94]

Such universalism was necessarily reflected also on those living outside the imperial domain. In relation to a tributary state as old as the Chosŏn, in particular, the Qing emperors cast themselves as the benevolent rulers of the Confucian world, an image that required them to accept Korean demands, at least to some degree. The aborted proposal for the Mangniushao post offers an example of how the Qing ruling ideology was projected in its foreign relations. The Chosŏn court's loyalty was very useful and important for justifying Qing rule, while its potential as a military threat to the Qing empire was minimal. Because of this carefully weighed positioning, one can argue that Qing universalism in the eighteenth century actually helped the Chosŏn king protect his territory and sovereignty. This peculiarity of the tributary relationship between the Qing and the Chosŏn led to the creation and maintenance of the borderland, whose logic did not permit the establishment of a military post. Instead, the same tributary relationship invited people and money to flourishing markets in this supposedly empty zone, as chapter 4 demonstrates.

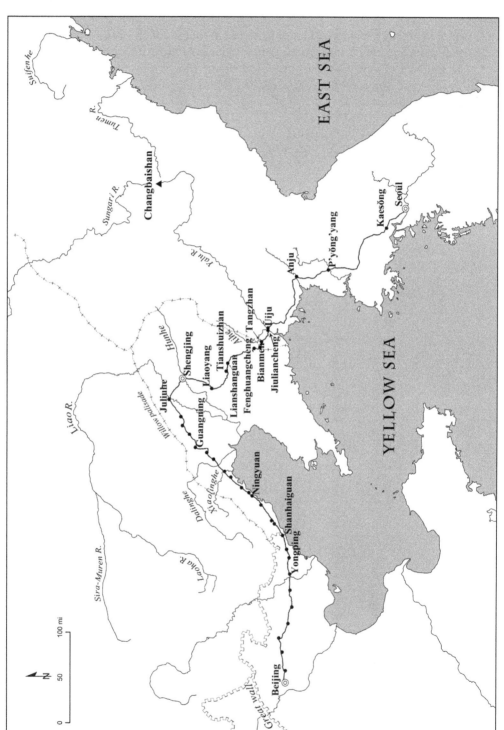

MAP 4. The Chosŏn tributary embassy's travel route

4

Movement of People and Money

On January 8, 1748, the Shengjing military governor Daldangga received a report that property belonging to a member of the Chosŏn embassy had been stolen as the group had passed Liaoyang, a city within Daldangga's jurisdiction.[1] According to the initial report delivered through Korean interpreters, the victim was Sahwan, a Korean packhorse driver serving the embassy on its journey to Beijing. He was also a servant of Yun Ch'angli, the Korean official in charge of the embassy's luggage. Sahwan reported what he had seen:

> When we arrived near Wanbaoqiao, a man riding a horse turned up all of a sudden shouting out loud. My horse was so frightened that it ran away. I hurried to catch up with the horse and found it standing in front of a house. There I saw one of the two packages of silver [that the horse had been carrying] on the ground, but the other package was gone. . . . We asked [the people in the house] about the silver, but they said they didn't know about it. Later, my colleagues searched through the house and found the silver package hidden in a pile of sorghum.[2]

Sahwan pointed to Song Erdazi, a Qing subject living in Wanbaoqiao, as the prime suspect. Song's testimony was, however, very different from the Korean servant's presentation of the case:

> When I had made a fire [inside my house] . . . the Koreans appeared at the gate, asking for a light for tobacco. Near the gate was a pile of firewood; it was very windy on that morning, so I did not give it to them. Then they asked me the way, so I opened the gate. Upon coming in, however, they started talking all of a sudden about their lost luggage, rummaging through my house with one hand while tying me up with the other. . . . As the day dawned, the Koreans returned, insisting that their silver had been found in the pile of sorghum in my house and tying me up again.[3]

This incident, which later became known as "Korean Sahwan's false accusation of theft," was reported by Daldangga to the Board of Rites in Beijing and eventually to the Chosŏn court in Seoul, and it troubled the Qing and Chosŏn courts for several years to come.

This chapter discusses the Chosŏn tributary embassy and their trade as the background of the Sahwan case and then examines the subsequent series of disputes involving the Shengjing military governor and the Chosŏn court. Two problems are of special concern here. First, the Qing and Chosŏn courts had established a tributary relationship that not only defined the nature of their political ties but also shaped their economic connections. Qing foreign policy guaranteed regular visits and the payment of tribute by the subordinate neighbor, and this regular ritual had an unexpected side effect: the creation of a variety of trading opportunities for Qing and Chosŏn merchants. Second, the empty buffer zone north of the Yalu River—maintained through the consensus of the Qing emperors and the Chosŏn kings—created a space and an opportunity for Koreans to make contact with local people in Qing territory. The frequent and regular contacts between the Chosŏn embassy and local Qing people led to the development of flourishing markets on the route from Fenghuangcheng to Shengjing.

In his analysis of the trade between Chosŏn Korea and Tokugawa Japan, James Lewis explains that "frontiers [such as Tsushima and Pusan] . . . [as] the sites of actual contacts" were as important as national centers in the formation of cultural perceptions and historical memory.[4] If Tsushima and Pusan were the contacting locations between Chosŏn Korea and Tokugawa Japan, it was Fenghuangcheng and Shengjing where Qing China and Chosŏn Korea met. Details of actual contacts at the boundary near the Yalu River and the Qing northeastern margin, in fact, revealed unknown dimensions of Qing-Chosŏn relations. A centralized perspective on Qing-Chosŏn tributary relations assumes that the courts in Beijing and Seoul had a single, direct connection and portrays other contacts, which took place in the periphery, as trivial, marginal, and even abnormal. For Beijing and Seoul, whose shared primary interest was to maintain proper tributary rituals, the incident involving Sahwan and Song Erdazi was merely an annoyance for both sides. From the perspective of the periphery, however, the practice of paying tribute not only served to maintain the political hierarchy between the Qing emperor and the Chosŏn king, but also affected the development of physical contacts and commercial exchange between people from the two countries. The tributary embassy provided a legitimate opportunity for many Korean profit seekers to cross the Yalu River and enter Qing territory, as well as for local Qing merchants and ordinary people to benefit from trade with the Chosŏn embassy.

This chapter also demonstrates the ways in which the empty, restricted area near the boundary and the peripheral margins of the empire were commercialized by the tributary relations. Fenghuangcheng and Shengjing witnessed the growth and thriving of trade and transportation related to the Chosŏn embassy in the eighteenth century. Local Qing people and Chosŏn merchants alike took advantage of the vacancy created at the boundary and developed various ways to exploit trade opportunities in the area. On the other hand, the frequent contacts between Chosŏn visitors and Qing locals sometimes turned into conflicts, mostly over money, and minor arguments sometimes developed into serious tensions between Beijing and Seoul. The tributary relationship attracted people and money to the Yalu River, but in the end the resulting contacts and conflicts caused Qing authority to be enforced to the Chosŏn court in Seoul. Tribute and trade combined to commercialize the Qing-Chosŏn boundary and some parts of the Qing northeast margin, yet this process was limited and controlled by the asymmetrical relations between the Qing and the Chosŏn.

THE CHOSŎN TRIBUTARY EMBASSY

The 1637 peace treaty between the Qing and Chosŏn courts required the Koreans to send royal embassies to the Qing to celebrate the winter solstice, New Year's Day, and the emperor's birthday, in addition to paying an annual tribute to Beijing. In 1645, when the Qing capital moved from Shengjing to Beijing, the Manchus allowed the Chosŏn court to combine other embassies with the winter solstice embassy because of the lengthened tribute route. This became known as the annual tribute or the regular embassy.[5] There were also various types of irregular embassies.[6] The composition of any given embassy varied according to the specific obligations and duties of the party. The leading members of the embassy were court officials, including the chief ambassador (K. chŏngsa), the vice ambassador (K. pusa), and the attendant secretary (K. sŏjanggwan). The chief ambassador was nominated from among members of the royal family or high officials, and he represented the Chosŏn king to the Qing emperor. The vice ambassador was in charge of the general office work of the embassy, while the attendant secretary supervised all affairs relevant to the embassy, notably regulations on smuggling.[7] In practice, however, these high officials did not directly manage the tributary mission because they were not permitted to communicate with Qing officials at will; every discussion had to be conveyed through written memorials. Go-betweens from the Office of Interpreters (K. Sayŏgwŏn) dealt with all practical matters. The chief interpreter essentially managed the mission, from trivial transactions with local merchants during the journey to important discussions with Qing officials pertaining to rituals at the imperial court. High court officials were thus in actuality simply nominal representatives, whereas the interpreters were the actual managers of the embassy.[8]

Tribute embassies also included military guards (K. kun'gwan) and other minor officials. These individuals were in charge of keeping records of the tribute and other goods, hiring porters and carts for transportation to Beijing, and protecting

FIGURE 9. *Sanhaegwan tongnasŏng* (eastern rampart of Shanhaiguan), circa 1784. Hand scroll, ink and color on paper, 35.4 × 45.3 cm. From *Yŏnhaengdo: Paintings of the Korean Envoys to Beijing during the Joseon Dynasty* (Seoul: Sungsil taehakkyo Hanguk Kidokkyo Pangmulgwan, 2009), 12. Used with permission.

the luggage from the predations of the local porters. Besides such minor officials, numerous retainers also served the embassy. The Chosŏn court sought to prevent an excessive number of people from joining the embassy, but since the number of retainers was not officially fixed, uncounted individuals were able to slip into the embassy entourage.[9] In addition to retainers, there were painters, astronomers, physicians, and others who usually had some connection with embassy officials. Moreover, numerous people joined the delegation to carry the tribute and the luggage and to lead the horses during the journey. With all of these participants, the total number of people in an embassy often exceeded three hundred.[10] By the early eighteenth century, the number had continued to grow; for example, 687 people crossed the Yalu River in the embassy of 1712.[11]

The Chosŏn embassy faced a long journey to the Qing imperial court. Traveling to Beijing from the Yalu River via Shengjing took a month.[12] Adding in the 1,070 *li* from Seoul to the Yalu River, the journey time totaled more than six weeks. Including the customary monthlong stay in Beijing, the whole round trip took at least four months and could easily last up to five or six months.[13] Although Beijing could be reached either by land or by sea, the land route was preferred because the sea-based journey was more dangerous. During the period when the Manchus were fighting Ming forces in Liaodong, the Chosŏn embassy traveled across the sea to the Ming court in Beijing. Once the Qing conquered China proper, the land route became the official travel route.

The final inspection of tribute embassies in Korea occurred in Ŭiju, a city on the Yalu River. A rigorous search for illegal group members was carried out, because the number of positions in the embassy was always significantly smaller than the number of people seeking entry into Qing territory. All of the tribute, people, and horses were checked. If anyone who was not officially listed was found in the embassy, the inspector in Ŭiju and the responsible embassy official were both punished.[14] However, this inspection was often meaningless, since no matter how meticulous the controls, it was impossible to prevent all illegal crossings. Pak Chiwŏn (1737–1805), who participated in the tribute embassy to Beijing for the commemoration of the Qianlong emperor's seventieth birthday in 1780, provides us with a description of the stunning sight of the embassy at the shore of the Yalu River.[15] Pak was particularly astonished by the great hassle created by the inspection, as embassy officials searched every item of luggage in order to prevent smuggling:

> People are asked for their name, residence, age, facial features, height, et cetera. The inspectors of the embassy and the Ŭiju office examine every single piece of luggage to check for any illegal items, such as gold, silver, pearls, ginseng, furs, or weapons. Attendants and servants take off their shirts and pants and open their luggage to show to the officials. Bundles of linens and clothes and various boxes are scattered all around the shore. Without these inspections, there is no way to prevent smuggling. However, the inspections inevitably create great inconvenience. Nonetheless, even this inspection is nothing but a ritual. Since the Ŭiju merchants sneak across the river prior to the inspection, what effect does it really have?[16]

Pak was surprised again after crossing the river. On his first night in Qing territory, he witnessed people setting up their tents to spend the night in an open field; others were busy cooking meals and tending to horses. Instead of viewing an unspoiled territory, as the Yongzheng and Qianlong emperors might have expected, Pak found a scene reminiscent of any common village.[17] Pak's vivid descriptions of the scenes at the Yalu River seem to contradict conventional assumptions about the Qing northeast, a region that held special meaning and value for the Qing imperial court and to which access was therefore supposedly rigorously prohibited. This sacred birthplace of the Manchus was supposed to be protected from all intruders, whether coming from China proper beyond Shanhaiguan or from Korea across the Yalu River. However, Pak's group of Chosŏn emissaries were left to their own devices for the first night after crossing the Yalu River and were not met by Qing officials until the next day.

After crossing the Yalu River, the Chosŏn embassy was led to pass through the designated gate at the foot of the Fenghuang mountain. This first Qing gate, which Koreans called Ch'aengmun, was located along the Willow Palisade, thirty *li* away from Fenghuangcheng, the Qing administrative office that was closest to the Chosŏn. The gate was 90 *li* away from the Yalu River and 120 *li* from Ŭiju.[18] Since there were no postal stations between the Yalu River and the gate of Fenghuangcheng, the embassy had to camp out for two days before arriving in Fenghuangcheng. Korean authors of travel diaries about journeys to Beijing often remarked that they entered Qing territory by crossing the Yalu River, but there was, in fact, an uninhabited area between the Yalu and the Qing gate. Pak Chiwŏn noted that when he crossed the river, the land seemed abandoned:

> The land near Jiuliancheng has . . . not only high mountains and deep waters, but also wide fields and rich woods. I expected to see a big village where houses are so crowded that the residents can hear each other's dogs and chickens. The land is seemingly very fertile and suitable for reclamation. . . . It could support the establishment of a huge military garrison. However, both we [the Chosŏn] and they [the Qing] have abandoned it to make an empty land [K. *han'gu*].[19]

Pak's description corresponds with Marion Eggert's explanation that "the Ŭiju border was considered a tripartite form, consisting of first the Yalu River, then a stretch of wilderness, and finally the palisade with its gate."[20] What Pak found, then, was not a clear-cut line dividing two neighbors; rather, it was a zone or a thick line. The land near the Yalu River remained empty, as the Qing and Chosŏn courts had agreed, but it also created unintended confusion about the exact limits of the two countries' territories, at least in the eyes of Korean travelers. While crossing the Yalu River, Pak Chiwŏn encountered a group of local people sailing across the river on their way back to Fenghuangcheng after logging timber in Changbaishan.[21] According to the Qing restriction policy, such a violation of the sacred mountain was a serious crime, but it nonetheless took place in front of the Korean visitors' eyes. Near Fenghuangcheng, Pak also met a group of people who were on their way to serve their military duty: "They were on donkeys, looking ragged and tired," he wrote. "I realized that [the Chosŏn boundary control] is more reliable whereas China's is very lax."[22] The strict regulations that the emperor issued in Beijing were seemingly failing to reach the empire's margins.

After passing through the vacant land, the Chosŏn embassy reached the Fenghuangcheng office. A Korean interpreter was sent ahead to the gate to report the arrival of the embassy, so the Fenghuangcheng senior commandant received the Korean visitors at the gate. Qing officials also checked the number of people in the embassy and the amount of luggage they had with them against the delivered documents. Any Koreans whose names were not listed were prohibited from passing through the gate.[23] However, there were numerous opportunities to evade this inspection. In 1806, for example, the Fenghuangcheng office allowed a given number of Koreans to come to the gate from Ŭiju in order to provide food and other necessities for the Chosŏn embassy. Despite the Qing court's warning to the Koreans not to abuse this opportunity to cross the river, Korean merchants considered it official permission to visit the Qing gate for trading.[24]

Dealing with the corruption of local Qing officials was an expected part of passing through the Fenghuangcheng gate. When the Korean embassy brought their tribute and luggage to the gate, its members usually presented a certain quantity of gifts to the Fenghuangcheng office. But these offerings eventually became a required "entrance fee" that grew every year as the Qing officials increased their demands. The exchange of "gifts" at the gate often developed into a fistfight between Korean interpreters and Qing soldiers and porters.[25] The abuses by the Fenghuangcheng officials grew more and more egregious, to the point that in 1811 court officials in Beijing formally accused them of having received Korean bribes for entry through the gate.[26] Two years later, Fenghuangcheng officials were criticized again for exacting bribes and entrance fees from the Koreans.[27] Korean aspirations to enter China caused the rampant corruption of Qing officials at the crossing point; but on the other hand, this corruption also made it possible for numerous unauthorized Koreans to continue to cross into Qing territory.

TRADING OPPORTUNITIES

Koreans participating in tribute missions were given an official right to do business during their journey to Beijing. During the Qing period, Korean embassies were officially permitted to carry up to eighty *kŭn* (C. *jin*) of ginseng, or the equivalent value in silver or other goods. A bundle (K. *p'o*) contained ten *kŭn* of ginseng, so the total trading allowance equaled eight bundles (K. *p'alp'o*). Later, the term *p'alp'o* came to stand specifically for the Chosŏn embassies' right to trade in China.[28] The *p'alp'o* trading right was granted to embassy officials, including the chief ambassador, the vice ambassador, the attendant secretary, military guards, and interpreters. It held more importance for interpreters than it did for high officials, because the former regarded the *p'alp'o* trading right as a substitute for their salaries, while the latter thought of it more as a bonus for serving the court.

Chinese silk was the main item that Korean merchants wanted to purchase when they visited the Qing empire. The Korean love for Chinese silk is described well in the stories of Zheng Shitai, a Beijing merchant who supplied Koreans with silk fabrics from Jiangsu and Zhejiang Provinces. Every year he ordered Chinese silk products worth as much as one hundred thousand *liang* of silver, all intended for his Korean customers. If the silk Zheng had ordered did not arrive in time, the Chosŏn embassy would actually postpone its departure from Beijing.[29] Winter hats made in Zhonghousuo, a town near Shanhaiguan, were among the other Chinese commodities that were popular with the Koreans. Hong Taeyong (1731–1783)

TABLE 2 The size of the *p'alp'o* trade.

	Rank (number of individuals)	Silver allowed per person (*liang*)	Total amount of silver (*liang*)
High officials	Chief ambassador (1)	3,000	3,000
	Vice ambassador (1)	3,000	3,000
	Attendant secretary (1)	2,000	2,000
	Military guards (7)	2,000	14,000
Subtotals	(10)		22,000
Interpreters (temporary positions)	Chief interpreters (2)	3,000	6,000
	High interpreters (2)	2,000	4,000
	Official for questions (1)	2,000	2,000
	Officials for local products (8)	2,000	16,000
	Officials for annual tributes (3)	2,000	6,000
	Officials for food (2)	2,000	4,000
	Manchu interpreter (1)	2,000	2,000
	Assistant interpreter (1)	2,000	2,000
	Ŭiju military officials (2)	2,000	4,000
Subtotals	(22)		46,000
Minor officials (temporary positions)	Physician (1)	2,000	2,000
	Writer (1)	2,000	2,000
	Painter (1)	2,000	2,000
Subtotals	(3)		6,000
Total	(35)		74,000

SOURCE: Yu and Yi, *Chosŏn hugi Chungguk kwa ŭi muyŏksa*, 57.

visited hat shops in Zhonghousuo and declared, "All of our Korean hats come from here."[30] Fifteen years later, Pak Chiwŏn confirmed that Koreans still purchased huge numbers of Chinese winter hats made in Zhonghousuo, adding, "If you calculate the amount of silver we bring to China on these winter solstice embassies [and other official missions] . . . it is no less than one hundred thousand *liang* of silver. In ten years the total comes to one million *liang*."[31] Silver was the currency most commonly used to buy Chinese products, but the Koreans also traded other items, such as paper, fans, hides, cotton fabrics, and furs. Besides silk, Korean visitors also purchased cotton, dyes, pepper, fruit, and pottery; most of these purchases they made at the Fenghuangcheng gate.[32]

Various opportunities for trading were available to the Chosŏn embassy between the Yalu River and the Fenghuangcheng gate.[33] From Ŭiju to the Fenghuangcheng gate, the embassy had to manage the transportation of the tribute and other luggage by itself. This seemingly inconvenient situation in fact provided the Korean merchants with a huge business opportunity. The Ŭiju office often sent extra horses to accompany the envoy in case of unexpected incidents during the journey, and these spare horses did not go to the Fenghuangcheng gate with empty carts. Korean merchants used them to carry their own commodities to trade with the local Chinese at the gate. The number of spare horses increased steadily, along with the frequency of this type of private trade. Officially, merchants were allowed to bring only a dozen horses, but a Chosŏn court official noted in 1686, "In these days private merchants and officials in the embassy take as many as one thousand horses."[34]

The area beyond the Fenghuangcheng gate on the way to Shengjing also provided the Koreans with plentiful opportunities for trade. Once the Chosŏn tribute was delivered to Shengjing, it was managed by Qing officials and soldiers. After the goods were handed over, a Chosŏn official with the title of military escort (K. *tallyŏnsa*) returned to Ŭiju with the part of the embassy that was not traveling on to Beijing. On his way back, he often used the horses, now relieved of their burdens, to carry the commodities he had acquired in Shengjing. Before 1705, the *tallyŏnsa* was selected from among the military officers in Ŭiju, but subsequently a merchant was appointed to the position. By the time the *tallyŏnsa* left Shengjing and returned to Ŭiju, he had often made too many purchases to carry in his own carts. He then hired local Qing people to deliver his goods to the Fenghuangcheng gate, where Koreans from Ŭiju were waiting to receive him. Those who came to meet the *tallyŏnsa* at the gate themselves never arrived empty-handed; they also did not want to miss the chance to trade Korean commodities with local people in Fenghuangcheng.[35]

These systemic appropriations by Korean merchants of the horses and services provided for the tribute embassy transformed the Qing gate into an active marketplace. Korean interpreters described the situation at the gate around 1715 as follows:

> In the past ten years, the city [of Fenghuangcheng] has grown, as the market developed and more people moved in. When the market opened, the city was full of carts and horses, carrying cotton from Jinzhou, Fuzhou, Haizhou, and Gaizhou; cotton fabrics from Shenyang and Shandong; and hats from Zhonghousuo and Liaoyang. Ships from the south [China] also came to the harbor of Niuzhuang. Beijing merchants came to the Fenghuangcheng gate with silk and other commodities. The shops on the streets looked like those in any city inside Shanhaiguan. The clothes and accessories worn by the merchants [at the Fenghuangcheng gate] were as splendid and lavish as those of high officials.[36]

In order to prolong the time available for conducting business in Fenghuangcheng, embassy interpreters often cooperated with private merchants and delayed the embassy's departure from the gate to the Yalu River. Korean officials complained about the widespread smuggling and hectic trade at the Fenghuangcheng gate:

> On their way back to the Chosŏn, officials in the embassy often hurry to leave and cross the Yalu River. These officials do not want to wait for [their servants who have

FIGURE 10. *Choyangmun* (Gate of Rising Sun), circa 1784. Hand scroll, ink and color on paper, 35.4 × 45.3 cm. From *Yŏnhaengdo: Paintings of the Korean Envoys to Beijing during the Joseon Dynasty* (Seoul: Sungsil taehakkyo Hanguk Kidokkyo Pangmulgwan, 2009), 14. Used with permission.

to move slowly to transport] the imperial gifts for the king, so they are the first ones to cross the Yalu River. They eventually leave behind [at the Fenghuangcheng gate] interpreters and retainers from the embassy, who are free to go back and forth between the gate and Ŭiju. They are given a lot of time to trade with Qing people.[37]

The departure of the high officials gave the rest of the embassy free rein to conduct trade. In this way, the Qing-Chosŏn tributary relations made their boundary wide open to Korean merchants.

THE TRANSPORTATION BUSINESS

If the Korean traders were mostly interpreters and Ŭiju merchants, their Qing counterparts were local merchants in Fenghuangcheng and Shengjing. The best opportunity for local people to work with the Koreans was in helping to transport the Chosŏn embassy's huge amount of baggage—the tribute for the Qing emperor and food and necessities for the embassy itself—across the Yalu River, through

Fenghuangcheng, and on to Shengjing. The local porters were mainly villagers who lived along the road between Fenghuangcheng and Shengjing, a route that included eight postal stations in the Shengjing region, which were known as the "eight eastern stations" (*Dong bazhan*).[38] Upon arrival in Shengjing, the Chosŏn tribute was handed over to the Shengjing Board of Revenue; a portion of it was left in Shengjing, and the rest was taken on to the imperial court in Beijing. The transport and care of the tribute now became the responsibility of Qing officials.[39] The Chosŏn tribute was not the only item to be delivered. The Korean visitors often wished to travel more comfortably, so they employed local people to drive them in horse-drawn carriages to Shengjing or even all the way to Beijing. By the nineteenth century, it was so common for members of the Korean embassy, even interpreters and traders, to rent carriages in Fenghuangcheng that "riding on a horse became a matter of shame."[40]

For the local people living in this remote margin of the Qing realm, the business of providing transportation for the Korean embassy presented an infrequent but very profitable opportunity. The transport business soon became an important part of the local economy. As a Korean visitor pointed out, "Local people [at the eight stations] were entirely dependent for their living on transportation of Korean luggage."[41] In 1660, a Korean traveler noticed that it was easier and cheaper to hire local porters in the winter, when they were not working in the fields.[42] By the late seventeenth century, wages for transportation were standardized: "It costs five *liang* of silver to have a piece of luggage carried from Fenghuangcheng [to Shengjing]. The same trip in the other direction was twice as expensive.... People from the eight stations make huge profits, so the streets are full of lavish houses." If a cart could carry several pieces of luggage at once, the wages that local porters earned were indeed substantial.[43] Pak Chiwŏn also recognized the economic benefits that Qing locals accrued from the Korean embassies. When he asked people living near the Fenghuangcheng gate about their livelihoods, he was told, "Our lives would be threatened without the visits from your country."[44]

The lucrative business of luggage transportation for the Chosŏn embassy soon attracted the attention of the Shengjing merchants, who in the late seventeenth century organized a group called the *lantou* to monopolize the Korean trade: "From 1689 onward, a local man in Liaodong named Hu Jiapei organized a transportation cartel called the *lantou*. Hu and other merchants took exclusive charge of carrying the luggage [of the Chosŏn embassies]."[45] These merchants were so rich that they were believed to "have a thousand slaves and keep numerous mistresses." Most importantly, they had a close relationship with Qing officials in the Shengjing Boards of Rites and Revenue. Seven of the twelve *lantou* merchants were, in fact, Shengjing officials. Therefore, even before the granting of official approval for the *lantou* business, the Shengjing office informed the Korean embassy that their luggage should be handled by the *lantou* merchants.[46]

The *lantou* cartel, operating under the protection of the Shengjing office, exploited the Chosŏn embassies. First, the *lantou* merchants intervened in the scheduling of the Chosŏn embassy's departure and dates of stay, so that the embassy often had to stay in Qing territory for several additional months, wasting funds and causing perishable goods to spoil. Second, the Qing merchants often provided poor service; for example, in 1690, when the Fenghuangcheng senior commandant came to the gate to receive the Chosŏn embassy, the *lantou* merchants, blaming the rain, did not show up to take the embassy's luggage. Without *lantou* transportation, the members of the Chosŏn embassy had to sleep in their carts in the rain.[47] Korean discontent with the *lantou* monopoly is well documented in Chosŏn records:

> Once the Chinese *lantou* merchants began to monopolize transportation, the delivery fee doubled. These greedy Chinese merchants volunteer to pay taxes to the Shengjing office and cooperate with the officials there, and in return they monopolize the benefits from the Korean trade. At the Qing gate, they intentionally delay the departure of the embassy [to Ŭiju] or tell the [Chosŏn] officials to return to Korea first, and then they trade freely [with the merchants].[48]

The *lantou* merchants developed a special connection with the Korean interpreters, who helped increase the former's influence over the Chosŏn embassies. When the Koreans arrived in Fenghuangcheng, the *lantou* held a lavish reception banquet to entertain the foreign visitors.[49] On the way back to Ŭiju, the attendant secretary and minor officials in charge of the luggage were invited to stay at an extravagant house owned by the *lantou* merchants.[50] It was arguably the Korean interpreters who monitored an embassy and provided information about it to the *lantou* merchants. One Korean official cynically noted, "There are fourteen *lantou* merchants," referring to the twelve Qing merchants plus the two embassy interpreters covertly collaborating with them.[51]

The monopoly of the *lantou* cartel was not favorable for Korean traders. When some of the Korean merchants purchased illegal commodities in Shengjing and were caught in the inspection in Fenghuangcheng, the *lantou* used this opportunity to curb Korean merchants from making transactions without its approval. The *lantou* merchants manipulated the Fenghuangcheng officials into complaining to the Chosŏn court about illegal Korean trade, an accusation that led to the dismissal of the Ŭiju magistrate on charges of neglecting the inspections at the Yalu River.[52] This incident demonstrates the influence of the *lantou* merchants: their power reached the Chosŏn court and affected Chosŏn inspections at the Yalu River.

The *lantou* cartel also exploited local Qing people at the eight eastern stations. While the *lantou* merchants charged the Korean embassy ten *liang* of silver for delivering a cart to Liaoyang, they paid local porters only two and a half *liang* and kept the remaining seven and a half *liang* for themselves. In 1712 the local people

FIGURE 11. *Chogong* (tributary ritual), circa 1784. Hand scroll, ink and color on paper, 35.4 × 45.3 cm. From *Yŏnhaengdo: Paintings of the Korean Envoys to Beijing during the Joseon Dynasty* (Seoul: Sungsil taehakkyo Hanguk Kidokkyo Pangmulgwan, 2009), 16. Used with permission.

sought to reclaim the profits from business with the Koreans by taking legal action against the *lantou* impositions.[53] In response to this litigation, and with the intent to protect their cartel, the *lantou* merchants bribed the Manchu officials in Shengjing, who eventually wrote a memorial to the Kangxi emperor requesting that the *lantou* organization be protected rather than abolished. The money for the bribe, surprisingly, came from the Chosŏn embassy.[54] In the end, the *lantou* won the lawsuit and maintained its monopoly over the provision of transportation services to the Korean embassy.

Continuing abuses by the *lantou* merchants finally led the Chosŏn king, Kyŏngjong (r. 1720–24), to ask the Yongzheng emperor to abolish the cartel. Soon the Qing and Chosŏn courts launched a joint investigation of Hu Jiapei and other *lantou* merchants in Fenghuangcheng. In 1723, Hu was finally deprived of his monopolistic right to the Korean trade and made to wear a cangue for three months after receiving one hundred lashes from a flogging leather (*bian*). Not only were the *lantou* merchants punished, but the Fenghuangcheng senior commandant was also disciplined for corruption and abuse of power. After the *lantou* cartel was dismantled, the Korean embassy was once again free to hire carts and horsemen directly from the local Qing population.[55] However, the breakup of the *lantou* did not come without a cost. Since the Shengjing and Fenghuangcheng offices lost two thousand *liang* of tax income and other benefits that they had received from the *lantou* merchants, the Qing officials turned to the Koreans with their grievances. To appease them, the Korean embassy agreed to hire only local porters recommended by the Fenghuangcheng officials.[56]

"DISHONORING THE STATE"

As early as 1700, it was known that some Koreans associated with the Chosŏn embassy were indebted to Qing merchants. Well aware that such a situation might cause further problems, the Chosŏn court ordered the decapitation of any Korean trader owing money to Qing subjects, regardless of the value of the debt.[57] However, even this harsh ruling failed to end credit transactions between Qing and Chosŏn merchants. Trading on credit became an issue again in 1706, when Qing merchants in Fenghuangcheng made an official complaint about Korean liabilities.[58] The following year, the Chosŏn court sent the accused debtors to Fenghuangcheng for interrogation, which revealed that only one out of the nine accused Koreans had actually borrowed any money. The rest were being falsely accused: the contracts with the accused Koreans had been forged and signed by the Qing accusers themselves. The Fenghuangcheng senior commandant, evidently backing his countrymen, told the Chosŏn officials that he was interested only in receiving the money owed and was not concerned with the fate of the debtors.[59]

It was in 1724, soon after the dissolution of the *lantou* cartel, that the enduring credit practices finally caused serious diplomatic tensions between the Qing and Chosŏn courts. In that year, the Shengjing officials found that Hu Jiapei and his eleven cosigners, the former *lantou* merchants, owed a substantial amount of money to the Shengjing office.[60] The money, which the *lantou* merchants had borrowed from the office over more than seventeen years, was now tied up in huge outstanding loans to numerous people, including thirty-eight officials in the Shengjing office and eighteen in the Imperial Household Department in Beijing. The greatest debtors, however, were Korean traders. There were 247 Korean debtors who together owed more than sixty thousand *liang* of silver.[61]

The Shengjing office reported the staggering Korean debts to the Yongzheng emperor, who eventually ordered the Chosŏn court to investigate the issue and to repay the money. However, the emperor's order to cross-examine the Qing accusers and the Chosŏn accused at Zhongjiang on the Yalu River was nearly impossible to follow. One of the problems was that there was no way to locate the hundreds of Korean traders who frequently changed their names and constantly moved back and forth across the Yalu River. Beyond the issue of locating the debtors, the Chosŏn court also had no intention of spending more than sixty thousand *liang* to pay off private debts. Clearing these debts on behalf of private traders would have set a precedent that would have opened the door for similar claims by the Qing in the future. After long discussions, the Chosŏn court decided to explain to the Shengjing office that the Korean debtors should, indeed, be decapitated on the shore of the Yalu River but that their private debts would not be taken care of by the state.[62] As a result of the Chosŏn court's repeated petitions, the Yongzheng emperor finally decided to dismiss the case of Korean debts to Qing merchants in 1728:

> The late Chosŏn king [Sukchong] was praised by the Kangxi emperor for his capability and modesty. He enforced the law properly to punish Korean debtors and acted fairly. I have heard that the present king [Yŏngjo] is weak and incompetent. . . . An investigation of debtors would be beyond his capacity. Ordering [the Chosŏn king] to undertake an impossible task is not appropriate to my intent to embrace foreigners. Therefore, it is not necessary to interrogate the criminals. I am generously waiving the silver that the Chosŏn subjects are supposed to pay. This decision is meant to bestow a favor on a foreign subordinate [*waifan*], not to ease regulations on foreigners to a greater extent than is the case for people in the inner land [*neidi*].[63]

In referring to the Chosŏn king as weak and incompetent, this imperial letter was surely insulting to the Koreans. After the embarrassing incident of "falling into debt to the Qing and dishonoring the state" (K. *Chŏngch'ae yokkuk*),[64] the Chosŏn court tried to implement rules limiting Korean trade with Qing merchants. Upset with the accusations made by the Yongzheng emperor, the Chosŏn king Yŏngjo blamed the credit problem on rampant trade activities. His court officials agreed that it was the private merchants sneaking along with the embassy to Shengjing who were causing all the trouble. The Chosŏn court was convinced that as long as merchants continued to join the tributary embassy traveling to Shengjing, humiliating problems such as financial obligations to Qing merchants would persist.[65] Finally, the court decided to authorize trade in Shengjing only for the embassy's interpreters. Soon thereafter, other types of trade, such as using extra horses at the Fenghuangcheng gate and joining the Korean *tallyŏnsa* group in Shengjing, were also prohibited. Yŏngjo ordered that the local Qing porters should deliver the tribute and the luggage from Fenghuangcheng all the way to Shengjing, an edict intended to eliminate any opportunity for Korean merchants to enter the gate and to reach Shengjing.[66] In short, the Chosŏn court sought to end debt problems by closing off all possibilities of trade for the tribute embassy between Fenghuangcheng and Shengjing.

However, these attempts were ineffectual, because the Korean trade with the Qing was already inextricably linked to the maintenance of the Chosŏn tribute embassy visits. In fact, the embassy needed a vast amount of silver in addition to the money required to prepare the tribute and gifts for the Qing emperor.

Whenever the Chosŏn embassy handed over the tribute, delivered documents, collected information, or discussed complicated issues with Qing officials in Beijing, the delegates had to present gifts or silver. It was the profits from the trade along the embassy's journey that made the tribute mission possible; the practice of the embassy visits would have been impossible without the substantial amount of silver gained from trade with Qing merchants. In other words, the trade and the tribute embassy existed in a symbiotic relationship, neither being possible without the other. Therefore, the growth of the trade with the Qing was a top priority for the Chosŏn tribute embassy, and abuses by merchants, such as shady credit practices, needed to be tolerated. As a result, Yŏngjo's efforts to regulate the Chosŏn embassy's trade were doomed to fail. Before long, smuggling was rampant from Ŭiju to the Fenghuangcheng gate and on to Shengjing, and silver continued to cross the Yalu River. Finally, in 1754, the Chosŏn court had to reauthorize trade with the Qing for Ŭiju merchants who served the tribute embassy.[67]

The markets in Fenghuangcheng and Shengjing continued to thrive during the eighteenth century. In 1780, Pak Chiwŏn reported that numerous Qing subjects waiting for the arrival of the Korean embassy at the Fenghuangcheng gate were pleased to meet the Korean interpreters and other retainers, who were in fact all merchants from Ŭiju. The two groups were familiar with each other thanks to the regular visits of the Chosŏn embassy. When Pak and his friend stopped by a civilian's house in Fenghuangcheng, they found it full of Korean packhorse drivers and servants having drinks.[68] From this point onward, all of the Korean luggage was to be carried on carts belonging to the local people, as King Yŏngjo had earlier ordered; this did not, however, stop Korean trade with the Qing, as the king had hoped. Instead, Korean visitors continued to bring their goods for trade to Fenghuangcheng.

The local Qing population actively contributed to the creation of a meeting place with the Koreans. Throughout the eighteenth century, Korean embassies continued to rely on local cart drivers for the transportation of their luggage. The end of the *lantou* monopoly did not ease the problems of carrying luggage to Beijing via Shengjing. In 1790, when the Chosŏn embassy had to rush to leave Shengjing in order to celebrate the Qianlong emperor's eightieth birthday in Beijing, Qing cart owners attempted to take advantage of the situation by raising cart fees to ten times their normal level. The accompanying Qing officials recognized the attempted exploitation and punished the cart owners, forcing them to lower their fees. Indignant at this decision, the owners responded by causing further trouble for the Korean embassy by hiring local gangsters to drive their carts. The leader of the cart drivers, who called himself a bannerman of the Plain Yellow Banner, frequently delayed the departure of the embassy by demanding "a break after every five *li* and a drink after every ten *li*." The Koreans were annoyed but could do nothing since they were dependent on the local people for their journey.[69] Chosŏn tribute paying and Qing profit seeking were inextricably intertwined to create a flourishing trade in goods and services in the Shengjing region.

THE ISSUE OF SILVER THEFT

Although it was the emperor sitting in Beijing who received the Chosŏn embassies and their tributes, it was the Shengjing military governor who had to deal with all practical matters related to the Korean visitors. A variety of Chosŏn affairs, ranging from control of illegal trade to the resolution of liabilities among merchants and the prevention of trespassing, fell under the auspices of the Shengjing office. Accordingly, when the Chosŏn embassy reported that some of its belongings had been stolen, the Shengjing military governor managed to connect the incident to the earlier arrest of ginseng poachers in an entirely different location in order to shape the implementation of the Qing Chosŏn policy. The military governor in question was Daldangga, who had failed to gain the emperor's permission to build a military guard post at the Yalu River in 1746. As discussed in chapter 3, Daldangga had sought to combat the problem of ginseng poaching by strengthening the Qing military presence in the area near the boundary, but his plan was thwarted by strong opposition from the Chosŏn court, which persuaded the emperor to veto the idea. It was less than a year after the frustration of the denied guard post proposal that Daldangga was informed of a Korean packhorse driver who had lost his silver near Liaoyang. The military governor, surely annoyed by the Chosŏn court, saw a good chance to exact revenge for the failure of his security plan.

The case of Sahwan and Song Erdazi, described at the beginning of this chapter, reached Daldangga after passing through several hands: first the village head of Wanbaoqiao, then the Liaoyang senior commandant, and finally the Fengtian prefect. The village head said that Song Erdazi, the man accused of stealing the silver of the Korean Sahwan, had been tricked into opening his door to the Koreans, and that his good intentions to help the foreign travelers had unexpectedly been met with assault. Song Erdazi recounted the ensuing situation in detail:

> Wu Er and Zhang Lian, who were staying in my house at the time, were also tied up and sent to the [local] office. . . . [The Koreans insisted] that their silver had been found in the pile of sorghum in my house and tied me up again. They did not even give us time to put hats on our heads or socks on our feet. . . . My house is located very close to the main street. Since they had hurried to catch up with me and soon reached me in front of my place, how could I have managed to remove a package of silver from the horse and hide it in the sorghum pile?[70]

According to the village head's report, the two individuals, Wu Er and Zhang Lian, who were working for Song at the time and staying at his place, had not put on proper clothes, hats, or socks before they were taken to the local office—evidence implying that they had been mistreated during the arrest.[71] One of Song's neighbors also reported that the Koreans had attacked him after he heard a scream and ran to Song's place: "The Koreans asked who I was. I said I was [Song's] neighbor. Then a Korean came with a bamboo stick and hit me on the head twice. My head was torn up. I was so scared that I ran back home." Later he showed his scar to a local official as evidence of the assault.[72]

Song Erdazi, Wu Er, and Zhang Lian were all residents of the area near the tribute route who had presumably been hired to transport the Koreans' luggage. What is striking in the accounts of this case is the apparent attitude of the Korean travelers toward the local porters who provided transportation services for them. Under the excuse of searching for the lost silver, the Koreans moved around in an intimidating crowd, forced their way into houses, searched through them, and attacked locals at will. It was these Korean foreigners, not Qing soldiers, who found the suspects, tied them up, and sent them to the office. It is true that there were only a dozen Qing soldiers accompanying the tribute embassy—too few to properly escort hundreds of Koreans—so the Koreans had to protect themselves. However, the primary reason why the Koreans felt able to act in such an arrogant way in the territory of the "superior country" was that they were at a remote margin of the empire, where Koreans appeared with regularity. In addition, the economic relationship between the Korean embassy and the local Qing population was that of employer and employee, another factor that emboldened the Koreans to behave imperiously, or even abusively, in this context. Furthermore, Korean interpreters forwarded Sahwan's allegation directly to the Shengjing Board of Rites, and Qing soldiers imprisoned Song Erdazi solely on the basis of the Korean servant's accusation without further investigation. All of these facts indicate that the Koreans were uniquely privileged in this remote region.

However, Daldangga had no intention of protecting the privileges Koreans enjoyed within his jurisdiction. The fact that Sahwan's testimony contradicted that of Song Erdazi raised his suspicions, so he decided to summon the suspects and to conduct his own questioning. Song Erdazi, Wu Er, and Zhang Lian were pressured to tell the truth with the threat of severe treatment if they failed to do so, but they continued to insist that they had not stolen any silver from the Koreans.[73] On the other hand, all of the Korean interpreters and Qing soldiers questioned by Daldangga answered that they had not themselves seen when and how Sahwan lost the silver, and that they had relied on his word only in reporting the theft. It also turned out that not one of the other Korean packhorse drivers had seen exactly how Sahwan lost his silver.[74]

Convinced that Sahwan held the key to resolving the affair, Daldangga called him back for further questioning. Daldangga asked Sahwan why he had changed his testimony concerning what he saw in front of Song Erdazi's house, why the other packhorse drivers had not seen the "man on horseback" he had mentioned, and whether he acted with violence while tying up the suspects. Surprisingly, Sahwan confessed that his testimony had been a lie:

> As it was getting dark, it became very windy. We arrived near Wanbaoqiao around the time of the rooster's crow. Desiring to smoke, I slackened the reins of my horse and struck a light. Not expecting it, my horse was so startled by the light that it ran away. I followed the sound of the hooves to the west, arriving in front of Song Erdazi's house. When I grabbed my horse, I found that one of the two bundles of silver had fallen to the ground, but the other one was gone. I was so scared that I began to cry. Then many of my colleagues joined me. I tried to light up the area to search for the silver bundle, but Song Erdazi would not give me a light. When I said I was lost, he opened the door. When I said I had lost some silver, he said he did not know anything about it. Then I said, "My horse was standing in front of your house and the silver was gone. If you did not take it, then who could have taken it?" My colleagues came to tie him up. . . . Later, I found the other silver bundle on the ground. By then people had already tied [Song and the others] up. If I had confessed that it was actually me who had scared the horse, causing it to run away and drop the silver on the ground, my lord would have blamed me not only for being reckless but also for falsely accusing innocent people. I was so scared that I lied about finding the silver in the pile of sorghum.[75]

After revealing that Sahwan had lost the silver himself and then falsely accused innocent locals of a crime, Daldangga sent all of the Koreans involved back to Korea, asking the Chosŏn king to resolve the case. He also proposed punishments for each of them. Sahwan had committed two crimes, namely, the fabrication of the theft of silver and the false accusation of an innocent party, so Daldangga suggested that he be beaten sixty times by a heavy flogging stick (*zhang*) and sentenced to penal servitude (*tu*) for a year. He recommended that Sahwan's lord, Yun Ch'angli, also be punished for blindly trusting his servant's word and falsely accusing innocent Qing subjects. According to Daldangga, the Korean interpreters were all guilty, too, because they had not conducted an appropriate investigation of the incident, but merely reported that a Korean servant's silver had been stolen. Finally, he declared that the Qing soldiers were not innocent either: they should be punished for having neglected to investigate the theft carefully and to report it immediately to their superior, in addition to having failed to provide the foreign embassy with proper escort service.

Daldangga suggested that the Chosŏn king deal with the Koreans involved in the case: "This incident happened because people from the small country are ignorant of what is right and wrong. I beg the emperor to show generous forgiveness and great kindness in allowing the Chosŏn king to punish the people concerned."[76] However, this seemingly generous offer to let Koreans discipline Koreans offered no comfort to the Chosŏn court. The Chosŏn officials took offense at the edict from the Qing Board of Rites, which blamed Yŏngjo for neglecting his duties.[77] Some court officials argued that in addition to the individuals involved in the false accusation of theft, the delegate who brought such an odious letter to the Chosŏn court should be punished.[78] In addition, the Chosŏn court distrusted Daldangga's intentions in the case. The Koreans believed that there were more pressing issues than the Sahwan case affecting the Qing-Chosŏn relationship, most notably the increasing number of illegal Qing settlers in the area near the Yalu River.[79] They suspected that Daldangga had attempted to take advantage of the Sahwan case to deflect attention from the problem of illegal settlers at the boundary—a phenomenon that, in the view of the Chosŏn, had far greater potential to damage the Qing-Chosŏn relationship in the long run. "The Qing authorities, especially Daldangga, are not trustworthy," was a common view among Chosŏn court officials discussing the sentences of Sahwan and the others concerned in the case.

BROADENING THE INVESTIGATION

The Koreans may have expected the incident of Sahwan's false accusation to end with the ruling that Sahwan and Yun Ch'angli be sent into exile. However, Daldangga had different plans. Prompted by the shocking realization that Koreans had dared to level false accusations against Qing subjects in Qing territory, the Shengjing military governor decided to reinvestigate similar cases that had happened earlier. Daldangga wrote a letter to the Qianlong emperor, describing two other cases akin to Sahwan's. According to his investigations, Sahwan was not the only Korean to have reported a loss of silver in Qing territory. One case had occurred in 1744, when a group of Koreans had passed near Langzishan and one of them, Yi Goroja, had reportedly discovered his silver missing and accused a local innkeeper of the theft. The case had not been resolved, Daldangga explained, because the suspected innkeeper had since died of an illness and Yi Goroja had returned to Korea without waiting for the results of the investigation.[80] The second case, involving a Korean interpreter, Yi Yunbang, similarly remained unsolved. This case had happened in 1745, when Yi Yunbang and eleven other members of the Chosŏn embassy had reported their silver missing near Shilihe. Once again, the Koreans had accused an innkeeper, but the thief had not yet been identified.[81]

Having observed the case of Sahwan, Daldangga did not believe that Yi Goroja and Yi Yunbang had really lost silver in Qing territory:

> The suspects have already been questioned several times, but they have never changed their original testimonies, bitterly insisting that they are innocent. It is not right at all that we rely only on the word of Koreans and suspect [our subjects] of being criminals. If we ask the Chosŏn king to collect testimony from the accusers, it is very likely that they will simply repeat what they said earlier. This case will not

be resolved in that way. An attempt to solve this case [based on the statements of Koreans] will end up having the same result as we saw in the case of Sahwan, who falsely accused Song Erdazi. Without cross-examination of Sahwan and Song Erdazi, the Korean servant would never have confessed the truth, and Yun Ch'angli would never have accepted responsibility for his crime.[82]

In order to figure out who was telling the truth, Daldangga insisted, cross-examination of the accusers and the accused was necessary: "The original testimonies of Yi Goroja and Yi Yunbang are confused and unreliable, so we need to wait for the truth. The suspects consistently claim their innocence, but their statements are also one-sided and should be double-checked against those of the accusers."[83] The Qianlong emperor endorsed Daldangga's suggestion, and the Shengjing Board of Rites asked the Chosŏn court to immediately send all concerned parties to Daldangga for interrogation.[84]

In the first instance, the Chosŏn court blamed Yi Yunbang and the Korean interpreters for these disputes, which it saw as arising from their careless accusations against Qing subjects without proper evidence. Nonetheless, the Chosŏn court also suspected Qing officials of greed and of seeking bribes from the Korean embassy; the court feared that the upcoming investigation of the previous cases of the Chosŏn embassy's lost silver would trigger even more demands from Qing officials.[85] In contrast to the Shengjing military governor, who thought that the Koreans, having carelessly lost their silver, had pinned the blame on innocent Qing subjects and managed to avoid the ensuing crises, the Chosŏn court considered all these troubles to have been caused by the corruption of Qing officials. In the end, the Chosŏn court consented to the Qing request on the condition that a Chosŏn official would be allowed to accompany the summoned Koreans and to conduct the investigation together with Qing officials. Accordingly, the vice minister of the Chosŏn Board of Punishment (K. *hyŏngjo ch'amŭi*), Kim Sangjŏk, was sent to Fenghuangcheng with the accusers.[86] King Yŏngjo gave a special message to Kim Sangjŏk: "It is not proper to punish innocent subjects of the superior country." The king advised Kim to do his best to conduct a thorough investigation of the case.[87]

In 1749, Daldangga's successor as Shengjing military governor, Alantai, reported the result of the investigation to the Qianlong emperor. Quoting the two Fenghuangcheng officials who carried out the joint examination with Kim Sangjŏk, Alantai reported that "the Qing subjects singled out as thieves provided evidence to prove their innocence, whereas the accusations of the Koreans were not verified." It turned out that Yi Goroja and his colleagues had quarreled with the innkeeper over the charge for their stay. Later, finding the group's baggage and a hundred *liang* of silver missing, a Chosŏn interpreter and a Qing soldier immediately arrested five Qing people staying in the inn and handed them over to the office. However, the baggage of the Koreans was later found inside the house along with other items, and only some of the silver was not recovered. Yi Yunbang's case was similar. After the early departure of four of the Korean travelers, the remaining eight discovered that their silver was gone. The Qing soldiers beat up and tortured the innkeeper before sending him to the office. The village head later reported that, in spite of several years of effort, he had found no evidence of the innkeeper's involvement in the theft.[88]

Alantai concluded that Yi Goroja and Yi Yunbang had plotted to level false charges of theft against innocent Qing subjects. To make matters worse, in the course of the reinvestigation it was revealed that Yi Yunbang had also attempted in vain to bribe a servant who was a witness of the case. Yi had given twenty-five *liang* of silver to the servant to give a false witness statement, but the servant subsequently disclosed the bribe to Qing officials. Yi Yunbang's attempted bribery undermined the efforts of Kim Sangjŏk, who had tried to settle the dispute as a representative of the Chosŏn court. The revelation convinced Alantai of the Korean's guilt, and he insisted that "the Chosŏn king should examine the process by which his Korean subjects made schemes [to falsely accuse Qing subjects] and discuss the sentences of these criminals." He also asked the Qianlong emperor to discipline the Qing soldiers who had failed to investigate the cases properly.[89]

In 1749, the Qing Board of Rites sent the Chosŏn court an imperial edict concerning punishments for the Korean criminals:

> Those people, including Yi Yunbang and Yi Goroja, arrested and falsely accused innocent people of the inner land [*neidi*] and also attempted to buy off a servant. Their crimes deserve a sentence of military servitude. However, imperial favor is blessing them, reducing their sentences to one hundred strokes with a heavy flogging stick [*zhang*] and penal servitude [*tu*] for three years. The silver used for the bribe should be sealed and sent back to the Chosŏn court.[90]

Three months later, the Chosŏn court reported to the Qing Board of Rites that all of the criminals had been punished, including the Chosŏn representative, Kim Sangjŏk, who had been sent to Fenghuangcheng for the cross-examination.[91] Severe punishments were meted out to all concerned, including the servants who had failed to take care of the silver and instead tried to avoid responsibility by accusing someone else, the interpreters who had too readily trusted the word of their servants and made little effort to discover the truth, and the representative of the Chosŏn court who had participated in the joint interrogation. Daldangga thus succeeded in setting a precedent that he hoped would deter future offenses by Koreans as well as enhance the authority of the superior country.

Despite Daldangga's revelation of the Koreans' false accusations in these cases, the Chosŏn embassy's reports of silver thefts in Qing territory were not always fabricated. Another case shows that some Koreans really did have property stolen from them during their journey and that someone had to take responsibility for their compensation. In 1746, the Liaoyang military commander reported that a

Korean servant, Yi Ch'ansuk, had lost a thousand *liang* of silver. As in the previous cases, Yi Ch'ansuk seemed to have lost the silver during his journey with the embassy to Beijing and suspected some of the innkeepers and cart drivers with whom he had been in contact. Unlike in the previous cases, however, Qing officials determined that Yi Ch'ansuk's silver truly had been stolen in Qing territory, but they failed to find the real thief. Who, then, should pay back the silver to the Koreans? After two and a half years of discussion, the Shengjing Board of Rites reached the conclusion that the Qing merchants who had contracted to transport the Korean embassy's luggage should take responsibility for the compensation:

> These merchants were affluent, so they were able to become the merchants [authorized to work with the Chosŏn embassy]. They were entrusted with the valuables of the Korean embassy and received a huge transportation fee. Nonetheless, they failed to care for the commissioned property and thus caused its loss. It is therefore appropriate that these merchants take responsibility for compensating the owners. They should be put in custody until they pay back the entire amount. Their release can be granted only after everything is paid. The money can be reimbursed later when the real criminal is arrested.[92]

In 1750, the Shengjing Board of Rites sent the specified amount of silver to Korea.[93] The Chosŏn court wrote a letter thanking the Qianlong emperor for his imperial kindness: "The great country has always taken care of the small country. Your Highness is now showing mercy even to a servant and allowing him to recoup his loss even though such a long time has passed. This is all thanks to the great kindness of the great country. This small country cannot hide its joy and gratitude."[94] To the Korean envoys, the local Qing residents on their travel route were merely innkeepers providing lodging for a night, porters transporting their valuables, merchants acting as trading partners, or even thieves eyeing their belongings. To the Chosŏn king, however, the Qing emperor and the Shengjing military governor represented the highest power in the world, authorities to whom he had to regularly pay homage and tribute, who commanded his obedience when they ordered him to arrest his own subjects and send them to the Qing, and whom he even had to thank for punishing his own people. The relations between the Qing and the Chosŏn thus varied greatly depending on whether their encounter took place in Beijing, Shengjing, or a local town on the far reaches of the empire.

. . .

Qing foreign policy guaranteed regular visits from the subordinate neighbor for the purpose of paying tribute, and the Chosŏn practice of sending tributary embassies created an opportunity for Koreans to make regular contact with Qing people. The various cases involving members of the Chosŏn embassy on the Fenghuangcheng–Shengjing route demonstrate that the practice of tribute payment, originally intended to preserve the political hierarchy between the Qing and

Chosŏn courts, also had an unexpected outcome, as a great number of Koreans, along with their money and goods, were attracted first to their boundary and then to the Qing northeastern margin. Korean travelers had to depend on the local Qing population for various services in order to make the journey to Beijing for an audience with the emperor. The tributary relationship and the practice of embassy visits were, therefore, the reason for all of the ensuing disputes over thefts and losses.

In this way, trade and tribute, two key elements of Qing foreign policy, complemented each other to form a commercial web spanning the boundary between the two neighbors. Equally, it is important to note that these commercial relations between the subjects of the Qing and those of the Chosŏn were framed by the asymmetrical power relationship between the suzerain court and the tributary state. The procedure for settling disputes, which was initiated, carried out, and concluded by the Qing court, demonstrates the political hierarchy inherent in the tributary relationship. Problems experienced by the Koreans, such as the rampant corruption among the Qing officials encountered by the Chosŏn embassies and the Chosŏn king's frustration with the punishment of his own officials, were never raised in discussions with the Shengjing military governor or the Qianlong emperor. The tributary relationship required commercial exchange, but this economic connection was built and maintained on the premise of a firm political hierarchy.

5

From Borderland to Border

On April 4, 1867, the vice minister of the Shengjing Board of Revenue, E-le-he-bu, reported to the Tongzhi emperor (r. 1862–74) that a steadily increasing number of civilian farmers were illegally cultivating prohibited land outside the eastern line of the Willow Palisade. According to his letter, the illegal settlers had even approached the Shengjing office and volunteered to pay taxes, following the precedent of Jilin, where illegal famers were already allowed to do so. E-le-he-bu had responded cautiously to the farmers' willingness to pay taxes, since their settlement in the prohibited area outside the palisade was a serious violation of Qing restriction policy in the northeast. He was also well aware that the area was located near the boundary with the Chosŏn and therefore required special consideration; he needed to check whether the settlement could cause problems with the Chosŏn court.[1] E-le-he-bu's report was forwarded to the six boards and the Grand Council for further discussion. The high officials in Beijing emphasized that Shengjing was the sacred birthplace of the Qing empire and that several thousand *li* of land and mountains there had always been protected by the palisade. Simultaneously, however, they recognized that there were numerous people living outside the palisade and that these people made their living by cultivating the land and logging timber. The officials were rightly concerned that if the illegal settlers were forced to evacuate the prohibited territory, they would lose their livelihoods and likely end up rebelling. The Qing court thus had to find a solution that would place these settlers under the state's authority but also protect the prohibited land near the boundary with the Chosŏn.[2]

As early as 1863, the Jinzhou garrison lieutenant general (*fudutong*), En-he, had informed the emperor of the situation in the area between the Willow Palisade and the Yalu River in the following way:

> Because of the wide land and the deep mountains in this region, thorough investigation and patrolling are nearly impossible. Trespassers have long been sneaking into the area, first to hunt and to log, and later to mine for gold and to cultivate land. These days, vagabonds from Zhili and Shandong are coming here and forming gangs to cause trouble. Previously they built houses and tilled the land only in the deep mountains, but now there is no limit to the illegal settlement, and it is spreading widely over hundreds *li* of land. Patrolling soldiers are few in number and weak in power, so they are unable to stop these criminals. The prevention of access to the area near the boundary is gradually becoming ineffectual; the land outside the palisade is being reclaimed without any official effort [by the state].[3]

En-he's last sentence provides a succinct description of the illegal settlement that was taking place at the Qing-Chosŏn boundary already in the late nineteenth century. No matter how much the Qing and Chosŏn authorities tried to restrict access to the area, the vast territory near the Yalu River had gradually filled with illegal farmers hungry for land.

This chapter examines the ways in which the Qing and Chosŏn courts discussed the increasing illegal settlement at the boundary where ginseng disappeared and how Korean immigrants north of the Tumen River led the two neighbors to a series of negotiations to establish the exact limits of their territories in the late nineteenth century. The chapter begins by tracing the changes in the Qing ginseng monopoly in the nineteenth century. As ginseng became scarce and people involved in its business expected little profit, the Qing court failed to maintain its monopolistic control over it. The depletion of ginseng in Manchuria came along with an influx of Chinese farmers in the restricted margins of the empire. From the nineteenth century on, the Qing prohibition of civilian settlement in the northeast gradually broke down; the growing number of Chinese immigrants effectively invalidated the state's restrictions. In addition, Russia undermined Qing rule over land and tribal people in Manchuria through a series of new treaties. Under the circumstances, the only way for the Qing court to uphold its territorial sovereignty in Manchuria was to encourage Chinese farmers to move to the region and thereby fill it with Qing subjects. The previously restrictive Qing Manchuria policy, consisting mainly of the stationing of banner soldiers and unwavering insistence on the evacuation of the region, was gradually replaced by a new plan of "recruiting civilians to populate, cultivate, and settle," a policy that was known as *yimin shibian*.

The second focus in this chapter is on the transformation of the nature of Qing-Chosŏn political relations and territorial boundaries. As early as the nineteenth century, the area near the Yalu and Tumen Rivers and Changbaishan had lost its fame for rich ginseng production. Instead of ginseng hunters, it was civilian farmers who were increasingly seen in the region. This supposedly empty land invited not only Chinese immigration but also Korean settlers, and consequently the Qing government began to claim jurisdictional authority over the Korean immigrants. Debates over the Korean settlers living north of the Tumen River became more complicated because they took place at the very time when Qing-Chosŏn relations were being reinterpreted and renegotiated. The Qing court of the late nineteenth century wanted to retain the absolute power over the Chosŏn court that it had held for centuries; newly emerging international relations in East Asia, however, caused the Chosŏn to reevaluate its traditional respect for the suzerain Qing power in order to protect Korean subjects living north of the Tumen River. This chapter demonstrates that this change in Qing-Chosŏn relations led to a revision of their previous conceptions and practices of boundary and sovereignty. The new environment surrounding the two countries no longer tolerated the borderland that the Qing and the Chosŏn shared, and instead led to the emergence of a clearly defined border.

DISAPPEARING GINSENG, INCREASING PEOPLE

Until the late eighteenth century, Manchurian ginseng continued to claim an important position in Qing state revenue. In 1753, the Qing state's total revenue from customs duties had been 4,330,000 *liang* of silver. In 1760 the Qing court issued six thousand ginseng permits and allocated a quota of six *liang* of ginseng per permit, 36,000 *liang* in total. This amount was equivalent to 1,440,000 *liang* of silver, since the market price of a *liang* of ginseng at the time was forty *liang* of silver.[4]

As table 3 shows, however, the number of issued ginseng permits plummeted and the ginseng business declined from the late eighteenth century onward. The primary reason for this trend was the overharvesting and subsequent depletion of ginseng stocks. The depletion was a predictable result of the continuous exploitation of this natural resource over the centuries. Shortages of natural resources in Manchuria throughout the period 1750 to 1850 applied not only to ginseng but also to pheasants, storks, pine nuts, and sable skins. This phenomenon indicates that it was imperial foraging, rather than Han Chinese poaching, that had played a primary role in resource depletion in Manchuria.[5] The government imposed various regulations in an effort to protect the resource base, such as enforcing "resting" periods for mountains, rivers, and forests; strengthening control over gathering operations; erecting walls and fences; dispatching patrols to strategic points to deter poaching; and arresting poachers, illegal cultivators, and black market operators.[6] However, the policy of resting ginseng-producing mountains, for example, amounted merely to a temporary halt in the issuance of ginseng-gathering permits and was thus ineffective in combating illegal poaching.[7] The depletion of ginseng stocks also wreaked

TABLE 3 Change in the number of ginseng permits from the 1760s to 1850s.

Year	Number of permits printed	Number of permits issued
1760	10,000	6,000
1777	6,000	2,900
1789	5,000	2,330
1799	2,287	Unknown
1846	1,752	Unknown
1852	753	632

SOURCE: Wang, "Qingdai dongbei caishenye," 191.

havoc on the state's control over gatherers, licensed merchants, and officials. It was a common practice that the Ginseng Office extended advance loans to gatherers to enable the latter to pay for their expenses; the gatherers were then expected to pay back the loans by selling their surplus ginseng. In actuality, however, every year, 30 to 40 percent of gatherers failed to meet their quota. Facing a shortage of collected ginseng, the Ginseng Office often had to borrow public funds and purchase surplus ginseng from licensed merchants. As the issuance of ginseng permits declined because of the depletion of the stocks, the Ginseng Office's debts increased.[8]

However, even the persistent shortfalls in ginseng resources and the decline in state income did not make the Qing government relax its strict prohibition against ginseng cultivation, which might have provided an alternative source. Fully grown, four- to five-year-old ginseng was hard to find, but younger ginseng was poor in quality and less valued on the market. Therefore, ginseng gatherers sought to transplant young wild ginseng plants into gardens, wait for them to reach maturity, and then harvest the mature ginseng for the state. However, the government was concerned that the widespread cultivation of ginseng would affect its state-controlled price, and it thus continued to outlaw the practice of ginseng cultivation and to punish ginseng farmers as severely as it did poachers.[9] In 1802, when the Jilin military governor proposed legalizing ginseng cultivation, the Jiaqing emperor retorted: "Ginseng grows from the energy of the soil [diling]. If anyone collects a big piece of the root, he should pay it [to the state]; if he cannot find a big one, it is fine for him to report the truth. Why should he use human efforts to cultivate it and cheat [the state]? Only wild ginseng growing in the mountains has medical effects; taking cultivated ginseng is useless."[10] Despite the emperor's distrust, cultivated ginseng became widespread: in 1810, for example, it represented 60 percent of the ginseng received by the state from Shengjing and 10 percent of the receipts from Jilin.[11]

As poor ginseng harvests caused financial ruin for the gatherers and devastating deficits for the Ginseng Office, the Qing government sought to support the ginseng monopoly through the booming business in sorghum liquor (*gaoliang jiu*). Distilled liquors were already produced as early as the Yuan dynasty; it was the Qing era, however, when the real growth in liquor consumption took place. Chinese liquor was made of sorghum, a grain growing widely in northern China and Manchuria. The sorghum liquor, which was cheap and easy to get drunk on, was particularly popular during the cold winter in Manchuria.[12] Concerned that its production consumed a large amount of food grains, however, the Qing court imposed a strict prohibition on distilling liquor. In 1726, the Yongzheng emperor lectured his subjects: "The price of rice rose because of the flood in Zhili Province, and I therefore already decreed a prohibition on distilling liquor in the regions outside the passes. However, liquor dealers reportedly run their business in Shengjing as well as at the boundary with Mongolia. Spending food grains on such a wasteful business should be thoroughly proscribed."[13] By the late eighteenth century, however, when the Qing government was no longer able to obtain the predetermined quota of ginseng from the gatherers, liquor dealers gradually joined the ginseng business as sponsors (*baoren*) of gatherers, taking responsibility for recruiting and provisioning them and guaranteeing the amount and quality of the ginseng they gathered. In 1800, the Shengjing Ginseng Office formally authorized the liquor business and began to collect taxes from the distillers. In 1807, liquor dealers' sponsorship of ginseng gatherers was officially legalized.[14]

Despite all these efforts, wild ginseng in Manchuria was exhausted to the extent that the government could no longer maintain its monopoly on ginseng collection and trade. The chronic shortage of ginseng caused a serious burden on liquor dealers, who had difficulty in securing the ginseng quotas and eventually refused to sponsor ginseng gatherers. Without the distillers, the government was unable to find takers for a sufficient number of ginseng permits to procure the predetermined quota of ginseng. The rate of depletion of wild ginseng in Manchuria accelerated; the number of ginseng permits issued continued to decline; and the merchants and gatherers could not meet the high ginseng quotas set by the state. All of these factors combined to spell the end for the Qing ginseng monopoly. In 1853, the Qing court finally announced the official end of the state monopoly on ginseng collection and trade.[15]

By the time ginseng disappeared in Manchuria to the extent that the Qing court had to give up the monopoly, circumstances in the northeast had changed radically in terms of both domestic politics and foreign relations. Prior to the middle of the nineteenth century, the wealthy provinces in the Yangzi Delta contributed their surplus to poorer provinces, such as Jilin and Heilongjiang. But these subsidies were greatly depleted due to years of warfare in the south, especially during the Taiping Rebellion (1851–64), which devastated the affluent Jiangnan region. The emptied provincial treasuries caused serious problems in Qing rule in Manchuria, as the poorly paid banner soldiers were unable to impose effective restrictions on the increasing illegal immigrants and to establish necessary public order within local societies.[16] Furthermore, as banner garrison troops in the northeast were mobilized to suppress rebellions in China proper, security in Manchuria was also jeopardized by foreign aggressors, notably Russia. By the mid-nineteenth century, Russia pushed forward a series of expeditions of the Heilongjiang River, where the Qing did not have military power to prevent Russian approaches. In 1858, when Qing forces were in the midst of fighting the Taiping rebels and were also strug-gling against British and French forces, Russia succeeded in forcing the Qing court to sign the Treaty of Aigun. Two years later, in 1860, the Convention of Beijing confirmed the "[opening of] the entire northern frontier of the Qing empire, from Manchuria to Xinjiang, to Russia's political and commercial influence." By requir-ing the Qing to cede all lands north of the Heilongjiang and east of the Ussuri to Russia, these two treaties enabled Russia to encroach on Qing Manchuria.[17]

By the 1850s, the Qing court continued its effort, in vain, to maintain the re-striction policy on civilian settlement in Jilin by repeating the old rhetoric of the "place of Manchu origins." However, local military commanders in the northeast had to find ways to meet the new financial shortfalls, and land was the most abun-dant and readily available resource. Eventually, the Jilin and Heilongjiang authori-ties began to make a series of proposals to Beijing that the restricted areas should be opened to civilian settlement, and by doing so, money and taxes be collected from the settlers. In 1859, Jilin military governor Jing-chun proposed the opening of the previously prohibited regions of the Suifen and Ussuri Rivers, because of the possible threat that the Russian ships might approach there. He suggested that "if [our] people can gather and settle in the region and take profits from timber log-ging, hunting, ginseng gathering, and fishing in the deep mountains, the Russians will retreat on their own." The Xianfeng emperor (r. 1850–61) agreed with Jing-chun, saying that "it is beneficial that China's subjects should live in China's vast land" (*yi Zhongguo zhi kuangtu, ju Zhongguo zhi minren, li zhi suozai*), by which people were to protect themselves and foreign aggressions be prevented.[18] The fol-lowing year, in 1860, the Qing court opened parts of southern Jilin for civilian settlement, a decision largely considered the first official lifting of the restriction policy in Qing Manchuria. From the 1860s to the 1880s, many prohibited areas in Jilin and Heilongjiang were gradually opened for settlement and the restrictions on civilian settlers became effectively nominal.[19]

The opening of the northeast and the increase in civilian immigrants required a transformation of the administrative system in Manchuria: the Qing govern-ment needed a new institutional structure to deal with the increasing civil af-fairs. In 1875, the acting Shengjing military governor, Chong-shi, suggested that the Shengjing government be restructured to match the administrative system of China proper and to make a necessary response to the increasing numbers of Chinese immigrants. The Guangxu emperor (r. 1875–1908) eventually approved his proposal, and the Shengjing military governor was granted authority over all affairs involving garrison troops as well as civilian settlers. While increasing the power of the military governor, this reform also sought to limit the privileges of banner garrisons and shift more administrative authority into the hands of civil officials. Between 1877 and 1883, Jilin also carried out an overall reorganization of its government through the efforts of the Jilin military governor, Ming-an. Throughout the 1870s and the 1880s, new county administrative offices for civilian affairs were established in various places in Shengjing and Jilin. As administrative power was transferred from banner garrisons to civil offices, the primary purpose of the government changed from protecting and nurturing the banner forces to supervising and governing Chinese immigrants.[20] It was these newly arrived Chinese settlers who began to occupy Manchuria when ginseng grew scarce and the Manchus lost their privilege.

FILLING THE EMPTY LAND

Just like other regions of Manchuria, the long-prohibited areas near the Chosŏn boundary faced a profound transformation in the nineteenth century, in terms of both environmental conditions and political relations. The region around the Yalu and Tumen Rivers and Changbaishan had claimed a reputation for rich production of high-quality ginseng, which caused the constant trespassing incidents between the Qing and the Chosŏn. After the exploitation for centuries, however, the old ginseng mountains in Shengjing and Jilin, especially those near the Chosŏn boundary, which had long been harvested, no longer produced much ginseng. And as the ginseng harvest shrank, the number of illegal ginseng hunters also dwindled. By the mid-nineteenth century, there were very few cases reported to Beijing or Seoul for trespassing related to ginseng poaching. Now, it was illegal timber loggers and farmers who were replacing the ginseng poachers and animal hunters in the land north of the Yalu and Tumen Rivers.[21] The emergence of civilian farmers in the restricted areas at the boundary brought substantial changes in the ideas and practices of this territory that the Qing and the Chosŏn had shared. As previous chapters show, it was ginseng that led the two neighbors to an agreement to keep the land at the boundary off-limits to civilian settlers. The Qing wanted to protect the Manchu privilege, which was signified as ginseng, while the Chosŏn hoped to avoid conflicts with the suzerain power by giving up this precious root despite its physical accessibility. When there was ginseng, the land at the boundary was to be restricted for the purpose of preserving both Qing hegemony and Chosŏn sovereignty. As ginseng disappeared and people began to settle there, however, the two neighbors had to reconsider their old agreement to maintain the empty land at the Yalu and Tumen Rivers—as well as their ideas about territory and boundary.

Two good examples from the 1840s illustrate the growth of illegal settlements of Chinese farmers near the Yalu River. In 1842, the Chosŏn provincial governor of Hamgyŏng reported to Seoul that Qing subjects were building houses and cultivating land across the Yalu River from the Chosŏn Kanggye and Manp'o. In response to the Chosŏn court's request to put a stop to illegal settlement at the boundary, the Shengjing military governor investigated three relevant locations, where 3,300 *mu* of cultivated land was found along with nearly a hundred thatched huts. Qing soldiers failed to arrest any of the illegal settlers, all of whom ran away, so the soldiers merely destroyed the unauthorized fields and lodgings. The incident reveals that Chinese immigrants were not intruding into the area near the Yalu River only for such temporary activities as ginseng poaching or timber logging; rather, they were establishing permanent settlements and engaging in cultivation. Strikingly, neither the Qing nor the Chosŏn had managed to check these violations until as much as 3,300 *mu* of land had been put under the plow. A similar situation was reported in 1846, only four years later, with the discovery that vast tracts of land in forty different locations across the Yalu River from Chosŏn Kanggye were being cultivated. This time Qing and Chosŏn officials undertook a joint investigation along the middle and lower parts of the Yalu River and arrested three hundred illegal settlers.[22]

Reports about rampant illegal settlement led to an increase in Qing patrols at the boundary with the Chosŏn. Most importantly, the Qing and the Chosŏn agreed to make joint patrols of the boundary a regular, biannual practice. The two governments carried out thirty-eight joint patrols during the years 1849 to 1867. However, all of these efforts to stop illegal settlement and to keep the area off-limits and empty were ineffectual. The Qing and Chosŏn soldiers reported no cases of illegal settlement between 1857 and 1867, but this apparent calm did not reflect the reality in the region.[23] In 1867, the Shengjing military governor Du-xing-a visited the area outside the palisade and met with Chosŏn officials at Zhongjiang to deal with illegal settlements near the Yalu River. Two years later, Du-xing-a sent a report to the emperor, saying that more than one hundred thousand people were living outside the palisade and had already claimed 96,000 *xiang* of land. His conclusion was that illegal settlers were now too numerous to be forcibly removed; the only possible solution was to "expand the perimeter of the palisade and legalize settlement in this region."[24] The Qing court finally had to figure out what to do with this supposedly vacant but actually inhabited land.

Du-xing-a's suggestion to move the palisade toward the Yalu River—that is, to develop the land at the Chosŏn boundary—was, in fact, not new at all. As discussed in chapter 3, two previous Shengjing military governors, Nasutu and Daldangga, had made similar proposals to develop the area near the Yalu River by establishing a new guard post outside the perimeter of the Willow Palisade, but both of their plans had been rejected. But in contrast to the Yongzheng and

Qianlong emperors, who had decided to acquiesce to the Chosŏn request not to develop the Yalu River region, the Guangxu emperor decided to invalidate the long-standing Qing agreement with the Chosŏn court regarding the management of their boundary. In 1875, the emperor imposed taxation on the already reclaimed land in Dadonggou, located at the mouth of the Yalu River, and also permitted household registration for illegal settlers, whether they were civilians or bannermen: "Small people have long settled in the relevant lands and are now volunteering to pay taxes. The court is willing to show them mercy and forgive their past crimes, helping them make their living."[25]

The next year, in 1876, the Chosŏn court was informed of an imminent plan for the Qing authorities to open new administrative offices near the Yalu River. Not surprisingly, the Chosŏn voiced strong opposition to the plan, as it had to the proposal to establish a military post at Mangniushao in 1746. The court stressed, once again, that development around the Yalu River had long been prohibited and that if offices were built in this land, "people from here and there could easily sneak in, and goods could be freely exchanged, which would soon lead to trouble."[26] Prompted by the Chosŏn court's opposition, the Guangxu emperor ordered local officials to investigate the situation, just as the Yongzheng and Qianlong emperors had done earlier. In his report of 1877, the acting Shengjing military governor, Chong-hou, explained that settlement at the Yalu River was rampant and immigration into the region could no longer be halted. From his point of view, state sanction of development in the area was inevitable.[27] For the purpose of dealing with civilian affairs related to Chinese immigrants in the region, in 1876 and 1877 Chong-hou established new county offices in Xiu'am, Fenghua, Kuandian, Tonghua, and Huairen, many of which were located outside the palisade.[28] The Chosŏn court's wish that the Qing and the Chosŏn preserve the empty buffer zone between them in order to protect the territory of each had become unrealistic under the strong pressures from Chinese immigration and settlement.

Once the land at the Yalu River was opened for settlement, prohibitions on inhabitation in the Tumen River region were lifted as well. Since being appointed as the acting Jilin military governor in 1877, Ming-an followed the precedents in Shengjing and reformed the Jilin government to build new civil offices and open land for Chinese immigrants. By 1881, administrative offices were newly opened in Dunhua and Yitong near the Tumen River. In addition to the Jilin military governor, the Guangxu emperor dispatched a Han Chinese official, Wu Dacheng (1835–1902), with the special mission of strengthening military defense and developing land in the regions of Sanxing, Ningguta, and Hunchun. First, promoting the military rank of Hunchun regiment colonel (*xieling*) to garrison lieutenant general (*fudutong*), Wu also built an office for land development (*zhaokenju*) in Hunchun, and enforced an active recruitment of Chinese farmers in Shandong to settle and cultivate land in this northeastern margin. Furthermore, he ordered his men to investigate the land north of the Tumen River.[29] In order to support Wu's efforts to develop land near the Chosŏn boundary, the Qing court also sent a letter to the Chosŏn court, saying, "This development is led by the [Qing] authorities, and therefore [the Chosŏn] local officials should not be worried."[30] By the 1880s, the areas around the Yalu and Tumen Rivers, which had for so long been closed off to civilian access, were formally opened for settlement and cultivation. The gates of the Willow Palisade lost their designated function of controlling people's movements in the restricted area. With the rapidly increasing number of immigrants, the last remainders of the empty space at the boundary between the Qing and the Chosŏn gradually disappeared.

It was not only Chinese farmers who searched for land near the Yalu and Tumen Rivers: a growing number of Koreans crossed the rivers and settled in the area north of the rivers. People living east of Changbaishan, in areas such as Musan, Hoeryŏng, Chongsŏng, and Onsŏng, crossed the Tumen River; those living on the west side of the mountains, especially in the Four Closed Counties, crossed the Yalu River. The Chosŏn court continued to prohibit its Korean subjects from crossing the Yalu and Tumen Rivers without state permission, and local officials were not allowed to get involved with affairs taking place across the rivers unless they were given an order from Seoul.[31] However, reports of Korean trespassing and illegal settlement north of the rivers continued. In 1866, a group of seventy men and women in Kyŏngwŏn crossed the Tumen before getting arrested and sent back by the Qing soldiers; as many as two hundred Koreans were reported to cross the Tumen and pass through Hunchun to the Russian territory. The Hunchun regiment colonel witnessed that growing number of Koreans immigrants coming to cross the Tumen:

> Many guard posts have reported that Koreans in a small group of three to five, or in a big group of several dozens with families, continue to come passing guard posts [in the Hunchun area]. They are heading to the south of Hunchun in search of gold or cultivable land. . . . [So far] no civilians have lived in Hunchun; no order to open land has been received. If they are not evicted now, it will be difficult to get rid of them later.[32]

Despite such warnings from local Qing officials, illegal Korean incursions and settlement remained on the rise. It was in the late nineteenth century that references to the so-called Kando (C. *Jiandao*)—a name indicating contemporary Yanbian in Jilin—first appeared. The Kando region was sometimes used to refer to all of Manchuria, but more typically the region north of the Yalu River was called Western Kando and the region north of the Tumen Northern Kando.[33] It has been said that Korean immigration towns in Western Kando appeared in the 1860s and 1870s.[34] The visible presence of Korean settlements north of the Yalu River was, in fact, officially recognized by the local Chosŏn authorities. In 1871, Cho Wihyŏn, the Chosŏn county magistrate (K. *kunsu*) of Huch'ang in P'yŏngan Province, sent his troops to evict Qing intruders who had entered Chosŏn territory illegally in order to log timber in Samsu and Kapsan. The next year, he dispatched three military agents north of the Yalu River to collect information about the areas of Ji'an, Tonghua, and the Hun River, also known as the Tunggiya River during the period when Möngke Temür had lived. Their travel report for July 5 to August 13, 1872—later titled *Diary of North of the River* (K. *Kangbuk ilgi*)—shows the conditions of Korean immigrants in Qing territory at that time.[35] According to the diary, six to seven thousand Koreans had crossed over to the north side of the Yalu and settled in the area around the Hun River outside the Willow Palisade. Most of the Korean immigrants who settled in Qing territory during the famine of 1869 to 1870 came to be called "false Qing subjects" (K. *kaho*), because they adopted Qing hairstyles and clothing.[36]

The north of the Tumen was also gradually filled with Korean immigrants. When the famine devastated Hamgyŏng Province, many people were forced to look for a source of livelihood elsewhere and crossed the Tumen River on search of land to cultivate. In addition to natural disasters, tax increases by corrupt local officials were another reason cited to explain why people had to leave their homes.[37] By this time, the punishments imposed by the Chosŏn court on trespassers became more lenient, creating yet another incentive for people to cross the river. A trespasser arrested in 1867, for example, was exempted from punishment altogether, and in general, if arrested intruders regretted their wrongdoing, they were simply released. In 1868, the Chosŏn court reduced the degree of punishment imposed on officials who overlooked transgressions within their jurisdictions, and by 1871, such officials were not disciplined at all, even if people under their direct command were caught crossing the river illegally.[38] In fact, there was a well-known case that the Chosŏn local authorities openly encouraged Koreans to cultivate land north of the river. In 1880, Hong Namju, a local official of Hoeryŏng, pointed out that the lands north of the Tumen, long empty and off-limits, were now opened for Chinese immigrants, while Korean entrances were still regrettably restricted. Hong argued that since the Hoeryŏng people suffered from severe famine, they should be allowed to cross the river for cultivation and settlement. Eventually, during the years 1880 to 1881, dozens of thousands of Korean farmers developed land, "hundreds *li* in length and dozens *li* in width," north of the Tumen. It was reported that people crossed the river every day as if the region to its north was not "outside" (K. *oeji*); more surprisingly, even Korean officials were dispatched to the area across the river to register land and collect taxes.[39] This remarkable phenomenon of Korean immigration to the north of the Tumen was soon to be recognized in both Beijing and Seoul.

Korean immigrants who settled north of the Yalu and Tumen Rivers in the late nineteenth century did so for several reasons: domestic pressures due to population growth, the shortage of land in the Chosŏn northern region, and the attraction of new settlements in Qing Manchuria.[40] Most of all, it was the change in Qing policy in the northeast that made Koreans see the previously prohibited land as a settlement opportunity. As the Qing lifted its restrictions on access to the northeastern region, the area at the boundary with the Chosŏn was also exposed to the increased flow of migrants. People from both sides of the Yalu and Tumen Rivers had always crossed the rivers, and trespassing was a topic that the Qing and the Chosŏn had discussed throughout their long history. However, the wave of trespassing and settlement that took place in the late nineteenth century was a wholly new phenomenon. While previous illegal incursions had generally been limited in duration, undertaken mostly for the purposes of ginseng poaching and hunting, the late nineteenth-century intruders entered the areas near the Yalu and Tumen Rivers with the intention of staying for the long term.

KOREAN SUBJECTS NORTH OF THE RIVER

It was primarily the growing influence of the Western powers and Japan in the late nineteenth century that initiated the change in Qing perceptions of neighbor Chosŏn, which the Qing had always seen as subordinate. When European ships appeared at Korean shores, the Qing and Chosŏn courts were asked to explain the exact nature of their relationship. The process that ensued was surely confusing for all concerned. In the 1860s, when French and American ships were involved in skirmishes off the coast of Korea, they assumed that the Qing, as the suzerain power, rather than the subordinate Chosŏn court, would take responsibility for the incidents. This assumption was supported by the Chosŏn court: it admitted its lack of experience and knowledge in foreign relations and asked the Qing to deal with the French in order to help the Chosŏn "live in eternal peace and reverently fulfill its tributary duties."[41] However, the Qing government responded, "Even though it is surely subordinate to us, the Chosŏn is independent in its national affairs."[42] In this confusing situation, Okamoto Takashi explains, both the Qing and the Chosŏn courts refused to take responsibility for dealing with the European powers, indicating that they understood their relationship differently from one another. The Chosŏn believed that its subordinate king was not allowed to establish relations with foreign countries without the recognition of the suzerain, while the Qing did not want to intervene in Chosŏn affairs, mostly to avoid trouble with the Western powers.[43] However, the Japanese attack on Taiwan in 1874 and Japan's annexation of the Ryukyu Islands in 1879 prompted the Qing court to take the Chosŏn issue more seriously. In 1881, while negotiating the establishment of official diplomatic relations between the Chosŏn and European countries, the Qing diplomat Li Hongzhang (1823–1901) attempted to legalize Korea's subordinate status vis-à-vis Qing China and obtain international recognition of this special relationship. By this time, Qing policymakers sought to change the traditional

Qing-Chosŏn relationship to include and accommodate more intervention of this kind. More than anything, as Kirk Larsen stresses, "Qing informal imperialism" was the outcome of the recognition that Qing-Chosŏn relations in the late nineteenth century had become multilateral, rather than bilateral, as they had been in the eighteenth century.[44]

Now, the issue of Korean immigrants north of the Tumen began to attract the attention of the Qing court. Before the early 1880s, the court seemed to pay little mind to reports of large numbers of Korean immigrants settling north of the Tumen River. Nor was there much of a response from the Shengjing or Jilin military governors, such as dispatching officials to evict the Korean trespassers or making an effort to send them back to the Chosŏn. However, soon after the land near the Tumen was open for Chinese farmers to settle, the Qing officials realized it had been already occupied by Korean immigrants. In the fall of 1881, acting upon Wu Dacheng's order, Hunchun officials investigated the areas around two hundred *li* north of the Tumen River and realized that several thousands of Korean farmers had developed as much as two thousand *xiang* of land. They also found that the number of Korean immigrants was continuing to grow, and that the Chosŏn officials of Hamgyŏng Province were even issuing land certificates to people in the area around Hunchun.[45]

Upon receiving such reports, the Jilin military governor Ming-an insisted that Chosŏn officials had no standing to discuss property matters in areas north of the Tumen River. He stressed that Korean immigrants were "children of the Heavenly Court" and therefore should be permitted to settle in Qing territory, instead of being sent back to the Chosŏn. He further claimed that these Koreans were China's subjects (*Zhongguo zhi min*), since they had settled on and cultivated China's land, and that they should be allowed to pay taxes to the Qing government and wear Chinese clothes. This following comment from the Board of Rites shows how the Qing court viewed Korean immigrants at this time:

> The people now under discussion have already cultivated China's land; therefore, they should be considered China's subjects. According to the report of the military governor [Ming-an], they should be allowed to receive land certificates and pay taxes. In addition, following a designated period of time they should be included in our territory and taught to follow our rules and wear our clothing. They can be given temporary permission to keep their customs for a while, just as people in Yunnan and Guizhou were allowed to do.[46]

Agreeing with his officials' suggestions, the Guangxu emperor ordered that Korean settlers be issued land certificates and allowed to pay taxes. He further concluded that the Korean immigrants should be placed under the jurisdiction of Hunchun and Dunhua. This decision implied that Korean settlers to the north of the Tumen River would be regarded as Qing subjects.[47]

This plan of naturalizing immigrant Koreans as Qing subjects was met with strong opposition from the Chosŏn court, which found it unacceptable. If it condoned such a practice on the part of the Qing, the Chosŏn court reasoned, the Russians and the Japanese would be likely to raise similar demands:

> [Chinese and Korean people] have different customs and cultures. Those people who crossed and settled in [Qing territory] were born and raised in our country [the Chosŏn]. It would be a problem on both sides of the boundary if these illegal settlers, after being assimilated with [the Qing people], did not observe [Qing] regulations and made trouble instead. The Chosŏn shares boundaries with Russia in the north and with Japan in the east; there are also some local people who trespassed [in these neighbors' territories] just like those who crossed the Tumen River. If these countries try to apply this precedent of the Heavenly Court [to their own boundaries], they will face the same troubles.[48]

Because of these concerns, the Chosŏn court insisted that the Guangxu emperor should order Qing officials in Hunchun and Dunhua to send the Korean immigrants back to their own country. The emperor eventually agreed to send Korean settlers back to the Chosŏn within a year: "It is proper that Korean wanderers who settled in Jilin should be sent back to their country. However, if they are immediately removed, they may not be able to make a living. Let them go back home within a year as a sign of my benevolence."[49]

Nonetheless, Guangxu's decision to send Korean immigrants back to the Chosŏn did not mean that the Qing government simply gave up its efforts to extend its administrative authority to Koreans living in Qing territory. On the contrary, it began to issue new regulations applicable to Korean immigrants. In 1885, the Bureau of Trade and Commerce of Jilin and Korea (*Ji Han tongshangju*) was established and given charge of all affairs involving trade, taxation, and cultivation. The Qing government also built new offices at several locations north of the Tumen River, especially those that lay across the river from the locations of Chosŏn administrative offices, such as Hoeryŏng, Chongsŏng, and Onsŏng. The primary job of these new offices was to "govern the Korean immigrants [*Hanmin*] and settle disputes between Koreans and Chinese [*Huamin*]." Qing officials designated an area of land as wide as seven hundred *li* north of the Tumen River exclusively for Korean immigrants, who were granted a tax exemption for five years. These policies to authorize Korean settlement north of the river caused rapid growth in the number of Koreans emigrating across the Tumen River, so that by 1886 as many as 12,490 Koreans in 2,350 households had moved to the Hunchun area.[50]

Meanwhile, the Chosŏn court's opposition to the Qing government's efforts to naturalize Korean immigrants as Qing subjects and its subsequent appeal to have such immigrants sent back to the Chosŏn did not necessarily reflect the interests of the actual people who were the subject of these discussions between Beijing and

Seoul. The Korean settlers north of the river believed that they had been forced to risk their lives and cross the river because of the long-lasting famine and perpetual hunger back home, and that they had had to endure many difficulties before settling down in the area. Not surprisingly, they did not want to give up their new homes. In 1883, when Qing officials in Dunhua informed Korean immigrants that they should go back to their own country after that year's harvest, the newcomers decided to "challenge the assumption inherent in the Qing demand," namely, that the area where they had settled lay outside Chosŏn territory.[51] They made the claim that this area was, in fact, part of Chosŏn territory.

This argument was first addressed in 1883 by the local people in Chongsŏng, who wrote a petition to the Qing officials in Dunhua. It was an extremely unusual action, in that no local Korean had ever made direct contact with the Qing authorities. Their letter explained that there were actually two different rivers, both called "Tumen" in Chinese pronunciation but written in different characters; these two rivers were, in fact, distinguished from one another in Korean pronunciation as "T'omun" and "Tuman." They further argued that the Qing and Chosŏn territories were separated by the T'omun, not the Tuman, and that the land between the two rivers belonged to the Chosŏn. Their evidence was the stone marker of Mu-ke-deng, which had been erected in 1712 as a part of the investigation of Changbaishan and which proclaimed that the boundary of the two countries was demarcated by the Yalu River in the west and by the Tumen River in the east. The local Koreans asserted that the "Tumen River" inscribed in the stele was actually the T'omun River, not the Tuman.[52] Two months later, following the local residents' petition, the Chongsŏng prefect sent an official letter to the Qing counterpart in Dunhua, repeating the same argument that the T'omun and the Tuman were two different rivers. Based on this claim, the Chongsŏng prefect refused to cooperate with the Qing government's plan to send Korean immigrants back to the Chosŏn.[53] Korean immigrants and the local Chosŏn authorities, for their part, firmly contended that the Tuman mentioned on the Mu-ke-deng's stele was the Hailanhe (K. *Haeran'gang*), another river located farther north from the Tuman, and that the land they settled in, therefore, was within Chosŏn territory. Finally, in 1885, the Chosŏn court proposed a boundary investigation to the Qing Board of Rites and the new office of foreign affairs, the Zongli yamen, asking that Qing officials be sent to the Tumen River.[54] Attaching a copy of the old map of the area and a rubbing of the stele to a letter to the Qing court, the Korean officials proposed a joint field investigation to check the stele and the origin of the Tumen and to clarify the boundary of the two countries.[55]

Were the Tuman and T'omun in fact different rivers? The *Songs of Flying Dragons* (K. *Yongbi ŏchŏn'ga*), published by the Chosŏn court in 1447, provides an explanation of the location of "T'omun," saying that "T'omun is the name of place north of the Tuman River, sixty *li* away from Kyŏngwŏn."[56] This explanation shows that in the fifteenth century the Chosŏn court distinguished between "T'omun" and "Tuman." During the investigation of Changbaishan in 1712, however, Chosŏn officials used the names "T'omun" and "Tuman" interchangeably. Pak Kwŏn, the Chosŏn counterpart of Mu-ke-deng, recognized the "Tuman" as the boundary, while the Manchu official called it the "Tumen," but they did not disagree regarding which river the names denoted. The Chosŏn court officials were also well aware that "the so-called T'omun River in the letter [from the Qing] is the Chinese pronunciation of the Tuman (K. *T'omun'gang chŭk hwaŭm Tuman'gang*)."[57] By the middle of the eighteenth century, the Chosŏn court was fully aware that the two rivers, the Tuman and the T'omun, were in reality one and the same river being called by two different names. In 1757, when the Qing court asked the Chosŏn court about the "Tuman" while investigating Korean trespassers, the latter court provided a detailed answer:

> The names of the Tuman and T'omun Rivers are very close. The river in the north of the small country is called Tuman by [Korean] people. The Tuman that those criminals referred to is nothing but the T'omun, a name used by the great country. Han Sanglim [one of the trespassers] said "T'omun," while Cho Chayŏng [the other trespasser] said "Tuman," but it is the same river with two names.[58]

In addition, a Korean map, officially commissioned by the Chosŏn court during the years 1777 to 1791 and titled "Map of the Northwestern Boundary" (K. *Sŏbuk kyedo*), demonstrates the contemporaneous Korean understanding that the T'omun and the Tuman were the same river.[59]

By the late nineteenth century, however, when the location of the Tumen River became a source of conflict with the Qing, the Chosŏn court either forgot or ignored the geographic knowledge that it had possessed in the eighteenth century and decided to accept the arguments made by the local residents in the area. Interestingly, this shows that the Koreans selected, recalled, and reinterpreted their own geographic knowledge of their territory in accordance with the new situation that they faced in the late nineteenth century. The Chosŏn court in the early eighteenth century had been willing to ignore the fact that the imperial emissary had located the Tumen riverhead in the wrong place, whereas the Koreans in the late nineteenth century endeavored to find the exact location of the same riverhead. The eighteenth-century Chosŏn court had been reluctant to share geographic information about the boundary with the Qing; by contrast, the late nineteenth-century Koreans took the initiative to clarify the boundary. The dramatic shift in the Chosŏn attitude shows that Korean ideas about territorial boundaries had undergone a profound change by the late nineteenth century, the era in which both parties' willingness to tolerate the existence of the borderland—that is, the ambiguity of the exact location of the boundary and the uninhabited buffer zone around it—was about to end.

It was the stone stele of Mu-ke-deng that provided the two sides with the source of their disputes over the exact location of the boundary. Officials from the two countries held very different interpretations of the stone marker built in 1712. Chosŏn officials stressed that Mu-ke-deng, the imperial emissary of the Kangxi emperor, had investigated the origins of the rivers specifically in order to clarify the Qing-Chosŏn boundary, and they maintained that the stele was the outcome of his research. Therefore, if there was any uncertainty about the boundary, Koreans claimed, the stele should be used as the standard of judgment. In contrast to the Chosŏn officials, who were firmly convinced of the authority of the stele, Qing officials did not think that the stele provided indisputable evidence of the location of the boundary.[60] While Chosŏn court officials were widely aware of Mu-ke-deng's investigation and the resulting stele, only a few individuals at the Qing court had paid attention to the stele's erection. The stele was not well known or much discussed among Qing scholars of geography, and this lack of information explains, in part, why Qing officials gave so little credence to it. Furthermore, most of the documents related to Mu-ke-deng's travels and investigation had already been lost, so that Qing officials did not have much evidence with which to verify the legitimacy of the stele. The Qing officials also emphasized that the name Tumen came from a Manchu word *tumen*, which means "ten thousand," and the river happened to be known by two names thanks to the use of different Chinese characters. From the Qing point of view, then, the boundary should be established on the basis of the origin of the river, not on the basis of an old, unreliable stone marker.[61]

DEMARCATING THE BORDER

It took two years before the Qing and Chosŏn governments finally launched a joint survey of the boundary. The question about the exact location of the Tumen riverhead was first raised by local Koreans, then shared with the Chosŏn local officials, and finally reached Seoul and Beijing. The Chosŏn authorities of Chongsŏng had first proposed such a survey to their Qing counterpart in Dunhua in July 1883; then, in August 1885, the Chosŏn court sent an official letter to the Qing Board of Rites and the Zongli yamen arguing that the Tuman and the T'omun were two different rivers and thus it was necessary to investigate the area. Finally, in September 1885, Li Hongzhang responded to the Chosŏn court, agreeing to conduct a joint Qing-Chosŏn survey.[62] Two months later, November 6, 1885, Qing inspectors went to Hoeryŏng to meet with their Chosŏn counterparts. The main issue to resolve was the question of whether the Tuman and the T'omun were in fact one and the same river. The Qing officials argued that they were, but their Chosŏn counterparts disagreed. Another disagreement concerned the question of what should be the reference point for determining the location of the boundary: the river or the stele. The Qing officials claimed that since the stream that passed east of the stele flowed into the Sungari River, not into the Tumen, the stele of Mu-ke-deng failed to provide accurate geographical information. In response, the Korean inspectors referred to the official documents exchanged between the two courts at the time when the stele was erected and insisted that Mu-ke-deng's investigation and stele were legitimate and reliable criteria for locating the boundary. Despite two months of surveying and discussions, the two sides did not reach an agreement: the negotiations failed, and the officials returned to their respective countries.[63]

Two years later, on April 29, 1887, the Qing and Chosŏn courts resumed the boundary survey. This time it was the Jilin military governor who insisted on the urgency of the survey, as Korean immigration and settlement had continued after the failure of the earlier survey effort and conflicts were increasing between Chinese and Korean residents over land cultivation, causing serious tensions in local societies.[64] In this second round of discussions, the Chosŏn officials withdrew their initial assertion that the T'omun and the Tuman were distinct rivers. In fact, the Korean inspector, Yi Chungha (1846–1917), had been aware that it was the same river during his first investigation of 1885. Eventually the Chosŏn court official, Kim Yunsik (1835–1922), sent a letter to the Yuan Shikai (1859–1916) as early as October 1886 admitting that "the T'omun and the Tuman were the same river with different names."[65] Instead, what became the main issue in the second boundary survey was the location of the Tumen River's source. The Chosŏn officials identified Hongtushan shui (K. *Hongt'osan su*), one of the streams flowing from Changbaishan, as the origin of the Tumen River, while the Qing counterproposed Shiyishui (K. *Sŏgŭlsu*), another stream from the mountain, as the source—a choice that, if used to determine the boundary, would allow the Qing to claim the entire Changbaishan range and, as the Qing official pointed out, "the sacred birthplace [*faxiang zhi ben*] will not be violated."[66] The Chosŏn refused to accept Shiyishui as the origin of the Tumen, asserting that "there is no evidence to prove it in any document." In the end, after another one and a half months of surveys and debates, the two sides again failed to reach an agreement about the boundary.[67]

The Qing and Chosŏn officials were all well aware of the significance of territorial boundaries and sovereignty, an issue that was newly raised in modern international relations. While Yi Chungha knew that Hongtushan shui was only a few *li* away from Shiyishui and the land between them was actually useless, he still insisted that Hongtushan shui be the boundary, because "even a tiny piece of state territory is so important."[68] The fact that the Chosŏn court demanded field investigations in order to demarcate the boundary demonstrates that the Koreans had begun to recognize the system of international relations in which a country is defined by distinct boundaries and territorial sovereignty. These changes in Korean views of the Qing are well reflected in a memorial from Chi Kyŏngyong, a local official in the northern region, to the Chosŏn court in 1884. First stating that the

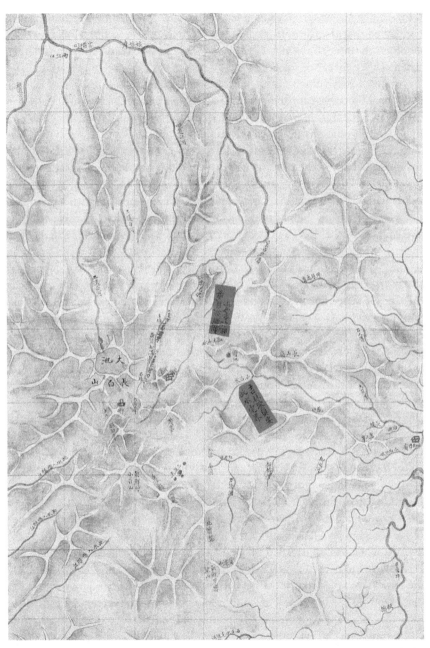

FIGURE 12. Changbaishan and the Tumen riverhead. Detail from *Paektusan chŏnggyebi chido* (maps of the stele of Changbaishan), 1887. Manuscript, 54.2 × 99 cm. Kyujanggak Institute for Korean Studies of Seoul National University, no. ko-ch'uk 26675. Used with permission.

Qing-Chosŏn boundary lay along the Hailanhe, not the Tumen River, Chi then contended that the Chosŏn should make an open claim to the Qing, especially since at the time "all the states in the world are in discussion with one another, whether they are big or small."[69]

Among Korean intellectuals, various conflicting ideas—strong nationalism, traditional Sinocentrism, and a limited understanding of the international world order—were held in an uneven fashion. As Andre Schmid stresses, Qing-Chosŏn boundary negotiations in the late 1880s demonstrate how the tributary relationship maintained its unique features, as well as how it was challenged and ultimately collapsed. Both sides frequently used old terms, such as "great country" (C. *daguo*; K. *taeguk*) and "small country" (C. *xiaobang*; K. *sobang*).[70] Using the same methods by which the Chosŏn kings had long appealed to the Qing emperor—emphasizing the old traditions of the tributary relationship between the two countries—the Korean inspector argued that all of the characters inscribed on the stele were included in the documents of the "Heavenly Court," representing an absolute verification that should not be disputed or disrespected.[71] As a representative of the Chosŏn court, Yi Chungha tried to challenge Qing authority to dispute the Chosŏn state's territorial sovereignty, but what he relied on in his negotiations with the neighboring country was the age-old rhetoric of the special relationship of the Chosŏn with the Qing. The expectation of imperial benevolence toward the Chosŏn was clearly revealed in Kim Yunsik's petition to Yuan Shikai for "borrowing [Qing] land for [Korean] settlement" (K. *ch'aji anch'i*), which asked the Qing for permission for the Korean farmers north of the Tumen to stay, while the Chosŏn authorities be given the right to collect tax from them. The tradition of asymmetrical relations between the Qing and the Chosŏn, and the recognition of territorial sovereignty, coexisted in Kim's impractical suggestion to borrow the Qing land for the Korean immigrants.[72] As Akizuki Nozomi points out, "By the 1880s, the Chosŏn court did not fully understand that the modern system of international relations was more or less in conflict with the tradition of Sinocentricism."[73]

During the 1880s and 1890s, the Qing court continued to undertake a major change in policy toward people and territory in the northeast. The new policy of encouraging people to settle at the northeastern margins eventually led to the invitation of Korean farmers into Qing territory north of the Tumen, a plan that was believed to benefit the Qing government through the collection of taxes and the improvement of security at the boundary. During the boundary surveys and discussions of the late 1880s, the Qing continued to invite Korean immigrants to Qing territory, making them into Qing subjects and requiring them to adopt Qing customs of dress and appearance.[74] As Yi Chiyŏng points out, the Qing at first considered Korean immigrants "foreigners living in our territory," while the Chosŏn regarded them as "our subjects living in foreign territory." Later, both sides argued that these Korean settlers were "our subjects in our territory."[75] These changes in the respective views of the Qing and the Chosŏn regarding the Korean immigrants in the area north of the rivers are another indicator of the transformation of their ideas about territory and sovereignty. The two states were no longer willing to accept the existence of an unclear buffer zone; instead, they sought to claim the right to rule both the people and the territory demarcated by a clear border. The Qing authorities tried to turn Korean immigrants into Qing subjects by listing them in Qing registers. For their part, the Chosŏn endeavored to resolve the problem of Korean settlers north of the Tumen, first, by claiming the territory as part of the Chosŏn realm, and later, by borrowing the land from the Qing for Korean immigrants. The series of Qing-Chosŏn boundary negotiations was provoked by illegal Korean immigration in the area that the two states had agreed to keep uninhabited, a phenomenon that led them to reconsider the empty buffer zone laying between them—more precisely, territorial sovereignty. This transition was clearly related to the emergence of the modern notion of national space as the core of a state's sovereignty. The empty buffer zone that blurred the exact limits of the two states' territories suddenly was undermining their power and authority and was thus no longer acceptable: "Sovereignty was something to be performed, and borders were to be implemented."[76]

It was the Sino-Japanese War of 1895 that officially ended the traditional tributary relationship between the Qing and the Chosŏn. The Qing army was defeated by Japanese troops, a clear affirmation that the Qing had no military or legal power to claim continued suzerainty over the Chosŏn. With the end of the war, the Qing court lost all of the exclusive privileges it had commanded from the Chosŏn court, including Korean tributary missions to the Qing emperor. The practices that had both embodied and symbolized the hierarchical relationship between the Qing and Chosŏn courts thus officially came to an end.[77] Four years after the end of Sino-Japanese War, in 1899, the Qing and Chosŏn courts reached the Treaty of Seoul, the twelfth article of which prohibited any further Korean trespassing in Qing territory, while guaranteeing the security of those Koreans who had already settled there.[78] In the meantime, the repatriation of Korean immigrants living north of the Tumen back to the Chosŏn was continuously delayed.

The Boxer Rebellion of 1900 expedited the fall of the Qing dynasty and prompted foreign expansion into China proper as well as into its peripheries. Taking advantage of the crisis, Russia quickly occupied Manchuria, including several locations near the Korean boundary. The Russian occupation of Manchuria provided Korea with an opportunity to extend its authority in the Kando region north of the Tumen River, as the Qing forces were largely constrained by Russian troops and Russia wanted to act favorably toward Korea in order to check Japanese movements in the Korean peninsula. The Korean government hoped to settle its boundary dispute with the Qing court by negotiating with Russia.[79] In an attempt to consolidate its rule over the Kando region, the Korean government sent a special inspector in 1902 to investigate the number of Korean households and people living there. However, the increasing competition between Russia and Japan in Manchuria dashed Korea's hopes of expanding its territory northward. By defeating Russia in the Russo-Japanese War of 1904 and making Korea into a Japanese protectorate in 1905, Japan took the lead in the boundary negotiations between China and Korea.[80]

In 1906, the Japanese established a police substation in Longjing and announced that Kando should be included in Korean territory; the following year, Japan further claimed that the Koreans had no obligation to follow Qing regulations. The Qing court rejected the Japanese claim that Kando was Korean territory, insisting on its exclusive right to rule the people and territory north of the Tumen River. On September 4, 1909, after several years of negotiations, China finally signed what became known as the "six treaties on the Three Eastern Provinces" (*Dong sansheng liu'an*), which allowed Japan to build railways and develop mines in Manchuria. One of the treaties was the "arrangement on the Tumen boundary between China and Korea" (*Tumenjiang Zhong Han jiewu tiaokuan*), also widely known as the Agreement of Kando, which secured China's territorial claims to the Kando region. This arrangement stated in its first article that "the China-Korean boundary is the Tumen and the origin of the river is Shiyishui," further explaining in following articles that Korean immigrants north of the Tumen should be governed by Chinese laws and included within the jurisdictions of Chinese officials.[81] By the time the Chinese-Korean boundary was finally confirmed, however, both the Qing and the Chosŏn courts were doomed. As the borderland they had shared for so long was replaced by a border, the old Qing and Chosŏn states were destined to disappear. The Qing empire and the Chosŏn kingdom could tolerate the existence of a borderland, but modern China and Korea needed a clear border between them.

. . .

Ginseng in Manchuria had been carefully managed throughout the Qing period by a well-developed system of imperial foraging. Such systemic exploitations of ginseng for centuries eventually brought about the depletion of wild ginseng to the extent that the state could not maintain its ginseng monopoly. And as ginseng disappeared in the Manchurian mountains, it was no longer ginseng poachers or illegal sable hunters who violated the restrictions on entering the region; instead, Chinese farmers came in search of land. Once providing wealth and prestige for the Manchus, Manchuria gradually came under the plow of Chinese farmers. As the Qing decided to open the northeastern margins to civilian settlement for the purpose of protecting their territory from foreign aggression, the flow of Chinese immigration reached the Yalu and Tumen Rivers, once a ginseng producing area that had been closed to civilian settlement. Under the strong pressure of

immigrants, the agreement between the Qing and the Chosŏn for the uninhabited empty zone at the boundary—one feature of the borderland—was no longer
maintained. Even as the Qing authorities tried to develop the land near the Tumen
River, they found it already occupied by Korean immigrants. Given the competition for land and people, they had to solve the ambiguity of the exact location
of the boundary—the other feature of the borderland. The joint investigations
of the Tumen riverhead in the 1880s were an announcement that the Qing and
the Chosŏn could no longer maintain the borderland that they had shared for
centuries. As the ideas and practices of territory and sovereignty transformed, the
borderland was replaced by a border.

Conclusion

Geography textbooks teach us that the Yalu and Tumen Rivers are the boundary between China and Korea. This seemingly straightforward fact was anything but clear during most of the long history of Chinese-Korean relations, because the territorial boundaries of these two countries, as well as their political relations, were subject to interpretation and negotiation. Just as the meanings of "China" and "Korea" have changed throughout history, so have perceptions of the boundaries between these two political entities evolved over time. The Chinese-Korean boundary has always been a place of encounters where people come into contact as well as conflict; simultaneously, their constant movements and interactions have led to the repeated rearrangement and redefinition of their countries' mutual relations. At some times, the boundary was a thick line, consisting of a vaguely defined zone within which the limits of territory and sovereignty were ambiguous and often overlapped. In other times, the two states sought to draw a sharp line to clearly divide their respective realms, a task that they found far from easy. Depending on the circumstances in which the neighbors found themselves, their boundary took the form of a frontier, a borderland, or a border. In this sense, the conceptions and practices of boundary between China and Korea are a reflection of their domestic politics and foreign relations. The Yalu and Tumen Rivers have been in the same place since time immemorial, but the Chinese and Korean ideas about them have been subject to continuous change.

Ginseng production in the region near the Yalu and Tumen Rivers and Changbaishan helps us trace the development of the boundary from frontier to borderland and finally to border. This precious root growing in the wildness of Manchuria and the Korean peninsula was an object of reverence due to its medical efficacy and commercial value. The Jurchens and the Koreans had an equal interest in the ginseng growing at their shared boundary. Once the Manchus established their state in Liaodong and claimed control over their territorial realm, the Yalu and Tumen Rivers became the boundary between the Jurchen/Manchu state and the Chosŏn. The natural resource of ginseng, as well as the territory in which it grew, became off-limits for the Koreans south of the rivers. The Jurchen-Chosŏn frontier, a vaguely defined zone where crossing the nominal boundary for the purpose of ginseng collection might have been overlooked, was more clearly demarcated, and trespassing for ginseng poaching in the neighboring state's territory began to be severely punished. The interest of the Qing in protecting the ginseng reserves around the Yalu and Tumen Rivers and their commitment to the strategic and cultural importance of Manchuria are clearly revealed in two separate projects regarding the boundary with the Chosŏn: the Changbaishan investigation and the military guard post at the Yalu River. These projects were initiated by the Qing court and promoted by Manchu officials for the goal of curbing unauthorized access to ginseng near the two rivers. After extensive examinations and discussions, the solution agreed upon by the two states was not the establishment of a clearly defined dividing line—a border—between their spatial realms. Instead, they decided to create and maintain a borderland, in which some parts of the boundary remained undefined and others were kept uninhabited by force. After centuries of unconstrained exploitation of the limited ginseng resources in Manchuria, ginseng became scarce. Trespassing for ginseng gradually disappeared at the boundary, but growing numbers of people began to settle in the land near the Yalu and Tumen Rivers. Instead of the privileged Manchus and ginseng hunters, Han Chinese settlers occupied Manchuria as well as the Chosŏn boundary. As the supposedly prohibited land at the boundary was occupied by illegal settlers, the Qing and the Chosŏn faced a serious challenge, compelling them to redefine their boundary as a clearly drawn line. Ginseng and people's movements in search of it thus shaped the nature of the Qing-Chosŏn boundary, causing its transformation from frontier to borderland to border.

Before the Manchus claimed rulership over Liaodong, the Ming, the Jurchens, and the Chosŏn had vague and porous frontiers. The history of the Jurchens is best illustrated through their close relations with the Ming and Chosŏn governments, with each of whom they intermingled politically and economically. While the Jurchens and the Koreans both paid tribute to the Ming court and acknowledged the superiority of the Son of Heaven in China, the Chosŏn claimed a status higher than that of the Jurchen "barbarians" by virtue of the official titles and trading opportunities they were granted. The Jurchen economy, based as it was primarily on hunting and gathering, made the Jurchens dependent on frontier markets with neighboring agricultural societies and eventually placed them in a vulnerable position in relation to the Ming and Chosŏn courts. The rise of the Jurchens in the late sixteenth century, however, caused a major rift in the three-sided relationship centered on Liaodong. Nurhaci began to challenge Ming authority after his successful unification of various Jurchen tribes and rival groups near his homeland. By the time Hong Taiji succeeded Nurhaci as the leader of the Aisin Gurun, it became obvious that the Jurchens no longer intended to regard their state's boundaries with Ming China and Chosŏn Korea as vague and porous. Instead, Hong Taiji wanted to protect his people and territory, preserve economic benefits for the Aisin Gurun, and enhance his authority even beyond the territorial realm of his Manchu state.

In order to accomplish these multiple goals, Hong Taiji focused on wild ginseng, a highly valuable natural resource growing near the boundaries with his neighbors and an essential element in the saga of the Jurchen people. The Jurchens had a long history of trading ginseng with the Ming Chinese at frontier markets, which provided them with a commercial opportunity to build their power in Liaodong. As they began to challenge Ming authority in Liaodong during the early seventeenth century, the areas in which this precious root grew came to serve as signposts dividing Jurchen territory from the neighboring Ming and Chosŏn states. Hong Taiji complained about Ming Chinese entering his territory and poaching ginseng, a carefully calculated action that made the plant off-limits to anyone other than the Manchus and helped the Aisin Gurun exploit the power of ginseng as a physical and cultural marker symbolizing Manchuness. But Ming China was not the only neighbor against whom Hong Taiji employed ginseng: the Jurchen ruler's most strenuous efforts were aimed at protecting this valuable commodity from Chosŏn Koreans. He made numerous complaints to the Chosŏn court about Korean encroachments for the purpose of ginseng poaching, claims that he then used to justify the attacks of 1627 and 1637 on the Chosŏn state. Hong Taiji thus protected the exclusive right of the Manchus to gather ginseng and succeeded in asserting his authority against the Chosŏn by redefining the nature of the boundary with the Chosŏn away from an ambiguous frontier. However, he did not succeed in drawing a clear-cut line to separate the two realms. The tributary relationship, achieved through Hong Taiji's two military campaigns, allowed his successors to create a borderland with the Chosŏn—more definite than the previous frontier, but still retaining elements of ambiguity.

The Qing-Chosŏn borderland rested on two principles: the asymmetrical tributary relationship, and the Qing restrictive policy on Manchuria. Ginseng continued to claim a special status in the Qing empire after the 1644 conquest of China. Access to ginseng was authorized only for Manchu aristocrats and banner members, and the profits from the ginseng harvest were reserved exclusively for the imperial court. The natural resources of Manchuria, as well as the hallowed land itself, were carefully preserved as symbols of the Manchus through a series of rules and regulations. One of the biggest threats to Manchuria and ginseng was, in fact, Korean trespassing in Qing territory. The tributary relationship established between the Qing and Chosŏn courts as a result of Hong Taiji's military campaigns did not stop local Koreans from crossing the Yalu and Tumen Rivers in search of ginseng. To the contrary, trespassing continued to disrupt relations between the two neighbors until the end of the nineteenth century. Korean trespassers were decapitated on the Yalu River in order to deter future criminals; Chosŏn officials were dismissed or demoted for failing to ensure adequate patrols at the boundary; and the Chosŏn king himself was blamed for neglecting his duty to serve the Qing emperor when cases of trespassing were discovered. In the early seventeenth century, as a part of a broader project of mapping the homeland of the Manchu imperial court, the Kangxi emperor proposed a joint survey with the Chosŏn authorities to establish the location of the origin of the Yalu and Tumen Rivers. This Qing survey initiative was not, however, well received by the Chosŏn court, which still held anti-Qing sentiments stemming from memories of inferior Manchu "barbarians" and devastating military defeats more than seventy years earlier. Despite their arduous surveying efforts in Changbaishan, Manchu and Korean officials ultimately failed to locate the origin of the Tumen River and ended up leaving the boundary at the upper Tumen River under-defined and unclear.

The process of the Changbaishan investigation and the debates surrounding it reveal the unique features of the respective conceptions of territory and sovereignty held by the Qing and the Chosŏn. The Qing reaction to the results of the investigation—namely, the incorrectly identified location of the Tumen River's source—tells us that the Kangxi emperor did not necessarily aim at clarifying the territorial boundary with the Chosŏn state. Instead, his primary interest in the northeast at the time, especially after the 1689 Treaty of Nerchinsk, lay in bringing the various tribal groups living there under Qing control and preventing further Russian influence over them. Kangxi's efforts to determine the boundaries of the empire and to fix them visually on maps were not necessarily aimed at containing Chosŏn Korea, a small neighbor who, in the early eighteenth century, was not regarded as posing any serious threat to Qing power. It was the loyalty of the Chosŏn, not a clear-cut demarcation of territorial limits, that the Qing sought to secure with the investigation of Changbaishan. However, the Chosŏn response to the investigation and to the resulting stone marker shows that Koreans had a very different perspective on their territory and sovereignty. The Chosŏn court's suspicions arose from its hostility toward the Manchus as well as from a desire to protect its lands from its powerful neighbor. Taking advantage of the relative lack of interest on the part of the Qing in territorial limits—based on the attitude that a superior power would not deign to fight with an inferior neighbor for a small piece of land—the Chosŏn decided to overlook the incorrect location of the Tumen riverhead. In other words, it was precisely the special relationship between the Qing and Chosŏn states, that is, their tributary relationship, that led the two neighbors to tolerate the unclear demarcation of their territories at the upper Tumen River. This ambiguity, intentionally left between their territories and authorized by the tributary relationship, was one of the key features of the Qing-Chosŏn borderland.

If the boundary at the upper Tumen River in the east was unclear, at the Yalu River in the west it remained empty, cleared of inhabitation. In the early eighteenth century, Qing officials in Shengjing in charge of inspecting the boundary with the Chosŏn attempted several times to station soldiers at a guard post near the Yalu River in order to deter both Qing and Chosŏn trespassers. However, the Chosŏn government launched an all-out effort to stop Qing officials and their soldiers from approaching Korean territory. After much discussion and debate, the Yongzheng and Qianlong emperors decided to accept the Chosŏn king's appeal not to station soldiers at the Yalu River, a conclusion that contrasted dramatically with the cruel attitudes of Qing rulers in the previous century toward Korean trespassers. As much as the Qing emperors desired to establish their claim to the Mandate of Heaven, they also wished to present themselves as benevolent, embracing rulers of all of their domestic and foreign subjects. For eighteenth-century Qing rulers, security at the boundary with an unintimidating neighbor was less important than gaining and maintaining the respect of an old tributary state. Here, again, the tributary relationship between the Qing and the Chosŏn was the defining factor behind the maintenance of an empty buffer zone at the Yalu River—the second key feature of the Qing-Chosŏn borderland.

In addition to the Qing emperor's desire to present himself to his subjects as a universal ruler, there was another reason the Qing agreed to retain the empty zone at the boundary with the Chosŏn: the primary goal of Qing policy in Manchuria was the protection of the northeastern region from Han Chinese. Throughout the Qing period, Jilin and Heilongjiang were kept off-limits to Han civilians in order to preserve the region as the sacred birthplace of the imperial court and the last bastion of the Manchus. Within the vast territory of Manchuria, access to the Yalu River and Changbaishan—the specific homeland of the Aisin Gioro family and the richest source of ginseng—was thoroughly restricted as early as the seventeenth century. Between the Willow Palisade—a physical array of gates and outposts enforcing the ban on unauthorized access to the northeastern region—and the region north of the Yalu River there remained a wide swath of empty land where people were not allowed to settle. Such a buffer zone allowed the Qing government to avoid contact and conflict with neighboring people; it also required the Chosŏn court to control and punish its own trespassing subjects, another way that the Qing showed the generosity of the great power to the tributary state. The Chosŏn authorities, in turn, made every effort to uphold the Qing regulations by striving to leave the areas around the Yalu and Tumen Rivers undisturbed. Restrictions of movement into Manchuria and the Chosŏn boundary were successfully enforced as long as Qing authority was absolutely dominant in the northeast and unconditionally respected by the Chosŏn court. Once Qing supremacy began to be challenged in the late nineteenth century, the idea of the untouched land at the boundary with Chosŏn territory came under pressure.

The empty zone at the Yalu River was never vacant in reality, however; instead, it continuously attracted people who engaged in a range of economic activities in the region. Ever since the complete surrender of the Chosŏn to the Manchus in 1637, the Chosŏn court took pains to observe the Qing demand to send tributary missions to the Son of Heaven in Beijing. Under various titles and within different types of missions, a great number of people joined the official embassy every year and crossed the Yalu River to enter Qing territory. During the journey from the last location in Chosŏn territory, Ŭiju, to the first entry point into Qing territory, Fenghuangcheng, several hundred Korean visitors participated in official rituals enacting Qing-Chosŏn relations and took advantage of a variety of trading opportunities with Qing merchants. In the remote areas at the empire's margin, where the Qing state sought to enforce a strict prohibition on entry and settlement, the Chosŏn visitors had to find forms of assistance other than the limited services provided by the Qing authorities in order to deliver their numerous tribute packages for the emperor and to transport necessities for themselves. As a result, the supposedly restricted zone unexpectedly gave a great number of Korean merchants an opportunity to cross the Yalu River under the excuse of assisting the embassy. In addition, local Qing people were eventually hired by the Chosŏn travelers as horsemen, cart drivers, innkeepers, and porters. Despite the state's efforts to limit contact between Qing and Chosŏn people, the Chosŏn tribute missions transformed this remote area into a lively place of trade and other forms of interaction. The growth of trading opportunities and transportation services and the subsequent debates and disputes show that the tributary relationship both defined the nature of the Qing-Chosŏn boundary and simultaneously provided enabling conditions for the contacts that occurred there. In short, the tributary relationship created the Qing-Chosŏn borderland as well as commercialized it.

A series of changes in Qing domestic politics and foreign relations in the late nineteenth century caused the disappearance of the Qing-Chosŏn borderland. For centuries, the Qing government had sought to maintain Manchuria and the area at the Yalu and Tumen Rivers as vacant and untainted, a goal that required immense state power in this distant location far away from the center of the empire. However, the vast, uninhabited territory at the boundary attracted from both sides increasing numbers of people hungry for land. In the late nineteenth century, by which time a huge number of civilian settlers had moved from China proper to the northeast and the threat of Russian encroachment in Manchuria was growing, the Qing relinquished the old governing principles of its Manchuria policy—the preservation of Manchuria as off-limits and the maintenance of an uninhabited buffer zone at the boundary with the Chosŏn. Subsequently, the Qing government began to encourage civilian settlement at the empire's margin to protect its territorial sovereignty against foreign powers. With the influx of people from both China proper and the Korean peninsula, the Qing-Chosŏn boundary became, for a while, a vague and porous contact zone—the distinctive feature of a frontier—in which a variety of people interacted. This change in the nature of the Qing-Chosŏn boundary occurred simultaneously with the rearrangement of the traditional hierarchy between the old neighbors. As Qing dominance was challenged by a series of military losses inflicted by foreign powers, Qing influence over Seoul and over the Yalu and Tumen Rivers also waned. The Qing court now had to frame its authority to control the boundary with the Chosŏn in the terms of modern international relations based on sovereign equality, rather than those of the traditional suzerainty envisioned by the Chinese world order. The transition from traditional tributary relations to modern international relations required the two neighbors to reenvision their borderland as a clear border.

The efforts of the two states to demarcate their boundaries and to build modern nation-states were, however, in conflict with the desires of the people crossing the rivers in search of land, wealth, and freedom, and they thus ended up creating another frontier between the nation-states. The most obvious evidence of the ethnic and cultural frontier between modern China and Korea, which emerged amid the clear-cut political borders drawn in the twentieth century, may be the existence of the contemporary population of Korean-Chinese (*Chaoxianzu*), who highlight the complicated history of Chinese and Korean boundaries and territorial sovereignty. Throughout their long relationship, then, the Qing and the Chosŏn saw frontiers, borderlands, and borders emerge between them, and this history lives on in modern China and Korea in the visible legacy of the *Chaoxianzu*.

INTRODUCTION

1. *Tongmun hwigo*, 1:912–16 (*kanggye*: 19b–26a).

2. *Tongmun hwigo*, 1:916–17, 919–20 (*kanggye*: 26b–28a, 33b–34b).

3. The New Qing History scholarship includes Crossley, *Translucent Mirror*; Elliott, *Manchu Way*; Rawski, *Last Emperors*; and Foret, *Mapping Chengde*. For explanation and critiques of the New Qing History, see Waley-Cohen, "New Qing History," 193–206.

4. Lattimore, *Manchuria: Cradle of Conflict*, 276. In addition to Owen Lattimore's work, Lee's *The Manchurian Frontier in Ch'ing History* made an important contribution to exploring Manchu distinctiveness, despite its strong support for the Sinicization of Qing Manchuria, in the sense that it emphasized the significance of Manchuria and non-Han people in Qing history.

5. Wakeman, *Great Enterprise*, 1:37–49; Crossley, *Translucent Mirror*, 47–50.

6. For some of the disagreements of Chinese scholars with the New Qing History scholarship, see Ding and Elliott, "21 shiji ruhe shuxie Zhongguo lishi."

7. For recent Chinese literature on Qing rules in the northeastern region, see Cong, *Zhongguo dongbeishi*, vol. 4; Li, *Dongbei tongshi*; Zhang, *Qingdai dongbei yimin*; Zhang and Zhang, *Qingdai dongbei bianjiang de Manzu*; Ding and Shi, *Qingdai peidu Shengjing yanjiu*; Huang and Luan, *Jilin tongshi*, vol. 2.

8. Edmonds, "Willow Palisade," 621.

9. For studies on Qing Manchuria in the context of Manchu difference, see Elliott, "Limits of Tartary"; Isett, *State, Peasant, and Merchant in Qing Manchuria*; Dan, *Remote Homeland, Recovered Borderland*.

10. Bello, "Cultured Nature of Imperial Foraging"; Bello, *Across Forest, Steppe, and Mountain*.

11. Schlesinger, "Qing Invention of Nature," 44, 157.

12. Rawski, *Early Modern China and Northeast Asia*, 1, 21.

13. Ledyard, "Yin and Yang in the China-Manchuria-Korea Triangle."

14. For Möngke Temür, see Kim, "Oŭmhoe ŭi Alt'ari Yŏjin"; Pak, *Myŏngch'o Chosŏn kwan'gyesa yŏn'gu*; Kawachi, *Mindai Joshinshi no kenkyū*; Liu, *Manzu cong buluo dao guojia*; Crossley, *Translucent Mirror*.

15. Robinson, "Residence and Foreign Relations in the Peninsular Northeast," 21–22.

16. For the ginseng trade during the early Manchu period, see also Inaba, *Manzhou fadashi*; Teng, "Mingdai Jianzhou Nüzhenren," "Ruguan qian Manzhou shehui jingji gailun," "Shilun Houjinguo de xingcheng, xingzhi ji qi tedian"; Iwaki, "China's Frontier Society"; Di Cosmo, "Manchu Conquest in World-Historical Perspective."

17. Imamura, *Ninjinshi*, vol. 2; Cong, *Dongbei sanbao jingji jianshi*; Song and Wang, *Qingdai dongbei shenwu*; Jiang, *Renshen diguo*.

18. Wang, "Qingdai dongbei caishenye"; Tong, "Qingdai Shengjing shenwu."

19. Symons, "Ch'ing Ginseng Management," 79.

20. For detailed analyses of Japanese historiography in the early twentieth century and the scholarship on Manchurian and Korean history (J. *Mansenshi*), see Tanaka, *Japan's Orient*; Nakami, "Nihonteki Tōyōgaku no keisei to kōzu"; Nakami, "Chiiki gainen no seijisei"; Terauchi, "Mansenshi kenkyū to Inaba Iwakichi." For a broader background of the intellectual history of East Asia in the early twentieth century, see various articles in Fogel, *Teleology of the Modern Nation-State*.

21. Inaba, *Manzhou fadashi*; Imamura, *Ninjinshi*, vol. 2. Imamura Tomo began his study of ginseng history in China, Korea, and Japan with the commission of the Japanese colonial government in Seoul (J. *Chōsen shōtokufu*) and completed the seven volumes of his book, which focused on philosophy, politics, economy, cultivation, medicine, miscellaneous records, and important terminologies, respectively, during the years 1934 to 1940.

22. Imamura, *Ninjinshi*, 2:107–11.

23. Fairbank, "A Preliminary Framework." With regard to the circulation of a Sinocentric understanding of Chinese foreign relations, it is necessary to point out that in the early 1960s, Nishijima Sadao also proposed "the theory of the East Asian world" (J. *Higashi Ajia sekairon*), an argument that traditional East Asian countries had created a cultural zone that shared Chinese characters, Confucianism, Chinese laws, and so forth, and that the Chinese emperor and foreign rulers were linked to one another through the political system of "tribute paying and enfeoffment." Nishijima, *Chūgoku kodai kokka to Higashi Ajia sekai*.

24. Rossabi, *China among Equals*; Hevia, *Cherishing Men from Afar*.

25. Di Cosmo, "State Formation and Periodization in Inner Asian History"; Millward, *Beyond the Pass*; Perdue, "Frontier View of Chineseness"; Kim, "Profit and Protection."

26. Di Cosmo, "Kirghiz Nomads on the Qing Frontier," 355.

27. Perdue, *China Marches West*, 403.

28. Reid, "Introduction: Negotiating Asymmetry," 3–4.

29. For examples, see Zhang, *Qingdai Zhong Han guanxi lunwenji*; Liu, *Zhong Chao guanxishi yanjiu*; Xu, *Zhong Han guanxishi*; Zhang, *Qingdai fanbu yanjiu*; Wei, *Zhong Han guanxishi yanjiu*; Huang, *Zhongguo gudai fanshu zhidu yanjiu*.

30. Haboush, "Contesting Chinese Time, Nationalizing Temporal Space"; Bohnet, "Ruling Ideology and Marginal Subjects."

31. Kye, "Huddling under the Imperial Umbrella," 59. Many Korean-language histories have explored the ways in which the Chosŏn court used the Korean elite's loyalty to the Ming to boost its own domestic legitimacy. Kye, *Chosŏn sidae haeoe p'abyŏng*; Han, *Chŏngmyo, Pyŏngja horan*; Hŏ, *Chosŏn hugi chunghwaron*.

32. Mark Mancall explains that the societies of the northwestern crescent, including Mongolia, Xinjiang, and Tibet, were ruled by the Court of Colonial Affairs (*Lifanyuan*) and resembled the Manchu homeland in Manchuria, whereas Korea, Japan, Vietnam, and the Ryukyu constituted the societies of the southeastern crescent and fell under the jurisdiction of the Board of Rites. Mancall, "The Ch'ing Tribute System: An Interpretative Essay." Nicola Di Cosmo provides a better translation of the Lifanyuan, "the court for the administration of outer provinces." Di Cosmo, "Qing Colonial Administration in Inner Asia," 289.

33. Ku, "Chŏng ŭi Chosŏn sahaeng insŏn."

34. Norman, *A Comprehensive Manchu-English Dictionary*. There is no evidence to trace the etymology of this word, but it is possible to guess that *Yalu* originally meant "boundary" for the Jurchen/Manchu people, and the Chinese *Yalu* and Korean *Amnok* originated from that.

35. *Injo sillok*, 15:50 (Injo 5/3/3), translation from Schmid, "Tributary Relations and the Qing-Chosŏn Frontier," 132. Many of the later letters of Hong Taiji to the Chosŏn court emphasized that "each party should observe the territories." *Taizong shilu* 3:22a (Tiancong 1/7/jiaxu); 3:26a (Tiancong 1/9/bingzi); 3:29b (Tiancong 1/12/renyin); 13:12a (Tiancong 7/2/jiashen); 23:22a (Tiancong 9/6/xinmao).

36. Ledyard, "Cartography in Korea," 298–305.

37. Schmid, "Tributary Relations and the Qing-Chosŏn Frontier," 127.

38. Schmid, *Korea between Empires*.

39. Zhang, *Qingdai Zhong Han guanxi*, 217–27.

40. Li, *Han Chung kukkyŏngsa yŏn'gu*, 166–68.

41. Yang and Sun, *Zhong Chao bianjieshi*, 596. Similar interpretations are also found in Chen, *Mukedeng bei wenti yanjiu*.

42. Some Korean scholars argue that the Chosŏn never reached an agreement with the Qing about the exact location of the Tumen riverhead; by the early twentieth century, Japan claimed sovereignty over Korea and handed the Kando territory to China in exchange for the privilege to develop mines in Manchuria. In particular, Kim Kyŏngch'un argues that the land between the Willow Palisade and the Yalu River was "no-man's-land" (K. *muin chidae*) within the actual Chosŏn jurisdiction and that it should therefore be deemed "Korea's lost territory." Kim, "Chosŏnjo hugi ŭi kukkyŏngsŏn."

43. Kim, *1880 nyŏndae Chosŏn Chŏng kukkyŏng hoedam kwallyŏn charyo sŏnyŏk*; Kim, *1880 nyŏndae Chosŏn Chŏng kukkyŏng hoedam ŭi yŏn'gu*.

44. Kang, "1712 nyŏn ŭi Cho Chŏng chŏnggye."

45. Pae, *Chosŏn hugi kukt'ogwan*; Pae, *Chosŏn kwa Chunghwa*.

46. Zhang, *Qingdai Zhong Han guanxi*, 254–64; Li, *Cho Chŏng kukkyŏng munje*, 187, 208; Zhang and Zhang, *Qingdai dongbei bianjiang de Manzu*, 246–53.

47. In fact, Sun Churi also calls the empty space "no-man's-land" (C. *wuren didai*). Sun, *Zhongguo Chaoxianzu*, 88–92.

48. Inaba, *Manzhou fadashi*, 345–46.

49. Pae, *Chosŏn kwa Chunghwa*, 324.

50. Winichakul, *Siam Mapped*, 75–79, 101.

51. Batten, *To the Ends of Japan*, 235–42.

52. Howell, "Ainu Ethnicity and the Boundaries," 142.

53. For similarities and differences between various borderlands, see Baud and Schendel, "Toward a Comparative History of Borderlands." For recent research trends in the study of borders, see Kolossov and Scott, "Selected Conceptual Issues in Border Studies."

54. Parker and Rodseth, "Introduction: Theoretical Considerations in the Study of Frontiers," 9–11. Malcolm Anderson also provides similar definitions: "frontier" refers to the widest meaning, such as a zone or a region, while "border" is applied to a narrow zone or line of demarcation. As the narrowest term, "boundary" is used to refer to the line of delimitation or demarcation. Anderson, *Frontiers*, 9. With regard to relations between Chosŏn Korea and Tokugawa Japan, James Lewis also explains that "'Frontier' [refers] to a zone or region bisected by a legal 'boundary' where the peoples on either side of the boundary interact with each other." Lewis, *Frontier Contact between Chosŏn Korea and Tokugawa Japan*, 7.

55. Adelman and Aron, "From Borderlands to Borders," 815–16. For further discussions and debates about the features of borderland, see Hämäläinen and Truett, "On Borderlands."

56. Perdue, "From Turfan to Taiwan," 28–29. In her studies of Liao history, Naomi Standen does not distinguish frontier from borderland, defining both as "a loosely defined geographical area straddling a borderline." According to Standen, people in tenth-century China did not necessarily understand borders as static entities, nor did they limit their movements within borderlines; instead, they "organized themselves according to administrative centers and allegiances." Standen, *Unbounded Loyalty*, 19–25.

57. It should be noted that the various features of frontiers, borderlands, and borders were apparent also in other regions of the Qing empire. The boundaries of Yunnan under Qing rule, for example, exhibited very different features—more those of a frontier than of a border—compared with the Qing-Chosŏn borderland in the eighteenth century. For a comparative approach to Qing boundary regions, see Millward, "New Perspectives on the Qing Frontier"; Giersch, *Asian Borderlands*; Herman, *Amid the Clouds and Mist*; Teng, *Taiwan's Imagined Geography*; Dai, *Sichuan Frontier and Tibet*.

CHAPTER 1 FROM FRONTIER TO BORDERLAND

1. Portions of this chapter were previously published in Korean as "Insam kwa kangyŏk: Hukŭm Chŏng ŭi kangyŏk insik kwa taeoe kwan'gye ŭi pyŏnhwa," *Myŏngch'ŏngsa yŏnggu* 30 (2008): 227–57.

2. *Sŏnjo sillok*, 28:24a (Sŏnjo 25/7/26); 66:8b (Sŏnjo 28/8/12).

3. *Sŏnjo sillok*, 69:17a (Sŏnjo 28/11/20). When they discussed their visit to Nurhaci in Fe Ala in 1595, the Chosŏn court repeatedly called the Jurchens "barbarous" (K. *kŭmsu*) and "wild people" (K. *hoin*; *no*; *talja*).

4. *Taizong shilu*, 15:13a–14a (Tiancong 7/9/guimao).

5. Chinese scholars refuse to call this region Manchuria, a name that is arguably tainted by the Japanese imperialist project of the twentieth century. Instead, they call it *Dongbei* (the Northeast), emphasizing China's historical and territorial rule over the area. Regarding

the origin of this geographic name, see Elliott, "Limits of Tartary," 604–7. In this sense, as Mariko Asano Tamanoi puts it, *Manchuria* represents "an effect of geopolitical imaginaries," not an actual territory. Tamanoi, *Crossed Histories*, 2.

6. Crossley, *Manchus*, 14–15; Li, *Dongbei tongshi*, 6–11.

7. Regarding the economic and geographic divisions of Manchuria, see Lattimore, *Inner Asian Frontiers of China*, 103–15; Lee, *Manchurian Frontier in Ch'ing History*, 3–4; Barfield, *Perilous Frontier*, 7–8; Di Cosmo, *Ancient China and Its Enemies*, 16–17.

8. Li, *Dongbei tongshi*, 1–6; Kim, *Yodong sa*, 50–61.

9. Farmed ginseng grows fourteen grams per year, whereas wild ginseng gains only one gram per year. Yu, *Uri mome choŭn insam kwa hongsam*, 155–56, 179–80. For ginseng's names and varieties, see Cong, *Dongbei sanbao jingji jianshi*, 2–18.

10. Heffern, *Complete Book of Ginseng*, 9–16; Court, *Ginseng*, 16–18, 23–30.

11. Quoted in Jiang, *Renshen diguo*, 26.

12. If the two lower extremities or "legs" are of equal length, the root is considered to be male. If the two legs are of unequal length, it is considered female. Heffern, *Complete Book of Ginseng*, 39.

13. For early records about ginseng and its medical efficacy, see Cong, *Dongbei sanbao jingji jianshi*, 19–25.

14. Li, *Bencao gangmu*, translation from Hou, *Myth and Truth about Ginseng*, 51.

15. Heffern, *Complete Book of Ginseng*, 22–23, 46.

16. Folktales and legends say that true wild ginseng is not supposed to be seen by humans. According to an ancient Chinese story, ginseng can emerge from the ground with the appearance of a human being; its blood is pure white in color, and just a few drops of it can bring a dead man back to life. Another folktale argues that ginseng can also cure sexual inadequacy, and that high-quality ginseng can restore fertility to a woman who has passed the age of childbearing. Heffern, *Complete Book of Ginseng*, 46–49.

17. Symons, *Ch'ing Ginseng Management*, 5–6.

18. Wang, "Renshen yuanliu kao," 16.

19. For ginseng's medical reputation and popular consumption in the Ming and Qing periods, see Jiang, *Renshen diguo*, 25–50.

20. Regarding the location of the Jurchen tribes in Manchuria, see maps in Imanishi, "Jušen koku iiki kō"; Wada, "Manshū shobu no ichi ni tsuite."

21. The Jurchens were one of the earlier peoples of Manchuria and were well known as the Jin, who controlled Manchuria and northern China during the years 1121 to 1234. When the Jin fell to the Mongols, many Jurchens remained in Manchuria and continued to follow their traditional lifestyle. Those who moved to northern China were later considered by the Mongols to be Chinese. Eventually, the Jurchens of Manchuria were alienated from Chinese culture and institutions, with only superficial political influence from the Yuan. Gertraude Roth Li speculates that the name "Jurchens" might come from the Jin dynasty Jurchen word *jusen*, but its meaning is unclear. Li, "State Building before 1644," 9. Regarding the early history of the Jurchens in Manchuria, see Serruys, *Sino-Jürčed Relations*, 1–16; Crossley, *Manchus*, 15–24.

22. From the 1430s to the 1470s, the Haixi Jurchens moved southward to the upper Liao and Sungari Rivers and formed the four Hūlun confederations: the Hada, the Ula, the Yehe, and the Hoifa.

23. Regarding the division of the three Jurchen groups, see *Da Ming huidian*, 107:7a–8b; Inaba, *Manzhou fadashi*, 100–112; Li, "State Building before 1644," 9–11.

24. Liaodong was a critical Ming military base used to curb the Mongols in the north. The Jurchens had the potential to threaten the Ming if they allied with the Mongols. Therefore, Ming policy toward the Jurchens in Liaodong aimed "to separate the Jurchens from the Mongol influence." No, "Myŏngdae Monggol kwa Manju," 49–50. For the early Ming policy against the Mongols in Manchuria and the steppe regions, see Wada, "Minsho no Manshū keiryaku: jō."

25. The Jianzhou Main Guard was built in 1403, the Morin (C. Maolian) Guard in 1405, the Jianzhou Left Guard in 1416, and finally the Jianzhou Right Guard in 1442. Wada, "Minsho no Manshū keiryaku: ge," 373–403; Serruys, *Sino-Jürčed Relations*, 18–28, 42–58; Kawachi, *Mindai Joshinshi*, 3–32; Li, "State Building before 1644," 11–14.

26. Kim, *Han Chung kwan'gyesa*, 2:590–93; Nam, *Myŏngdae Yodong chibae*, 195–221. The Ming also organized the Mongols in Liaodong into three guards—Döen, Taining, and Fuyu—and conventionally called them the "three Uriangkha guards." Later, the Fuyu were absorbed by the Korchin Mongols and the Döen and the Taining merged with the Five Khalka Mongols. Wada, "Minsho no Manshū keiryaku: jō," 321–24.

27. For a detailed discussion of the building of the Liaodong Frontier Wall, see Inaba, *Manzhou fadashi*, 125–30; Teng, "Mingdai Jianzhou Nüzhenren"; Cong, *Zhongguo dongbeishi*, 4:607–30; Nam, *Myŏngdae Yodong chibae*, 245–62.

28. Inaba, *Manzhou fadashi*, 109–10. Wada Sei also quotes the same phrase to explain the limited boundary of Ming authorities in Liaodong. Wada, "Minmatsu ni okeru Ōryokukō," 503.

29. Gertraude Roth Li agrees that Ming authority was largely circumscribed by the Liaodong Frontier Wall: "There is no reason to suppose that Ming officials' fantasies regarding its guards bore much relationship to the local power structure and subdivisions." Li, "State Building before 1644," 14. Kim Han'gyu also argues that the Ming military commissions did not reflect reality on the Liaodong frontier so much as "a Ming illusion of local autonomy." Kim, *Yodong sa*, 532–33.

30. *Da Ming huidian*, 107:8a–b; Inaba, *Manzhou fadashi*, 143–60; Kim, "Myŏngdae Yŏjin," 4–8, 21–27. Jurchen trading practices show that salt consumption continued to increase in Jurchen society. Considering the fact that vegetarians need more salt than meat eaters, this increase in Jurchens' salt intake indicates that Jurchen society was transitioning from a foraging economy to an agricultural economy.

31. Wang, "Guanyu Manzu xingcheng zhong de jige wenti"; Teng, "Ruguan qian Manzhou shehui jingji gailun"; Liu, *Manzu cong buluo dao guojia*, 62–77; Iwai, "China's Frontier Society."

32. *Ming Taizong shilu*, 40:2a (Yongle 3/3/guiyou); 52:3b (Yongle 4/3/jiawu).

33. Guangning was designated for the Uriangkha coming from the Zhenbei Pass; Kaiyuan for the Haixi Jurchens from Guangshun; and Fushun for the Jianzhou Jurchens. As the number of Jianzhou Jurchen traders increased, new markets in Qinghe, Aiyang, and Kuandian were opened. Cong, *Zhongguo dongbeishi*, 4:1064; Kim, "Myŏngdae Yŏjin," 28–32.

34. Qi, "Lun Qingdai changcheng," 79–81; Cong, *Zhongguo dongbeishi*, 4:1071.

35. Kawachi, *Mindai Joshinshi*, 592–96. For the total six months during the summer of 1583 and the spring of 1584, for example, the number of furs traded at the passes of Zhenbei and Guangshun reached 47,243. Kawachi, *Mindai Joshinshi*, 642–50.

36. Inaba, *Manzhou fadashi*, 172–74; Cong, *Dongbei sanbao jingji jianshi*, 37–43.

37. Kim, "Myŏngdae Yŏjin," 41–46.

38. Cong, *Zhongguo dongbeishi*, 4:1073–75, 4:1082–83.

39. No, "Myŏngdae Monggol kwa Manju," 56.

40. Lee, *Songs of Flying Dragons*, 152–54.

41. The name Uriangkha is found among both Mongol and Jurchen tribes. For an explanation of the Uriangkha Mongols, see Crossley, "Making Mongols," 80. Even though their names are denoted by the same Chinese characters (*Wuliangha*), the Uriangkha Mongols were a completely different group from the Uriangkha Jurchens. In Ming records, the Uriangkha refer largely to the three Mongol guards—Döen, Taining, and Fuyu—in Liaodong; in contrast, Chosŏn records use this name of Uriangkha (K. *Ollyanghap*) for the Jurchens to Korea's north. Wada Sei explains that the Uriangkha on the Tumen River were a different tribe distinguished from the Jurchens, while the latter were more civilized than the former. Wada, "Minsho no Manshū keiryaku: ge," 377–78. According to Yi Inyŏng, the Uriangkha who appeared in Chosŏn records were the Jurchens who lived near the Tumen River and they were largely equivalent to the Morin Jurchens. Yi, *Han'guk Manju kwan'gyesa*, 73. On the other hand, Kim Kujin explains that the Uriangkha, which he calls "Orangk'ae," and the Odori were roughly equivalent to the Jianzhou Jurchens who cultivated land on the Yalu and Tumen Rivers, while the Udike corresponded to the Haixi Jurchens on the Sungari and Mudan Rivers, who made their living through both land cultivation and animal husbandry. The Wild Jurchens were those who lived in the northeastern part of Manchuria. Kim, "Chosŏn chŏn'gi Yŏjinjok," 293–95.

42. *Ming Taizong shilu*, 25:6b (Yongle 1/11/xinchou).

43. *Yongbi ŏch'ŏn'ga*, 7:21b.

44. On Möngke Temür, see Kim, "Oŭmhoe ŭi Alt'ari Yŏjin"; Pak, *Myŏngch'o Chosŏn kwan'gyesa*, 169–201; Wada, "Minsho no Manshū keiryaku: ge," 403–77; Kawachi, *Mindai Joshinshi*, 33–107; Crossley, *Translucent Mirror*, 76–81.

45. Kawachi, *Mindai Joshinshi*, 45–54; Pak, *Myŏngch'o Chosŏn kwan'gyesa*, 170–79; Cho, "Ipkwan chŏn Myŏng Sŏn sidae," 18–19. In 1409 the Yongle emperor included the Jianzhou Left Guard in the jurisdiction of the Nurgan commission. Möngke Temür joined the Yongle emperor's expedition against the Mongols in 1421 but later returned to Omohoi. He continued to pay tribute to the Ming court and to receive gifts and rewards while raiding Chosŏn towns for food, iron, and other goods. *T'aejong sillok*, 19:32a (T'aejong 10/4/5); 20:32a (T'aejong 10/12/29).

46. *Manzhou shilu*, 1:10b–11a. The Qing record, commissioned by the Qianlong emperor, attempted to reconstruct the early history of the Manchus by linking Möngke Temür to Nurhaci in Hetu Ala and completely erasing the historical connections between Möngke Temür and the Chosŏn. But in fact, the genealogy from Möngke Temür to Nurhaci is not so clear; Nurhaci seems to have used the surname Tong in order to create a connection with the Jianzhou Jurchens, and later historians at the early Qing court fabricated an imaginary figure, Fuman, to complete the fake genealogy. Kawachi, *Mindai Joshinshi*, 733–34.

47. *Da Ming yitongzhi*, "Nüzhen," 89:4b.

48. Yang and Sun, *Zhong Chao bianjieshi*, 137. The argument that Möngke Temür allowed Ming authority to reach the Tumen River is also found in Diao and Cui, "Ming qianqi Zhong Chao dongduan"; Wang, "Guanyu Mingdai Zhong Chao bianjie."

49. Robinson, "Residence and Foreign Relations in the Peninsular Northeast," 18–19.

50. *Sejong sillok*, 79:9b (Sejong 19/11/3); 82:13b (Sejong 20/8/1).

51. Kim, "Ch'ogi Morin Orangk'ae yŏn'gu," 205–10.

52. In 1433 Chosŏn king Sejong expressed a strong commitment to the northern region: "Oŭmhoe [Hoeryŏng] has been within our territory. If Fanca moved to other place and another strong people settled in Oŭmhoe, we would not only lose that territory, but have to deal with another enemy." *Sejong sillok*, 6:17a (Sejong 15/11/19).

53. *Sejong sillok*, 116:9b (Sejong 29/intercalary 4/20).

54. Yi Inyŏng points out that in addition to these difficulties of management, the increasing threats from Esen's Oirat Mongols were likely to make the Chosŏn abandon the military bases on the Yalu River. Because Esen intimidated the Jurchens in Liaodong, the Chosŏn worried about the prospect of the Jurchens' moving south toward Chosŏn territory and decided to change its defense policy in the north. Yi, *Han'guk Manju kwan'gyesa*, 68–69.

55. Regarding the general history of Ming and Chosŏn relations, see Clark, "Sino-Korean Tributary Relations under the Ming."

56. *Sejo sillok*, 16:7a (Sejo 5/4/14, 15).

57. Han, *Chosŏn chŏn'gi sujik Yŏjinin*, 155–71.

58. Yi, *Han'guk Manju kwan'gyesa*, 29–56; Yi, "Chosŏn wangjo sidae ŭi pukp'yŏnggwan yain," 116–24.

59. Jurchen visitors to Korea were required to cross the Tumen River, because the Ming emissaries crossed the Yalu River on their visits to Seoul. The Chosŏn court did not want the Ming to become aware of Korean contacts with the Jurchens. Han, "Chosŏn ch'ogi sujik Yŏjinin yŏn'gu."

60. Yi, "Chosŏn wangjo sidae ŭi pukp'yŏnggwan yain," 129–35; Cho, "Ipkwan chŏn Myŏng Sŏn sidae," 52–53; Robinson, "From Raiders to Traders," 97–99.

61. *T'aejong sillok*, 11:21b (T'aejong 6/5/10).

62. *Chosŏn Sŏnjo sujŏng sillok*, 17:1b (Sŏnjo 16/2/1). The Chosŏn court records used various names for the Jurchens in the north, such as "protecting fence" (K. *pŏlli*) or "surrounding walls" (K. *pŏnbyŏng*). Han, *Chosŏn chŏn'gi sujik Yŏjinin*, 190–91.

63. *Yŏnsangun ilgi*, 46:18a (Yŏnsangun 8/10/18).

64. Robinson, "From Raiders to Traders," 97.

65. Chŏng, "Chosŏn ch'ogi yain kwa Taemado," 256. For further discussion on the relations between the Ming, the Chosŏn, and the Jurchens, see Chong, "Making Chosŏn's Own Tributaries."

66. Li, "State Building before 1644," 40.

67. Wakeman, *Great Enterprise*, 1:49–50.

68. Li Chengliang's story provides the best evidence of the entangled history of the Jurchens, Han Chinese, and Koreans in Liaodong. Li was probably a descendant of Korean immigrants to Liaodong. It is also likely that his ancestors were Jurchens who moved from the Yalu River area to Liaodong. Rising in the Ming army through military merit, Li eventually controlled Liaodong from 1570 to 1591. The Chosŏn court recognized that "people living in Liaodong and Guangning know no other name than Li Chengliang." *Kwanghaegun ilgi*, 6:3a (Kwanghaegun 1/7/2); *Mingshi*, "Li Chengliang liechuan," 6190; Crossley, *Manchus*, 50–51.

69. For details on the relocation of the Haixi Jurchens and the formation of the four Hūlun confederations, see Cong, *Zhongguo dongbeishi*, 3:723–40.

70. Li, "State Building before 1644," 26–27; Kim, *Kŭnse Tong Asia kwan'gyesa yŏn'gu*, 29–30.

71. *Taizu shilu*, 1:10b. Regarding the close relationship Nurhaci enjoyed with Ming Liaodong officials, especially Li Chengliang, see Crossley, *Manchus*, 48–53.

72. In his letter to the Ming, Nurhaci expressed his concern that the Japanese would invade the territory of the Jianzhou Jurchens, "since Chosŏn has been already invaded and our land is adjacent to it." Informed of Nurhaci's offer, the Chosŏn court decried it as "a vicious trick of cunning barbarians." *Sŏnjo sillok*, 30:16a (Sŏnjo 25/9/17). Kye Seung points out that Nurhaci's making his offer to the Ming, not to the Chosŏn, is evidence that at that point he still fully recognized Ming authority. Kye, "Imjin waeran kwa Nurŭhach'i," 367.

73. Li, "State Building before 1644," 28–30; Kim, *Kŭnse Tong Asia kwan'gyesa yŏn'gu*, 35.

74. Cong, *Zhongguo dongbeishi*, 4:1083–85.

75. *Kwanghaegun ilgi*, 6:78a (Kwanghaegun/1/4/21).

76. Quoted in Iwai, "China's Frontier Society," 10–11.

77. Iwai, "China's Frontier Society," 16–17.

78. Wang, "Renshen yuanliu kao," 18. For details on Nurhaci and the ginseng trade, see Cong, *Dongbei sanbao jingji jianshi*, 43–51.

79. *Taizu shilu*, 3:8b–9a (Wanli 33/3/yihai).

80. Wang, "Renshen yuanliu kao," 19.

81. Cheng, *Chouliao shuohua*, 2:27a.

82. *Taizu shilu*, 2:7b–8a (Wanli 16/4).

83. Di Cosmo, "Manchu Conquest in World-Historical Perspective," 54.

84. Imamura, *Ninjinshi*, 2:191–92.

85. Cong, *Zhongguo dongbeishi*, 4:1087.

86. *Ming Shenzong shilu*, 444:3a (Wanli 36/3/dingyou).

87. Iwai, "China's Frontier Society," 18.

88. Li, "State Building before 1644," 37.

89. Di Cosmo, "Manchu Conquest in World-Historical Perspective," 52.

90. The Chosŏn court informed the Ming commander of Liaodong about Nurhaci's letter, because the Koreans were worried that it could cause trouble with the Ming court, which had prohibited direct contact between the Koreans and the Jurchens. *Sŏnjo sillok*, 65:38b–39a (Sŏnjo 28/7/25).

91. *Sŏnjo sillok*, 69:18a–b (Sŏnjo 28/11/20).

92. *Sŏnjo sillok*, 71:41a (Sŏnjo 29/1/30).

93. Kim, *Kŭnse Tong Asia kwan'gyesa yŏn'gu*, 36; Hwang, "Yi Sŏngnyang sagŏn," 22–23.

94. *Sadae mun'gwe*, 46:29a–30b (Wanli 33/11/1), in *Imjin waeran saryo ch'ongsŏ*, 7:389–92.

95. *Kwanghaegun ilgi*, 6:14b (Kwanghaegun 1/3/10); Inaba, *Kōkai-kun jidai no Man-Sen kankei*, 51–58.

96. *Manbun rōtō*, 1:9–10.

97. *Taizu shilu*, 3:15a–b. Hwang Chiyŏng points out that during the agreement ceremony, the participants drank the blood of an animal sacrifice, a practice that Xiong Tingbi later denounced as degrading to the Ming court's dignity. Hwang, "Yi Sŏngnyang sagŏn," 16–17.

98. *Ming Shenzong shilu*, 455:7b (Wanli 37/2/xinsi).

99. *Taizu shilu*, 5:12a–13b.

100. *Taizu shilu*, 6:31b–32a (Tianming 4/8/jisi). For a detailed explanation of the founding of the Aisin Gurun, see Teng, "Shilun Houjinguo de xingcheng, xingzhi ji qi tedian."

101. *Manbun rōtō*, 4:87–88 (Tiancong 1/6/21); *Taizong shilu*, 3:18b (Tiancong 1/6).

102. *Manbun rōtō*, 4:111–12 (Tiancong 1/12/9); *Taizong shilu*, 3:29a (Tiancong 1/12/renyin).

103. As Yuan did not respond to Hong Taiji's first request for presents, four months later the desperate khan even cut his demands by half. *Taizong shilu*, 3:11b–12a (Tiancong 1/4/jiachen).

104. *Taizong shilu*, 5:11b–12a (Tiancong 3/6/yichou).

105. *Manbun rōtō*, 4:2–5; *Taizong shilu*, 2:1b–3a (Tiancong 1/1/bingzi).

106. *Manbun rōtō*, 4:22–28 (Tiancong 1/4/8); *Taizong shilu*, 3:2b–3a (Tiancong 1/4/jiachen). However, it is also noteworthy that Hong Taiji did not demand that Yuan give him the same respect as he did the Ming emperor. He asked Yuan to write his, Hong Taiji's, name in an official letter one character lower than the Ming emperor's name, but one character above the names of other Ming officials. Hong Taiji's request shows that at this time he had not yet challenged Ming supremacy; rather, he sought Ming recognition of the Jurchen state as an independent country. *Manbun rōtō*, 4:22–28 (Tiancong 1/4/8).

107. *Taizong shilu*, 3:13a (Tiancong 1/5/dingchou).

108. Crossley, "*Manzhou yuanliu kao*," 772–73.

109. *Taizong shilu*, 18:3b–6a (Tiancong 8/3/jiachen).

110. Regarding the origin of the names Jurchen and Manchu, see Chen, "Shuo 'Manzhou'"; Wang, "Guanyu Manzu xingcheng"; Elliott, *Manchu Way*, 39–88.

111. *Taizong shilu*, 61:4b (Chongde 7/6/xinchou).

112. *Sejong sillok*, 113:29a (Sejong 28/8/26).

113. *Sejong sillok*, 113:27b (Sejong 28/8/14).

114. *Sejong sillok*, 113:29a (Sejong 28/8/26).

115. *Chungjong sillok*, 97:13b (Chungjong 36/12/28); *Myŏngjong sillok*, 8:41a (Myŏngjong 3/9/2).

116. *Chungjong sillok*, 66:57b (Chungjong 24/11/22).

117. *Myŏngjong sillok*, 8:42a (Myŏngjong 3/9/3).

118. *Sŏnjo sillok*, 69:17a (Sŏnjo 28/11/20).

119. Kim, *Kŭnse Tong Asia kwan'gyesa yŏn'gu*, 83–85.

120. Hong Taiji's first invasion of the Chosŏn was closely related to his war strategy against the Ming. On the same day on which he sent Amin to attack the Chosŏn, he also sent two of his men, Fanggina and Untasi, to Yuan Chonghuan to list his seven vexations with the Ming. *Manbun rōtō*, 4:2–5 (Tiancong 1/8); *Taizong shilu*, 2:1b–3a (Tiancong 1/1/bingzi).

121. *Taizong shilu*, 4:10a (Tiancong 2/5/yiyou).

122. *Injo sillok*, 25:51b (Injo 9/intercalary 11/24).

123. *Taizong shilu*, 10:20a–b (Tiancong 5/intercalary 11/gengzi).

124. *Taizong shilu*, 14:9a–10b (Tiancong 7/6/bingyin).

125. *Taizong shilu*, 15:13a–14a (Tiancong 7/9/guiwei). Similar warnings and complaints are found in the letters sent to the Chosŏn court in the records of the following dates: Tiancong 8/10/renzi; Tiancong 9/7/guiyou; Tiancong 9/10/renyin; Tiancong 9/12/bingxu; Tiancong 10/4/jichou.

126. *Injo sillok*, 31:68a (Injo 13/11/20).

127. *Injo sillok*, 31:76a (Injo 13/12/30). A similar, but slightly different, letter is found in the Jurchen record as well. *Taizong shilu*, 27:3b–5b (Tiancong 10/1/renxu).

128. For the political significance of ginseng in Jurchen society, see Cong, *Dongbei san-bao jingji jianshi*, 51–59.

129. *Manbun rōtō*, 4:5 (Tiancong1/1/1), quoted in Schlesinger, "Qing Invention of Nature," 39.

130. In 1631, Hong Taiji refused to receive the Chosŏn court's gifts, claiming that the Koreans had sent less than they had promised. The khan, however, insisted on presenting ginseng to the Korean emissary Pak Nanyŏng, even though Pak did not want to take it. *Taizong shilu*, 8:4a–5a (Tiancong 5/1/gengzi). Various occasions on which Hong Taiji continued to gift ginseng to the Korean king and his envoys are found in *Taizong shilu*, 14:9a (Tiancong 7/6/yichou), 23:3b (Tiancong 9/3/renshen), and 25:20b (Tiancong 9/10/renchen).

131. Prior to his departure for Korea, the Chongde emperor sent a letter to the Ming official in Guangning explaining that he would attack the Chosŏn to punish them for their crimes, which included the Chosŏn neglecting to pay tribute to the Qing, refusing to repatriate Qing escapees, and failing to prevent Koreans from trespassing. *Taizong shilu*, 37:26a (Chongde 2/7/renchen).

132. Hong Taiji left Shenyang on December 29, 1636 (Chongde 1/12/3) and crossed the Yalu River on January 5, 1637 (Chongde 1/12/10). The Chosŏn king Injo surrendered to the Qing army on February 24, 1637 (Chongde 2/1/30). *Manbun rōtō*, 7:1477–1503; *Injo sillok*, 34:23a (Injo 15/1/30).

133. *Qingshi gao*, 526:14580; Kim, *Han Chung kwan'gyesa*, 2:719–20.

134. *Da Ming huidian*, 105:4a; Imamura, *Ninjinshi*, 2:15–23.

135. Hevia, *Cherishing Men from Afar*, 121.

136. *Injo sillok*, 41:12b (Injo 18/10/15).

137. *Injo sillok*, 46:3a (Injo 23/2/10).

138. *Hyŏnjong sillok*, 4:45a (Hyŏnjong 2/9/18); *Hyŏnjong kaesu sillok*, 8:19b (Hyŏnjong 4/2/13).

139. *Taizong shilu*, 61:3a (Chongde 7/6/xinchou).

140. *Taizong shilu*, 54:8a–9b (Chongde 6/1/bingxu).

CHAPTER 2 MAKING THE BORDERLAND

1. Some material in this chapter previously appeared in "Ginseng and Border Trespassing between Qing China and Chosŏn Korea," *Late Imperial China* 28, no. 1 (2007): 33–61.

2. *Tongmun hwigo*, 1:966–74 (*pŏmwŏl*: 3b–20a); Yi, "Samdogu sagŏn."

3. *Shengzu shilu*, 246:6b–7b (Kangxi 50/5/guisi).

4. For an overview of the Shunzhi period, see Dennerline, "Shun-chih Reign"; Wakeman, *Great Enterprise*, vol. 2.

5. Spence, "K'ang-hsi Reign," 120.

6. Ibid., 136–47.

7. Ibid., 150–60. For a detailed explanation of the Kangxi emperor's campaigns against Galdan, see Perdue, *China Marches West*, chapter 5.

8. Regarding the Qing cartographic projects, see Yee, "Reinterpreting Traditional Chinese Geographical Maps," 35–70; Perdue, "Boundaries, Maps, and Movement," 263–86;

Millward, "'Coming onto the Map,'" 61–98; Elliott, "Limits of Tartary," 603–46; Hostetler, *Qing Colonial Enterprise.*

9. Perdue, "Boundaries, Maps, and Movement," 264–65; Hostetler, *Qing Colonial Enterprise,* 22–25.

10. "The Russians have become our neighbors bordering several rivers and there are Central Asians in these regions who pay tribute to them, as well as forts, towns, and troops equipped with good weapons." Quoted in Hostetler, *Qing Colonial Enterprise,* 39.

11. Perdue, "Boundaries, Maps, and Movement," 267–71.

12. Hostetler, *Qing Colonial Enterprise,* 64–71.

13. Perdue, "Boundaries, Maps, and Movement," 277.

14. Sun, *Kang Yong Qian shiqi yutu huizhi,* 46–52.

15. Hostetler, *Qing Colonial Enterprise,* 79–80.

16. Elliott, "Limits of Tartary," 624.

17. Millward, "'Coming onto the Map,'" 61–62.

18. Ding and Shi, *Qingdai peidu Shengjing yanjiu,* 12–16.

19. Isett, "Village Regulation of Property," 127–28; Isett, *State, Peasant, and Merchant,* 24–30.

20. For the history of imperial touring in China, see Chang, *Court on Horseback,* 34–71.

21. Yongzheng traveled there once in 1721, when he was the imperial prince. Qianlong made four visits to the northeast, in 1743, 1754, 1778, and 1783. Jiaqing visited twice, in 1805 and 1818. Daoguang's visit in 1829 was the last tour by the Qing emperors. For details of the imperial eastern tours of Kangxi, Yongzheng, and Qianlong, see Wang, *Qingdi dongxun;* Chang, *Court on Horseback,* 72–113; Elliott, "Limits of Tartary," 607–12.

22. Chang, *Court on Horseback,* 23.

23. Ding and Shi, *Qingdai peidu Shengjing yanjiu,* 228–39.

24. Song, "Chŏng Kanghŭije tongsun"; Yi, "Chŏng ch'ogi Changbaeksan t'amsa."

25. Bello, "Cultured Nature of Imperial Foraging in Manchuria"; Bello, *Across Forest, Steppe, and Mountain,* 96–100.

26. For the history of the *Neiwufu* and its organization, see Torbert, *Ch'ing Imperial Household Department;* Qi, *Qingdai Neiwufu.*

27. The Manchu word *butha* means an activity of hunting and gathering of animals and fishes. During the Qing period, it was also used to indicate the various tribes who lived on hunting and gathering in the Heilongjiang area, such as the Solon, Dagur, and Oronchon.

28. For the details of the Shengjing branch, see Ding and Shi, *Qingdai peidu Shengjing,* 86–89.

29. *Shengjing shenwu dang'an shiliao,* 26 (Kangxi 6/9/27).

30. *Qinding Da Qing huidian shili,* 1215:690b.

31. Wang, "Qingdai Dasheng Wula zongguan yamen," 19–36.

32. Cong, *Dongbei sanbao,* 67.

33. In 1750, the ginseng tribute was finally removed from the Butha Ula. By this time other duties of the Butha Ula superintendent were also transferred to the Jilin military governor. By the late eighteenth century, the primary responsibility of the Butha Ula was to assure the tribute of pearls, honey, and pine nuts for imperial demands. *Qinding Da Qing huidian shili,* 1215:691a; Huang and Luan, *Jilin tongshi,* 2:231–35.

34. *Qinding Da Qing huidian shili*, 232:722b. In fact, Hong Taiji had briefly allowed officials with merits, not only *beile* princes, to collect ginseng, but this practice did not last long. *Taizong shilu*, 65:904a (Chongde 8/7/wuwu).

35. *Qinding Da Qing huidian shili*, 232:746a.

36. Cong, *Dongbei sanbao*, 71–72.

37. *Shengjing shenwu dang'an shiliao*, 26 (Kangxi 23/1/24; Kangxi 23/3/17); Imamura, *Ninjinshi*, 2:206; Cong, *Dongbei sanbao*, 74–82; Jiang, *Renshen diguo*, 66–80.

38. Symons, "Ch'ing Ginseng Management," 10–11; Wang, "Qingdai dongbei caishenye," 189–90. On the other hand, Cong Peiyuan explains the final year of banner privilege of ginseng gathering was 1699, not 1709. Cong, *Dongbei sanbao*, 81.

39. Imamura, *Ninjinshi*, 2:195–99.

40. *Shengjing shenwu dang'an shiliao*, 105 (Kangxi 51/3/27). The Qing efforts to stop illegal ginseng harvesting were not successful. In 1694 the Heilongjiang military governor Sabsu reported that as many as thirty to forty thousand ginseng poachers could be found in the regions of Ningguta and Ula. *Shengjing shenwu dang'an shiliao*, 63–64 (Kangxi 33/7/17).

41. Kim, "Paektusan ko," 256–64.

42. Inaba Iwakichi explains that the Aihu is a name of the upper stream of the Tumen River. Inaba, *Kōkai-kun jidai no Man-Sen kankei*, 63.

43. *Taizu shilu*, 1:1b–3b. For a detailed analysis of the legend of the Manchu progenitor, see Crossley, "*Manzhou yuanliu kao*."

44. Elliott, "Limits of Tartary," 608. As a symbol of the Manchus, Changbaishan appeared with great frequency in the literary works of Manchu writers and poets, and Baishan became the most common name for Manchu authors. Guan, "Qingdai Manzu zuojia wenxue."

45. *Shengzu shilu*, 69:3a–b (Kangxi 16/9/bingzi). Detailed information about the 1677 investigation of Changbaishan is found in Gioro Umene's report *Golmin šanyan alin-i eje-tun* (*Changbaishan zhi*). This Manchu document was first published in 1785 and is currently preserved at the Bibliothèque nationale de France. For an analysis of Umene's report, see Yi, "Ch'ŏng ch'ogi Changbaeksan t'amsa."

46. Elliott, "Limits of Tartary," 607–14.

47. Schmid, *Korea between Empires*, 216–18.

48. According to *Samguk yusa*, the son of the King of Heaven, Hwan'ung, descended to Paektusan to build his sacred city and married a female bear, Ungnyŏ. They had a son named Tan'gun, who later founded the Chosŏn. The founder of the Koguryŏ, Ko Chumong, was also arguably born near the south side of Paektusan. In addition, the Parhae was established in the area north of Paektusan. For further discussion regarding the association of Paektusan with the ancient kingdoms in Korean history, see Kim, "Paektusan ko," 264–72.

49. *T'aejong sillok*, 28:15a (T'aejong 14/8/21).

50. *Sejong sillok*, 76:24b (Sejong 19/3/13).

51. *Sŭngjŏngwŏn ilgi*, vol. 204 (Hyŏnjong 8/10/3).

52. Li, *Cho Chŏng kukkyŏng munje*, 271–73; Li, "Chaoxian wangchao de Changbaishan renshi."

53. *Sŏnjo sillok*, 914:4b (Sŏnjo 38/12/14).

54. For the Chosŏn court's debates regarding whether the four counties near the Yalu River should be maintained, see Yi, *Han'guk Manju kwan'gyesa*, 59–85; Pang, *Han'guk ŭi kukkyŏng hoekchŏng*, 198–216.

55. Kang, *Chosŏn hugi Hamgyŏngdo*, 31–32.

56. For details on Nurhaci's and Hong Taiji's campaigns against the Warka and Hūrha people and the latter's incorporation into the Eight Banners, see Cong, *Zhongguo dongbeishi*, 3:793–804; Matsuura, *Shinchō no Amūru seisaku to shōsū minzoku*, 224–26.

57. Pae, *Chosŏn hugi kukt'ogwan*, 64–77.

58. *Sukchong sillok*, 1:26b (Sukchong 1/11/13).

59. *Sukchong sillok*, 13:28 (Sukchong 8/11/24).

60. *Sukchong sillok*, 13:28 (Sukchong 8/11/24).

61. Kang, *Chosŏn hugi Hamgyŏngdo*, 35.

62. *Sukchong sillok*, 31:30b–31b (Sukchong 23/5/18).

63. Zhang, *Qingdai Zhong Han guanxi*, 188–94; Li, *Cho Chŏng kukkyŏng munje*, 69–70.

64. *Injo sillok*, 48:6b (Injo 25/2/29).

65. Li, *Cho Chŏng kukkyŏng munje*, 73–74; Wang, "Qingchao qianqi yu Chaoxian bianwu jiaoshe," 133–38.

66. Kang, *Chosŏn hugi Hamgyŏngdo*, 43–44.

67. Kim Kyŏngnok explains that Kangxi's fining of the Chosŏn king demonstrates a double standard, in that the emperor regarded the Chosŏn as an independent country but simultaneously treated it as part of his own domain. Kim, "Chosŏn ŭi tae Chŏng insik," 157.

68. A similar tension surfaced between the Ming Taizu and the Chosŏn T'aejong in the early fifteenth century. As part of efforts to limit Korean ambitions toward Liaodong, Ming Taizu took issue with the Korean king's letters, which arguably used disrespectful characters in reference to the emperor. Pak, *Myŏngch'o Chosŏn kwan'gyesa*, 5–63. Fuma Susumu explains that Kangxi's reprimand of the Chosŏn court was related to the traditions of rites and punishment in Chinese foreign policy. Both the Ming and the Qing sought to punish the Chosŏn when it did not seem to follow the proper rites for the emperor, so minor errors in letters addressed to the imperial court were often used as excuses by suspicious emperors to accuse Koreans of insubordination. Fuma, "Min Shin Chūgoku no tai Chōsen gaikō," 315–25, 336–46.

69. The final amount of the fine was reduced to five thousand *liang* after the Korean embassies bribed a Manchu official on the Board of Rites with one thousand *liang* of silver. Fuma, "Min Shin Chūgoku no tai Chōsen gaikō," 340–43.

70. *Kangxi qijuzhu*, 2:1341 (Kangxi 24/6/25); 1343 (Kangxi 24/7/8).

71. *Tongmun hwigo*, 1:903 (*kanggye*: 1a–b).

72. *Tongmun hwigo*, 1:904 (*kanggye*: 2a–3a).

73. *Shengzu shilu*, 246:6b–7b (Kangxi 50/5/guisi).

74. *Sukchong sillok*, 9:9a (Sukchong 6/3/5).

75. Kang, *Chosŏn hugi Hamgyŏngdo*, 50.

76. *Sukchong sillok*, 24:2a (Sukchong 18/1/18).

77. *Tongmun hwigo*, 1:905–906 (*kanggye*: 5b–6a).

78. *Sukchong sillok*, 51:16a (Sukchong, 38/3/8).

79. For Mu-ke-deng's work as the Butha Ula superintendent, see Zhang, *Qingdai Zhong Han guanxi*, 195–96; Wang, "Qingdai Dasheng Wula zongguan yamen," 53–65.

80. For a detailed description of Mu-ke-deng's first attempt to investigate Changbaishan, see Schmid, "Tributary Relations and the Qing-Chosŏn Frontier," 133–41; Li, *Cho Chŏng kukkyŏng munje*, 140–48.

81. *Tongmun hwigo*, 1:907 (*kanggye*: 8a–b).

82. Yu, "Paektusan chŏnggyebi," 515–16.

83. Despite allowing Pak to abandon the journey, Mu-ke-deng said he would continue his own mission "because I have received the imperial edict. Heaven will help me because the emperor is the Son of Heaven. I should not be worried." *Tongmun hwigo*, 1:907 (*kanggye*: 8a).

84. For an image of the stele inscription, see Zhang, *Qingdai Zhong Han guanxi*, 197.

85. Yu, "Paektusan chŏnggyebi," 517–20; Tao, "Qingdai fengji Changbaishan," 75–76.

86. *Tongmun hwigo*, 1:907–908 (*kanggye*: 9b–10a).

87. For Mu-ke-deng's third visit in 1713 and his discussions with Chosŏn officials, see Ledyard, "Cartography in Korea," 301–2.

88. *Sukchong sillok*, 54:5a (Sukchong 39/6/2), quoted in Ledyard, "Cartography in Korea," 302.

89. *Pibyŏnsa tŭngnok*, 6:543–44 (Sukchong 39/6/6), quoted in Ledyard, "Cartography in Korea," 302.

90. *Sukchong sillok*, 52:37a (Sukchong 38/12/7).

91. The Koreans believed that a personal appeal to Mu-ke-deng could help them avoid potential criticism from the Qing court about their unwillingness to build the fences. For the Chosŏn court's letter to Mu-ke-deng, see *Tongmun hwigo*, 1:907 (*kanggye*: 8b–9a); Zhang, *Qingdai Zhong Han guanxi*, 199–201; Yang and Sun, *Zhong Chao bianjieshi*, 197–203.

92. Yu, "Paektusan chŏnggyebi," 516.

93. Ibid., 525.

94. In 1712, when a group of Chosŏn envoys visited Beijing and met with Mu-ke-deng, the Manchu official said, "Since the project of building stone fences along the boundary may cause trouble for local people in Chosŏn, it is not necessary to hurry." In addition, he reported to the emperor incidents of abuse of Koreans by Qing officials in the trading markets in Kyŏngwŏn and Hoeryŏng. This favorably impressed the Chosŏn envoys to the imperial court. See Chʻoe, *Yŏnhaengnok* [1712], 40:79; Kim, *Nogajae yŏnhaeng ilgi* [1712], 33:202.

95. *Sukchong sillok*, 53:7b (Sukchong 39/1/22).

96. Zhang, *Qingdai Zhong Han guanxi*, 217–27.

97. Haboush, "Contesting Chinese Time," 115–41.

98. Schmid, "Tributary Relations and the Qing-Chosŏn Frontier," 138, 141.

99. Translation from Elliott, "Limits of Tartary," 616.

100. Elliott, "Limits of Tartary," 616–17.

101. *Qinding Manzhou yuanliu kao*, 1:1–2a.

102. Crossley, "*Manzhou yuanliu kao*," 765–66.

103. *Sŭngjŏngwŏn ilgi*, vol. 1189 (Yŏngjo 37/1/30).

104. *Sŭngjŏngwŏn ilgi*, vol. 1189 (Yŏngjo 37/3/25).

105. Another official pointed out that "the birthplace of our dynasty is in Kyŏnghŭng, 400 to 500 *li* away from Paektusan. In none of the classics or official histories is it stated that Paektusan is our sacred birthplace. Only a few people say this, and it is thus not trustworthy." *Yŏngjo sillok*, 109:12b (Yŏngjo 43/intercalary 7/10).

106. *Yŏngjo sillok*, 109:13a (Yŏngjo 43/intercalary 7/10).

107. Kang, *Chosŏn hugi Hamgyŏngdo*, 103–6; Li, *Cho Chŏng kukkyŏng munje*, 279–84; Li, "Chaoxian wangchao de Changbaishan renshi."

108. On the Chosŏn court's debates over the prospect of reopening the Four Closed Counties in the region of the Yalu River, see Kang, *Chosŏn hugi Hamgyŏngdo*, 240–42; Pae, *Chosŏn hugi kukt'ogwan*, 223–25; Kwŏn, *Chosŏn hugi P'yŏngando*, 193–96; Hŏ, *Chosŏn hugi chunghwaron*, 223–30.

109. *Chŏngjo sillok*, 5:6a–6b (Chŏngjo 2/1/13). In fact, King Chŏngjo also agreed that it was not appropriate to abandon fertile land hastily because of trespassing incidents, but he nonetheless decided not to allow restoration of the Four Closed Counties for the time being.

110. Cho, "Chosŏn hugi ŭi pyŏn'gyŏng ŭisik," 159–72; Mun, "Hakutōzan teikaihi to jūhasseiki Chōsen no kyōikikan," 54–59.

111. Cho, "Chosŏn hugi ŭi pyŏn'gyŏng ŭisik," 178–80; Kang, *Chosŏn hugi Hamgyŏngdo*, 245. Andre Schmid points out that the metaphors of "three thousand *li*" (K. *samch'ŏlli*) and "eight provinces" (K. *p'aldo*) that Chŏng used reflected a sense of space and the finiteness of the territorial realm. Schmid, *Korea between Empires*, 201–206.

112. Kwŏn, *Chosŏn hugi P'yŏngando*, 197–99; Yamamoto, *Daishin teikoku to Chōsen keizai*, 28–41.

113. Kang, *Chosŏn hugi Hamgyŏngdo*, 246.

CHAPTER 3 MANAGING THE BORDERLAND

1. Portions of this chapter were previously published in Korean as "Ongjŏngje wa Sŏnggyŏng chiyŏk t'ongch'i," *Myŏngch'ŏngsa yŏn'gu* 34 (2010): 143–77; "Ongjŏng Kŏllyung nyŏn'gan Manguch'o sagŏn kwa Chŏng Chosŏn kukkyŏng chidae," *Chungguksa yŏn'gu* 71 (2011): 69–97.

2. *Tongmun hwigo*, 2:1184–85 (*pŏmwŏl*: 20a–21b). Yi Sŏngyong's report is dated on Yongzheng 5/4/21.

3. *Tongmun hwigo*, 2:1185 (*pŏmwŏl*: 22a–b).

4. Winichakul, *Siam Mapped*, 75.

5. *Shengzu shilu*, 2:25a–26b (Shunzhi 18/2/dingsi). For the report of the Fengtian civil governor (*fuyin*) Zhang Shangxian describing the conditions in Liaodong in 1661, see Edmonds, "Willow Palisade," 613.

6. Cong, *Zhongguo dongbeishi*, 4:1465–67; Reardon-Anderson, *Reluctant Pioneers*, 20–24.

7. Li, *Dongbei tongshi*, 488; Ding and Shi, *Qingdai peidu Shengjing*, 65–103; Huang and Luan, *Jilin tongshi*, 2:206–19; Isett, *State, Peasant, and Merchant*, 32–34. Some scholars explain that Kangxi's decision to end the recruitment policy was related less to the increase of Han immigration to Liaodong and more to the corruption in granting many official ranks and titles to unqualified people. Tsukase, *Manchuria shi kenkyū*, 123–24.

8. In contrast to military governors in China proper, who possessed the purely military function of commanding banner troops, those in Manchuria supervised civil affairs as well. The Qing court appointed bannermen to the military governors in Manchuria, believing them to be more reliable than Han civil officials. The Qing preference for bannermen as military governors was also evident in other regions, such as Central Asia, where massive Han settlement could arguably have threatened security at the empire's margins. See Lee, *Manchurian Frontier*, 59–69; Isett, *State, Peasant, and Merchant*, 35–36.

9. *Shengjing tongzhi,* "Shengjing quantu," 4a–b.

10. Cong, *Zhongguo dongbeishi,* 4:1286.

11. *Shengzu shilu,* 5:22b–23a (Shunzhi 18/12/renshen).

12. The fences were made of soil and planted with willow branches. Some areas of the wall in Jilin were built with clay, with willow branches piled on top and tied with ropes. For details on the Willow Palisade's physical features, see Edmonds, "Willow Palisade," 600–604; Cong, *Zhongguo dongbeishi,* 4:1389–90; Li, *Dongbei tongshi,* 489–90; Zhang and Zhang, *Qingdai dongbei bianjiang,* 295–301.

13. For the names, locations, and personnel of each gate on the Willow Palisade, see Edmonds, "Willow Palisade," 604–10.

14. *Shengjing tongzhi,* 51:16a–22a.

15. Cong, *Zhongguo dongbeishi,* 4:1392–96; Li, *Dongbei tongshi,* 490–91; Huang and Luan, *Jilin tongshi,* 2:282–95.

16. Wang, "Dui Qingdai fengjin dongbei zhengce"; Zhang, "Liutiaobian, yinpiao yu Qingchao dongbei fengjin xinlun."

17. *Qinding Da Qing huidian shili,* 233:20; Cong, *Zhongguo dongbeishi,* 4:1397–99; Isett, *State, Peasant, and Merchant,* 29–30, 34–36.

18. *Shengzu shilu,* 69:3a–b (Kangxi 16/9/bingzi).

19. Zhang, "Qing qianqi dui Yalujiang fengjinqu de guanxia," 57.

20. Gao, *Hucong dongxun rilu, juan xia,* 3b–4a.

21. Symons, "Ch'ing Ginseng Management," 77–78.

22. *Shengjing shenwu dang'an shiliao,* 116–17 (Yongzheng 2/4/17).

23. *Qinding Da Qing huidian shili,* 232:725b.

24. Wang, "Qingdai dongbei caishenye," 190–91. One of the licensed ginseng merchants reportedly made a huge profit from his ginseng business, amounting to as much as three hundred thousand *liang* of silver. See Cong, *Dongbei sanbao,* 83–89; Jiang, *Renshen diguo,* 83–91.

25. *Shengjing shenwu dang'an shiliao,* 125–28 (Qianlong 1/10/20).

26. *Qinding Da Qing huidian shili,* 232:726a.

27. Land route permits were issued in Shengjing, valid for the route Shengjing–Xingjing–Hoifa–Elmin–Halmin. Water route permits were issued in Jilin and Ningguta and were used from Jilin Wula to Ussuri and Suifenhe. The center of the ginseng monopoly was Shengjing: each year the ginseng permits were sent from the Board of Revenue to Shengjing, then onward to Jilin and Ningguta; all unused permits were returned to the Board of Revenue to be destroyed. Imamura, *Ninjinshi,* 2:203; Tong, "Qingdai Shengjing shenwu," 45.

28. Permits to return from the mountain (M. *alin ci bederere temgetu bithe*) were to be presented after the collection. There was a permit for the escorting soldiers (M. *fiyanjilara temgetu bithe*; C. *yapiao*), who were brought into the mountains for protection. There were also permits issued to merchants (M. *fulgiyan temgetu bithe*; C. *hongpiao*). Tong, "Qingdai Shengjing shenwu," 45–46; Schlesinger, "Qing Invention of Nature," 123–30.

29. Imamura, *Ninjinshi,* 2:214–16; Cong, *Dongbei sanbao,* 89–96; Jiang, *Renshen diguo,* 91–104.

30. The state regulations concerning ginseng poaching became more detailed over time. In 1663 it was decreed that illegal poachers were to be killed, and in 1666, that anyone who provisioned illegal poachers was also to be killed. In 1676, a leader of illegal poachers and an

expense supplier were executed, and officials who neglected these wrongdoings were exiled; in 1714, a second conviction of poaching was punished by severing the Achilles tendon, and bannermen involved in ginseng poaching were banished and removed from banner registers. Imamura, *Ninjinshi*, 2:226–32; Symons, "Ch'ing Ginseng Management," 25–32.

31. *Yongzhengchao manwen zhupi zouzhe quanyi*, 2:1630 (Yongzheng 6/4/26).

32. *Yongzhengchao manwen zhupi zouzhe quanyi*, 1:325–26 (Yongzheng 1/9/10).

33. *Gongzhongdang Yongzhengchao zouzhe: Manwen yuezhe*, 29:310–11.

34. *Shengjing shenwu dang'an shiliao*, 230 (Qianlong 36/7/29); 232 (Qianlong 36/12/18).

35. *Yongzhengchao manwen zhupi zouzhe quanyi*, 2:1630 (Yongzheng 6/4/26).

36. *Yongzhengchao manwen zhupi zouzhe quanyi*, 1:613 (Yongzheng 2/1/18).

37. *Tongmun hwigo*, 2:1184 (*pŏmwŏl*: 19a–20a).

38. *Yongzhengchao manwen zhupi zouzhe quanyi*, 2:1521 (Yongzheng 5/10/10).

39. *Yongzhengchao manwen zhupi zouzhe quanyi*, 2:1522 (Yongzheng 5/10/10)

40. *Tongmun hwigo*, 2:1186 (*pŏmwŏl*: 23b).

41. *Tongmun hwigo*, 2:1188 (*pŏmwŏl*: 27a–b).

42. *Tongmun hwigo*, 2:1189 (*pŏmwŏl*: 30a–b).

43. *Tongmun hwigo*, 2:1189–90 (*pŏmwŏl*: 30b–31a).

44. *Tongmun hwigo*, 2:1191 (*pŏmwŏl*: 33a). Regarding the bannermen's legal privileges, see Elliott, *Manchu Way*, 197–200.

45. *Tongmun hwigo*, 2:1186–87 (*pŏmwŏl*: 24b–25a); *T'ongmun'gwan chi*, 10:9b–10a.

46. *Yongzhengchao manwen zhupi zouzhe quanyi*, 2:1635–36 (Yongzheng 6/5/28).

47. For the idea of the division between the inner and outer territories, see Yi, "Chunghwa cheguk ŭi p'aengch'ang kwa ch'ukso."

48. When hearing of the case, the Chosŏn court decided not to report it to the Qing court, because these Qing intruders worked for the Fenghuangcheng authority, which was responsible for examining the Chosŏn envoy at the entrance into Qing territory. The Chosŏn was worried that a complaint about such a minor issue as Qing intruders in Chosŏn territory could cause trouble in more important matters, such as the envoy's entrance into and journey through Qing lands. *Sukchong sillok*, 45:32b (Sukchong 33/7/20).

49. *Sukchong sillok*, 50:44b (Sukchong 37/7/30).

50. As discussed in the previous chapter, the Kangxi emperor's emissary Mu-ke-deng had failed in his first attempt to survey Changbaishan in 1711. The Koreans worried that if they asked the Qing court to stop Qing subjects from crossing the boundary, the Qing might use the request as an excuse to resume the Changbaishan survey. As a result, the Chosŏn court decided to report to the emperor that these Qing ginseng hunters had gotten lost and accidentally crossed the river with no intention of violating the Chosŏn territory. Li, *Cho Chŏng kukkyŏng munje*, 177–78.

51. *Tongmun hwigo*, 2:1178 (*pŏmwŏl*: 7b–8a).

52. *T'ongmun'gwan chi*, 9:60b.

53. *Tongmun hwigo*, 2:1183 (*pŏmwŏl*: 18b); *Qinding Da Qing huidian shili*, 511:4a.

54. *Tongmun huigo*, 2:1183–84 (*pŏmwŏl*: 18b–19a); *Qinding Da Qing huidian shili*, 511:5b.

55. *Sukchong sillok*, 55:19b–20a (Sukchong 40/8/8).

56. *Sukchong sillok*, 55:38b (Sukchong 40/12/3).

57. *Pibyŏnsa tŭngnok*, 6:662 (Sukchong 40/6/7).

58. *Tongmun hwigo*, 1:909 (*kanggye*: 13a).

59. *Tongmun hwigo*, 1:910 (*kanggye*: 14b).

60. *Shengzu shilu*, 257:548a (Kangxi 53/1/wuchen). The position of the Hunchun regiment colonel was promoted to that of a garrison lieutenant general (*fudutong*) later in 1870. The Hunchun garrison was maintained until 1909, when the Qing ended the military governorship in Manchuria. *Hunchun fudutong yamendang*, 1:1–4.

61. *Sukchong sillok*, 55:40a (Sukchong 40/12/23).

62. Li, *Cho Chŏng kukkyŏng munje*, 187.

63. Ibid., 190–97.

64. *Tongmun hwigo*, 1:911 (*kanggye*: 16a).

65. *Yŏngjo sillok*, 29:42a (Yŏngjo 7/6/20).

66. *Tongmun hwigo*, 1:911 (*kanggye*: 16a–17b).

67. *Tongmun hwigo*, 1:912 (*kanggye*: 18a–b).

68. *Shengjing shenwu dang'an shiliao*, 142–44 (Qianlong 3/2/20).

69. For the acculturation of the bannermen in the eighteenth century, see Elliott, *Manchu Way*, 275–344.

70. The imperial decree included eight articles, prohibiting, inter alia, unauthorized entrance to Shanhaiguan, Han Chinese land cultivation, and illegal ginseng poaching. For details on the restrictions proposed by the left vice minister of the Board of War, Šuhede, and the Shengjing military governor E-er-tu, see *Gaozong shilu*, 115:17b–25a (Qianlong 5/4/jiawu); Liu, *Manzu de shehui yu shenghuo*, 211–24; Wang, "Dui Qingdai fengjin dongbei zhengce."

71. *Gaozong shilu*, 294:10a (Qianlong 12/7/jiawu); 428:15a (Qianlong 17/12/bingshen); 676:19a–b (Qianlong 27/12/jihai); 983:11a (Qianlong 40/5/yichou). In the *Qing Shilu*, the expression "the place of origin" (*genben zhi di*) was first used for various places, including Xi'an, Nanjing, Beijing, and Shengjing. By the Qianlong period, however, it came to refer exclusively to Shengjing, drawing an obvious connection between identity and space—the Manchus and Manchuria. Elliott, "The Limits of Tartary"; Yi, "Chŏngdae Kŏllyunggi Manjujok ŭi kŭnbon."

72. For background on the Eight Banners livelihood problem in the eighteenth century, see Im, *Qingchao baqi zhufang xingshuishi*, 89–126; Elliott, *Manchu Way*, 305–22; Reardon-Anderson, *Reluctant Pioneers*, 46–58.

73. *Gaozong shilu*, 143:7a (Qianlong 6/5/guiwei).

74. *Tongmun hwigo*, 1:918 (*kanggye*: 31a–32b).

75. *Tongmun hwigo*, 1:912–13 (*kanggye*: 19b–20a).

76. *Tongmun hwigo*, 1:914 (*kanggye*: 23a–b).

77. *Tongmun hwigo*, 1:913 (*kanggye*: 20b).

78. *Tongmun hwigo*, 1:914 (*kanggye*: 23b).

79. *Tongmun hwigo*, 1:914 (*kanggye*: 22a).

80. *Yŏngjo sillok*, 63:11a (Yŏngjo 22/3/28).

81. Li, *Cho Chŏng kukkyŏng munje*, 203–5.

82. In fact, Chosŏn court officials debated for some time whether or not to confront the Qing about the Mangniushao post. Some argued that it would be inappropriate to act before the Shengjing military governor had informed the Chosŏn of any decision; others felt that the Chosŏn should take immediate action based on the Qing decision to move the gate. Yŏngjo decided to write directly to the Qianlong emperor to avoid the possible

complications his letter might encounter if forwarded in the usual fashion via several different levels of Qing bureaucracy. See *Yŏngjo sillok*, 63:12a (Yŏngjo 22/intercalary 3/5); 63:13b (Yŏngjo 22/intercalary 3/15); 63:14b (Yŏngjo 22/intercalary 3/21); 83:17a–18a (Yŏngjo 22/4/19).

83. *Yŏngjo sillok*, 63:17a–18a (Yŏngjo 22/4/19); *Tongmun hwigo*, 1:916 (*kanggye*: 26b–27a).

84. *Yŏngjo sillok*, 63:17a–18a (Yŏngjo 22/4/19); *Tongmun hwigo*, 1:916 (*kanggye*: 26b–27a).

85. *Gaozong shilu*, 270:26b–27a (Qianlong 11/7/jiyou).

86. Grand Councilor Bandi was dispatched to investigate the conditions near Mangniushao and subsequently sent to his emperor a secret memorial in the Manchu language. For the full text of Bandi's memorial, see Yun, "Cho Chŏng kwan'gyesa yŏn'gu," 369–70.

87. *Gaozong shilu*, 271:10a (Qianlong 11/7/jiayin); *Tongmun hwigo*, 1:918 (*kanggye*: 31a); *Yŏngjo sillok*, 64:28a (Yŏngjo 22/10/29).

88. *Tongmun hwigo*, 1:919 (*kanggye*: 32b).

89. *Tongmun hwigo*, 1:920 (*kanggye*: 34a).

90. It was Qianlong's successor, the Jiaqing emperor, who recognized this change. In 1800, Jiaqing emphasized that the areas outside the eastern line were strategically important because it was "the boundary with the Chosŏn," and he ordered his officials to report on the decrease in the number of outposts. However, for various reasons the number of outposts declined further, to three inside the eastern line and eighteen outside it by 1846. *Shengjing tongzhi*, 51:16a–19a; Ku, "19 segi Sŏnggyŏng tongbyŏnoe," 265–72.

91. Edmonds, "Willow Palisade," 620.

92. "Liutiaobian," in *Shengjing tongzhi*, 13:3a–b, translation from Edmonds, "Willow Palisade," 599.

93. Edmonds, "Willow Palisade," 600.

94. On Qing universalism, see Crossley, *Translucent Mirror*.

CHAPTER 4 MOVEMENT OF PEOPLE AND MONEY

1. Portions of this chapter were previously published in Korean as "Nandu: Chŏng Chosŏn chogong kwan'gye ŭi pyŏn'gyŏng chŏk ch'ŭkmyŏn," *Taegu sahak* 96 (2009): 1–37; "Kŏllyung nyŏn'gan Chosŏn sahaeng ŭi ŭn punsil sagŏn," *Myŏngch'ŏngsa yŏngu* 33 (2010): 139–66.

2. The incident took place on Qianlong 12/12/7 and was reported to Daldangga on the following day (Qianlong 12/12/8). The full text of this incident, "Korean Sahwan's false accusation of theft," exists in both Chinese and the Manchu language. The Chinese text is available in *Junjichu hanwen dangzhe*, no. 002300, preserved in the Taiwan Palace Museum; the Manchu text is found in *Junjichu manwen lufu, waijiao lei, Zhong Chao xiang*, microfilm no. 12, 00273, held in Beijing First Historical Archive.

3. *Junjichu manwen lufu*, microfilm no. 12, 00273.

4. Lewis, *Frontier Contact between Chosŏn Korea and Tokugawa Japan*, 7.

5. Chun, "Sino-Korean Tributary Relations," 90–91; Ledyard, "Korean Travelers in China," 3–5; Zhang, *Qing Han zongfan maoyi*, 15–17; Liu, "Qingdai Zhong Chao zongfan guanxi," 25–36.

6. Irregular embassies took place on the following occasions: appreciation of imperial grace; congratulations for imperial enthronements or for the successful suppression

of rebellions; comfort in the event of the emperor's illness; condolences on the deaths of empresses; obituary notices for the deaths of Korean kings, queens, or princes; and courtesy visits during the imperial eastern tours to Shengjing. Gari Ledyard estimates that the Korean embassy visited the Qing capital three times per year, but Zhang Cunwu counts fewer than two visits a year. Ledyard, "Korean Travelers in China," 5; Zhang, *Qing Han zongfan maoyi*, 40.

7. Zhang, *Qing Han zongfan maoyi*, 18–20.

8. Regarding Chosŏn interpreters and the *Sayŏgwŏn*, see Kim and Yi, "*T'ongmun'gwan chi* ŭi p'yŏnch'an." For an analysis of their identity as second-class individuals (*chungin*), see Hwang, *Beyond Birth*, 106–60.

9. *Qinding Da Qing huidian shili*, 39:3a.

10. According to Zhang Cunwu, the average number of people in each embassy was about three hundred, and the number of horses was about two hundred. Zhang, *Qing Han zongfan maoyi*, 24.

11. Out of these 687 people, 363 would go to Shenyang, and the remaining 324 would travel to Beijing. Out of a total 591 horses, only 232 were required for the journey to Beijing; the remaining 359 horses went to Shengjing. Ch'oe, *Yŏnhaengnok* [1712], 39:448–49.

12. The tribute embassy that Kim Ch'angŏp joined in 1712 departed from Seoul on November 30 (Kangxi 51/11/3) and crossed the Yalu River on December 23 (Kangxi 51/11/26). The group reached Fenghuangcheng two days later; Shengjing on January 2, 1713 (Kangxi 51/12/6); Shanhaiguan on January 14 (Kangxi 51/12/18); and, finally, Beijing on January 23 (Kangxi 51/12/27). The distance from Ŭiju to Beijing was about two thousand *li*, a one-month journey. Gari Ledyard has laid out the dates of departure and arrival of thirty embassy visits from 1488 to 1887 in "Korean Travelers in China," 29–40.

13. Im, "Yonhaengnok ŭi tae Ch'ŏng ŭisik," 117–18.

14. *T'ongmun'gwan chi*, 3:32a.

15. Pak Chiwŏn, who served as an attendant to his cousin Pak Myŏngwŏn, wrote a diary, *Yŏrha ilgi*, after visiting Shengjing, Beijing, and Jehol. In this diary, he described the conditions of eighteenth-century China in great detail, covering topics such as the state of the roads, fortresses, housing, people's daily lives, Qing politics, the economy, and religion. For a general introduction to Korean travel diaries about journeys to Beijing, see Ledyard, "Korean Travelers in China."

16. Pak, *Yŏrha ilgi* [1780], 53:259–60.

17. Ibid., 53:267.

18. *Qingji Zhong Ri Han guanxi shiliao*, 3:1065–66.

19. Pak, *Yŏrha ilgi* [1780], 53:266.

20. Eggert, "Borderline Case," 66.

21. Pak, *Yŏrha ilgi* [1780], 53:263.

22. Ibid., 53:273.

23. *T'ongmun'gwan chi*, 3:38a.

24. *Qingdai Zhong Chao guanxi dang'an shiliao xubian*, 50–51.

25. Pak, *Yŏrha ilgi* [1780], 53:281–83.

26. Generally, two hundred *liang* of silver was paid by Korean interpreters and subsequently distributed to several Qing officials. *Qingdai Zhong Chao guanxi dang'an shiliao xubian*, 72–73.

27. Ibid., 78–79. In fact, bribery had taken place in Fenghuangcheng since the seventeenth century. Prince Inp'yŏng, who frequently went back and forth between Seoul and Beijing, said in 1656 "I am following precedent" when he presented gifts to Qing officials according to their ranks. Inp'yŏng, *Yŏndo kihaeng* [1656], 22:61.

28. *Man'gi Yoram*, 1:205a–b. The permitted contents of the *p'alp'o* changed over time as foreign trade conditions fluctuated. In 1682, when the flow of ginseng from Korea to Japan was extremely high, the Chosŏn court ordered its envoys to Beijing to cease taking ginseng to China and carry silver instead. At this time, one *kŭn* of ginseng was equivalent to twenty-five *liang* of silver in Korea. In 1752, when silver imports decreased, the *p'alp'o* content changed again to a mixture of silver and other goods, such as paper, hides, and cotton. In 1797, ginseng was once again permitted to be taken to China. For details on the *p'alp'o* trade, see Kang, *Chosŏn hugi sangŏp chabon*; Ch'a, "Chosŏn hugi insam muyŏk"; Yu, "Chosŏn hugi tae Chŏng muyŏk"; Kim, "Chosŏn hugi tae Chŏng muyŏk"; Liu, "Qingdai Chaoxian shituan maoyi zhidu shulüe."

29. Kim, *Nogajae yŏnhaeng ilgi* [1712], 33:71–72; Hong, *Tamhŏn yŏn'gi* [1765], 42:114–16. It was Zheng Shitai's father who first began doing business with Koreans visiting Beijing. By the mid-eighteenth century, the Chosŏn embassies still purchased their Chinese silk products from the Zheng family, which virtually monopolized the Korean trade in Beijing. For detailed information about the Zheng family and its trade with Korean embassies, see Hatachi, "Shinchō to Rishi Chōsen to no chōkō bōeki ni tsuite." For a general overview of the Korean embassy in Beijing, see Matsuura, *Kinsei Chūgoku Chōsen kōshōshi*, 31–52; Matsuura, "Minshin jidai Pekin no kaidōkan," 359–79.

30. Hong, *Tamhŏn yŏn'gi* [1765], 42:229.

31. Quoted in Ledyard, "Hong Taeyong and His 'Peking Memoir,'" 88.

32. Hong, *Tamhŏn yŏn'gi* [1765], 42:206.

33. The Qing-Chosŏn relationship provided two types of trading opportunities: trade in the course of the tribute embassy's visits, and trade at Zhongjiang on the Yalu River and at Hoeryŏng and Kyŏngwŏn near the Tumen River. In terms of their size and duration and the number of participants, the markets at Zhongjiang, Hoeryŏng, and Kyŏngwŏn were far less significant to the Chosŏn economy than was the tribute embassy trade. Yu and Yi, *Chosŏn hugi Chungguk kwa ŭi muyŏksa*, 25–26.

34. *Pibyŏnsa tŭngnok*, 3:946 (Sukchong 12/5/4).

35. *T'ongmun'gwan chi*, 3:31b–32b; *Man'gi Yoram*, 1:202a–b.

36. *T'ongmun'gwan chi*, 3:62b–63a. A similar description is found in Kim Ch'angŏp's 1712 travelogue: "The area (K. *pyŏn'gye*) looked like a city. The people in Fenghuangcheng depend entirely on Korean trade for their living." Kim, *Nogajae yŏnhaeng ilgi* [1712], 33:379.

37. *Pibyŏnsa tŭngnok*, 8:411–13 (Yŏngjo 4/7/3). Ch'oe Tŏkchung made a similar observation in 1712. According to him, when the embassy finished its journey and returned to Ŭiju, several hundred people and horses were waiting to cross the river at the same time. The high officials insisted on crossing first, while others, including porters and horses loaded with luggage, were forced to wait until the following morning. Under such circumstances, a thorough inspection to check the number of people, horses, and packages and the contents of the latter would have been decidedly difficult. Ch'oe, *Yŏnhaengnok* [1712], 40:122–23.

38. The eight postal stations were Fenghuangcheng, Xuelizhan, Tongyuanbao, Lianshanguan, Tianshuizhan, Langzishan, Liaoyang, and Shilihe. *Shengjing tongzhi*, 33:15b–16a.

39. Yu and Yi, *Chosŏn hugi Chungguk kwa ŭi muyŏksa*, 34–35.

40. Kim, *Yŏnwŏn chikchi* [1832], 70:321.

41. O, *Pyŏngin yŏnhaeng ilsŭng* [1686], 29:152.

42. Cho, *Ch'wibyŏnggong yŏnhaeng ilgi* [1660], 20:211.

43. Sŏ, *Yŏnhaeng illok* [1690], 24:176.

44. Pak, *Yŏrha ilgi* [1780], 53:319.

45. *Kyŏngjong sillok*, 10:10a–b (Kyŏngjong 2/10/19).

46. Sŏ, *Yŏnhaeng illok* [1690], 24:176; 232–33.

47. Ibid., 24:225.

48. *T'ongmun'gwan chi*, 3:61b–62a.

49. Ch'oe, *Yŏnhaengnok* [1712], 39:452–53. Ch'oe did not appreciate the banquet that the *lantou* provided for the Korean visitors, because he correctly suspected that the Qing merchants aimed to make more money by showing hospitality to the Koreans.

50. Ch'oe, *Yŏnhaengnok* [1712], 40:120–21.

51. Kim, *Nogajae yŏnhaeng ilgi* [1712], 33:392.

52. Ibid., 33:447–48.

53. Ch'oe, *Yŏnhaengnok* [1712], 40:94–95.

54. In order to win the lawsuit and secure a decision favorable to their business, the *lantou* merchants had to bribe Qing officials in Beijing as well as Shengjing. The merchants obtained the money for the bribes by asking the Korean embassy to pay its transportation fee, up to ten thousand *liang* of silver, in advance. The Korean interpreters, who sided with the *lantou* merchants, forced the Chosŏn officials to acquiesce to *lantou* demands. Upon arrival in Shengjing, the interpreters also urged the military escort to leave quickly for Ŭiju, because the *lantou* did not want the local Qing merchants to meet the Korean merchants in Shengjing. This early departure was very disadvantageous for military escort's business interests. Kim, *Nogajae yŏnhaeng ilgi* [1712], 33:447–48.

55. *Kyŏngjong sillok*, 13:13a–b (Kyŏngjong 3/10/23).

56. *Man'gi Yoram*, 1:208b–209a.

57. *Pibyŏnsa tŭngnok*, 4:897 (Sukchong 26/5/1).

58. *Pibyŏnsa tŭngnok*, 5:533–34 (Sukchong 32/3/28).

59. *Pibyŏnsa tŭngnok*, 5:665–67 (Sukchong 33/5/27).

60. The merchants had borrowed 60,000 *liang* of silver from the Shengjing office but repaid only 10,000 *liang* of the principal and 18,000 *liang* in interest, leaving about 50,000 *liang* of the principal and 27,050 *liang* of interest unpaid. During the investigation, the Shengjing office also found that Hu and other merchants had exaggerated the value of their assets from 6,735 *liang* to almost 90,000 *liang*. They then bribed officials in the Shengjing office and in this way succeeded in securing the loans.

61. *Yongzhengchao manwen zhupi zouzhe quanyi*, 1224–25.

62. *Pibyŏnsa tŭngnok*, 8:29–32 (Yŏnjo 3/3/27).

63. *Shizong shilu*, 61:4b–5b (Yongzheng 5/9/wuwu); *Yŏngjo sillok*, 15:4a (Yŏngjo 4/1/10).

64. *Yŏngjo sillok*, 39:21a (Yŏngjo 10/12/12).

65. *Pibyŏnsa tŭngnok*, 8:497–98 (Yŏngjo 4/11/4).

66. *T'ongmun'gwan chi*, 3:32b; *Yŏngjo sillok*, 15:3b (Yŏngjo 4/1/10).

67. Yu and Yi, *Chosŏn hugi Chungguk kwa ŭi muyŏksa*, 114–20; Yu, "Chosŏn hugi tae Ch'ŏng muyŏk."

68. Pak, *Yŏrha ilgi* [1780], 53:279.

69. Sŏ, *Yŏnhaenggi* [1790], 50:446–447.

70. *Junjichu manwen lufu*, microfilm no. 12, 00273.

71. Ibid.

72. Ibid.

73. According to the report of Kim Sangjŏk, who carried out a joint investigation with Qing officials of another case of theft in 1739, an investigation at that time consisted mostly of coercing suspects to confess through torture. *Yŏngjo sillok*, 69:34b (Yŏngjo 25/4/19).

74. *Junjichu hanwen dangzhe*, no. 002300.

75. Ibid.

76. Ibid.

77. The letter from the Qing Board of Rites undoubtedly pointed at the Chosŏn king's negligence while asking the king to investigate the wrongdoings of Yun Ch'angli and others: "The officials in the embassy should be punished for overlooking such an incident. It cannot be said that the king is completely innocent, since he selected and sent those officials." *T'ongmun'gwan chi*, 10:35b.

78. The criminals were sentenced to severe punishments, as listed in a letter from the Chosŏn court to the Qing Board of Rites. The primary offender, Sahwan, was sent into island exile. Three official emissaries as well as Yun Ch'angli, who was accused of forcing his servant to make a false confession, were also exiled. *T'ongmun'gwan chi*, 10:35b; *Yŏngjo sillok*, 68:3a (Yŏngjo 24/7/17).

79. *Yŏngjo sillok*, 68:3b (Yŏngjo 24/7/23, 25).

80. Langzishan was one of the eight stations between the Fenghuangcheng gate and Shengjing. Yi Goroja and five other men stayed overnight in a local person's house and found their silver missing the following morning. The Koreans arrested four local people as suspects and handed them over to the Qing local office. *Junjichu hanwen dangzhe*, no. 002307.

81. The Korean travelers had stayed in a local inn and had tied their baggage together so it would not get stolen. When they heard voices shouting that there was smoke in the house, they immediately went outside. At dawn, four of the Korean travelers left. Yi Yunbang and others who remained later found their silver missing. They beat up the innkeeper before tying him up and sending him to the local office. Officials had tried to cross-examine Yi Yunbang and the innkeeper, but Yi had already returned to Korea. *Tongmun hwigo*, 2:1427–28 (*ch'ujing*: 1a–3b).

82. *Junjichu hanwen dangzhe*, no. 002307.

83. Daldangga listed the names of the Koreans who should present themselves at his office: "Those who should be summoned to the Qing include the following: Yi Goroja and the five others who stayed near Langzishan in 1744; Yi Yunbang and the eleven others who stayed near Shilihe in 1745; the Korean interpreter who first reported the incident; another Korean who wrote the testimony on behalf of Yi Yunbang." *Junjichu hanwen dangzhe*, no. 002307.

84. *T'ongmun'gwan chi*, 10:36a.

85. *Yŏngjo sillok*, 68:29a (Yŏngjo 24/11/14).

86. The Chosŏn court's insistence that a Korean official join the investigation of its subjects in Qing territory was, in fact, not unprecedented. In 1666, when a group of Koreans

had entered Qing territory and committed murder there, the Kangxi emperor had allowed the Chosŏn court to send an official to Fenghuangcheng to discuss the case with Shengjing officials. See *T'ongmun'gwan chi*, 10:36a; *Tongmun hwigo*, 2:1429 (*ch'ujing*: 5a–6b). For details on the process of Qing-Chosŏn joint investigation in Fenghuangcheng, see Wang, "Qingchao qianqi yu Chaoxian bianwu jiaoshe."

87. *Yŏngjo sillok*, 69:18a (Yŏngjo 25/2/23).

88. *Tongmun hwigo*, 2:1431 (*ch'ujing*: 10a–b).

89. *Tongmun hwigo*, 2:1431–32 (*ch'ujing*: 10b–11a).

90. *T'ongmun'gwan chi*, 10:37b.

91. Kim Sangjŏk did not bring silver with him to Fenghuangcheng, an action that was different from the past practice of bribing Qing officials in order to settle disputes between the two countries. The Chosŏn king praised Kim's integrity but did not succeed in saving him. The Korean records indicate suspicion that Kim may have been victimized in the case because he did not buy off Qing officials during the reinvestigation in Fenghuangcheng. See *Yŏngjo sillok*, 68:29a (Yŏngjo 24/11/14); *Tongmun hwigo*, 2:1432 (*ch'ujing*: 11b–12a).

92. There is no record explaining how Yi Ch'ansuk came to lose such a large amount of money. There is only a report from a year later, saying that "a cart driver and an innkeeper were questioned, and they will be released after the arrest of the real criminal." See *Tongmun hwigo*, 2:1434 (*ch'ujing*: 16b).

93. The two merchants who transported the Korean embassy's luggage were members of Bordered White Banner. When they paid the silver, not only did the Shengjing office verify whether the amount was correct, but the amount was also confirmed through discussions with the Chosŏn court and by asking Yi Ch'ansuk himself whether the lost silver had been pure silver or merely 80 percent pure. See *Tongmun hwigo*, 2:1433–34 (*ch'ujing*: 14b–15a).

94. *Tongmun hwigo*, 2:1434 (*ch'ujing*: 15b–16a).

CHAPTER 5 FROM BORDERLAND TO BORDER

1. *Tongmun hwigo*, 4:3488 (*kanggye*: 4b–5b). E-le-he-bu's letter is dated on Tongzhi 6/2/30.

2. *Tongmun hwigo*, 4:3490–91 (*kanggye*: 6a–9b). The Shengjing military governor Du-xing-a's report to the emperor in 1867 has the same content. For Du-xing-a's report, see Lin, *Qingji dongbei yimin shibian*, 182.

3. Lin, *Qingji dongbei yimin shibian*, 180–81.

4. Wang, "Qingdai dongbei caishenye," 191.

5. Bello, *Across Forest, Steppe, and Mountain*, 96–100.

6. Schlesinger, "Qing Invention of Nature," 123–32.

7. After realizing that the resting policy had been unsuccessful, the Qing court decided to end it and issued permits to gather ginseng in the Shengjing area every year. *Qinding Da Qing huidian shili*, 232:723b.

8. Jiang, *Renshen diguo*, 104–113.

9. Imamura, *Ninjinshi*, 2:234.

10. Quoted in Jiang, *Renshen diguo*, 124.

11. Jiang, *Renshen diguo*, 116–21.

12. Kawakubo, "Shindai Manshū ni okeru *shaoguo*," 304–5.

13. *Shizong shilu*, 42:19b–20a (Yongzheng 4/3/xinyu). Later the Qianlong emperor repeated his father's prohibition on liquor production, pointing out that "liquor distilling is the worst way of wasting food grains, but the most popular in the five northern provinces." *Gaozong shilu*, 42:12a–13b (Qianlong 2/5/bingshen).

14. *Shengjing shenwu dang'an shiliao*, 247–48 (Jiaqing 5/7/12); Imamura, *Ninjinshi*, 2:209–11; Kawakubo, "Shindai Manshū ni okeru *shaoguo*," 311; Cong, *Dongbei sanbao*, 97–104.

15. Tong, "Qingdai Shengjing shenwu," 47–48; Jiang, *Renshen diguo*, 143–47.

16. Lee, *Manchurian Frontier*, 116–19; Yang and Sun, *Zhong Chao bianjieshi*, 210–19.

17. Fletcher, "Sino-Russian Relations," 332–48; Tsukase, *Manchuria shi kenkyū*, 138–44, 152–56.

18. *Wenzong shilu*, 294:9b–11a (Xianfeng 9/9/jimao).

19. Tsukase, "Chūgoku tōhoku tōchi no henyō"; Lin, *Qingji dongbei yimin shibian*, 78–79; Gao, *Jindai Zhongguo dongbei*, 105–13.

20. Lee, *Manchurian Frontier*, 119–27; Yang and Sun, *Zhong Chao bianjieshi*, 219–24; Tsukase, *Manchuria shi kenkyū*, 144–52, 161–68.

21. Akizuki, "Ōryokukō hokugan no tōjun kaishō," 120; Yamamoto, *Daishin teikoku to Chōsen keizai*, 30–37.

22. Akizuki, "Ōryokukō hokugan no tōjun kaishō," 120–27; Ku, "19 segi Sŏnggyŏng tongbyŏnoe," 273–81.

23. The new boundary patrol included the following: the construction of three new outposts near the Yalu River; an increase in the number of stationed officers and soldiers; the rotation of stationed soldiers every six months; checks on the outside of the eastern line of the Willow Palisade every four seasons; and the dispatch of an imperial inspector from Beijing to check the adequacy of boundary security every three years. Ku, "19 segi Sŏnggyŏng tongbyŏnoe," 282–97.

24. *Tongmun hwigo*, 4:3496 (*kanggye*: 20b–21b); Akizuki, "Ōryokukō hokugan no tōjun kaishō," 128–31; Lin, *Qingji dongbei yimin shibian*, 182–83.

25. *Tongmun hwigo*, 4:3507–508 (*kanggye*: 43b–44b).

26. *Tongmun hwigo*, 4:3508–509 (*kanggye*: 45a–46a).

27. *Tongmun hwigo*, 4:3509–510 (*kanggye*: 47b–49a).

28. After Chong-shi died in 1876, the Shengjing military governorship succeeded to his brother, Chong-hou, who continued to reform the Shengjing government and built new offices for civilian affairs. Tsukase, *Manchuria shi kenkyū*, 146–47.

29. *Tongmun hwigo*, 4:3512 (*kanggye*: 52a–b); Tsukase, *Manchuria shi kenkyū*, 146–47; Kim, "O Taejing kwa 1880 nyŏndae," 6–22.

30. *Dezong shilu*, 136:16a–17a (Guangxu 7/9/wuxu).

31. Akizuki, "Hwa i chilsŏ esŏŭi kyŏnggye chidae," 282–85.

32. Quoted in Kim, *1880 nyŏndae Chosŏn Chŏng kukkyŏng hoedam ŭi yŏn'gu*, chapter 1:1.

33. Zhang, *Qingdai Zhong Han guanxi*, 178; Li, *Han Chung kukkyŏngsa*, 151–56.

34. Kim, "Chosŏn hugi Hanin," 180–93; Kim, "Puk Kando chiyŏk Hanin," 179–80.

35. The Korean soldiers departed Huch'ang on July 5, 1872 (Kojong 9/5/30) and returned on August 13 of the same year (Kojong 9/7/10). For a full Korean translation of the diary, see Ch'oe, *Kando kaech'ŏk pisa*, 11–86. For a detailed analysis of the diary and of Korean immigrants in the Qing, see Kim, "Korean Migration in Nineteenth-Century Manchuria."

36. Li, *Cho Chŏng kukkyŏng munje*, 236–41.

37. Yi, "19 segi mal Chŏngjo ŭi tae Kando Chosŏnin," 260.

38. Kim and Kim, "Chosŏn hugi Hanin ŭi pukpang iju," 175–86; Li, *Cho Chŏng kukkyŏng munje*, 230–32.

39. Sun, *Zhongguo Chaoxianzu*, 121–25; Kim, *1880 nyŏndae Chosŏn Chŏng kukkyŏng hoedam ŭi yŏn'gu*, chapter 1:2.

40. Yang and Sun, *Zhong Chao bianjieshi*, 225–32; Lian, "Qingdai dui Yalujiang bei'an Chaoxian yimin de zhengce."

41. Quoted in Kim, *Last Phase of the East Asian World Order*, 51.

42. Quoted in Larsen, *Tradition, Treaties, and Trade*, 23. This confusion persisted into the 1870s. In 1872, when a Japanese diplomat asked the Qing government, "The Chosŏn is your subordinate, is it not? You should take the lead regarding trade agreements on behalf of the Chosŏn," the Qing replied, "The Chosŏn is the subordinate [*fanshu*], but it is independent in its domestic and foreign affairs, in which we have never intervened." In 1877, the Qing court also responded to Japan, "Everyone knows that [the Chosŏn] is subordinate to China, and everyone also knows that it is an independent country." *Qingshigao*, 526:14597–98.

43. Okamoto, *Miwan ŭi kihoek*, 93–95.

44. Larsen, *Tradition, Treaties, and Trade*, 11–15.

45. Kim, *1880 nyŏndae Chosŏn Chŏng kukkyŏng hoedam kwallyŏn charyo sŏnyŏk*, 112–16; Yang and Sun, *Zhong Chao bianjieshi*, 225–32; Sun, *Zhongguo Chaoxianzu*, 144–56.

46. *Dezong shilu*, 143:17a–18b (Guangxu 8/2/renxu).

47. Yang and Sun, *Zhong Chao bianjieshi*, 232–38.

48. Kim, *1880 nyŏndae Chosŏn Chŏng kukkyŏng hoedam kwallyŏn charyo sŏnyŏk*, 157–62.

49. *T'ongmun'gwan chi*, 12:4a.

50. Yi, "19 segi mal Chŏngjo ŭi tae Kando Chosŏnin," 264. For details on the numbers of Korean immigrants and their reclaimed land north of the Tumen River, see Kim and Kim, "Chosŏn hugi Hanin ŭi pukpang iju," 187–204.

51. Schmid, *Korea between Empires*, 208.

52. Kim, *1880 nyŏndae Chosŏn Chŏng kukkyŏng hoedam kwallyŏn charyo sŏnyŏk*, 215–20.

53. Ibid., 221–27.

54. Ibid., 397–99; *T'ongmun'gwan chi*, 12:8b.

55. Zhang, *Qingdai Zhong Han guanxi lunwenji*, 179–80; Schmid, *Korea between Empires*, 209; Sun, *Zhongguo chaoxianzu*, 182–96.

56. *Yongbi ŏch'ŏn'ga*, 7:23b. Peter H. Lee's English translation, *Songs of Flying Dragons*, does not include this explanation regarding "T'omun." It is attached to a footnote about "Tumun goronbori," one of the Jurchen tribal leaders who followed the Chosŏn T'aejo. Based on this record in the *Songs of Flying Dragons*, Kang Sŏkhwa argues that the Tuman and the T'omun are in fact two different rivers. It was only because of a lack of geographic knowledge about the north, Kang says, that the Chosŏn court could not distinguish the two rivers in the eighteenth century. He adds that "the Chosŏn court's misunderstanding does not influence the fact that there were two different rivers." Kang, *Chosŏn hugi Hamgyŏngdo*, 56–58.

57. *Pibyŏnsa tŭngnok*, Sukchong 38/2/30.

58. *Tongmun hwigo*, 2:1103–104 (*pŏmwŏl*: 26b–27a).

59. Pae, *Chosŏn hugi kukt'ogwan*, 248–66.

60. Kim, *1880 nyŏndae Chosŏn Ch'ŏng kukkyŏng hoedam kwallyŏn charyo sŏnyŏk*, 264–70, 291–97.

61. With regard to the Mu-ke-deng's stele, Qing officials were suspicious that it might be a forgery or that the Koreans might have relocated it. Their distrust in the stele was due the fact that few official documents about its establishment in 1712 remained, and the wooden fences that Mu-ke-deng had ordered to be built had rotted away. Schmid, *Korea between Empires*, 210; Li, *Han Chung kukkyŏngsa*, 125–29; Kim, *1880 nyŏndae Chosŏn Ch'ŏng kukkyŏng hoedam ŭi yŏn'gu*, chapter 1:3.

62. Yang and Sun, *Zhong Chao bianjieshi*, 249–64.

63. Zhang, *Qingdai Zhong Han guanxi*, 182–86; Yang and Sun, *Zhong Chao bianjieshi*, 265–90; Yang, *Han'guk kukkyŏngsa*, 70–90; Akizuki, "Chō Chū kankai kōshō," 94–95.

64. Kim, *1880 nyŏndae Chosŏn Ch'ŏng kukkyŏng hoedam ŭi yŏn'gu*, chapter 2:1.

65. Kim, *1880 nyŏndae Chosŏn Ch'ŏng kukkyŏng hoedam kwallyŏn charyo sŏnyŏk*, 619–23; *T'ongmun'gwan chi*, 12:10b–11a.

66. Kim, *1880 nyŏndae Chosŏn Ch'ŏng kukkyŏng hoedam kwallyŏn charyo sŏnyŏk*, 931–36.

67. Li, *Han Chung kukkyŏngsa*, 145–47; Zhang, *Qingdai Zhong Han guanxi*, 187–88; Yang and Sun, *Zhong Chao bianjieshi*, 317–42; Yang, *Han'guk kukkyŏngsa*, 91–102.

68. The Qing official responded, "The territory is equally important for us." Kim, *1880 nyŏndae Chosŏn Ch'ŏng kukkyŏng hoedam kwallyŏn charyo sŏnyŏk*, 771, 798.

69. Akizuki, "Chō Chū kankai kōshō no hottan to tenkai," 85–90.

70. Schmid, *Korea between Empires*, 209–10. For example, the twenty-third article of the regulation for commerce between Fengtian and Chosŏn, signed in 1883, still articulated that the Chosŏn should call the Qing "the heavenly court" or "the superior country." *Kojong sillok*, 20:92b (Kojong 20/12/3).

71. Zhang, *Qingdai Zhong Han guanxi*, 184.

72. Kim, *1880 nyŏndae Chosŏn Ch'ŏng kukkyŏng hoedam ŭi yŏn'gu*, chapter 3:1.

73. Akizuki, "Chō Chū kankai kōshō," 101.

74. Jiang, "Qing zhengfu yimin shibian zhengce," 190. Regarding the Qing government's registration of Korean immigrants, see Yang and Sun, *Zhong Chao bianjieshi*, 369–74.

75. Yi, "19 segi mal Ch'ŏngjo ŭi tae Kando Chosŏnin," 277.

76. Schmid, *Korea between Empires*, 214.

77. Ku, *Han'guk kŭndae tae Ch'ŏng chŏngch'aeksa*, 219–20, 227–35; Larsen, *Tradition, Treaties, and Trade*, 231–37.

78. The Treaty of Seoul of 1899 was mostly a commercial agreement, but it also recognized the Great Han Empire (*Taehan cheguk*) and Kojong as its emperor. For the contents of the treaty and China's position in Korean commerce, see Larsen, *Tradition, Treaties, and Trade*, 250–63.

79. Li, *Han Chung kukkyŏngsa*, 165–72.

80. Yang and Sun, *Zhong Chao bianjieshi*, 413–45; Sun, *Zhongguo Chaoxianzu*, 204–12; Akizuki, "Hwa i chilsŏ esŏŭi kyŏnggye chidae," 305–16.

81. Yang and Sun, *Zhong Chao bianjieshi*, 513–26; Sun, *Zhongguo chaoxianzu*, 212–24; Yang, *Han'guk kukkyŏngsa*, 114–29.

BIBLIOGRAPHY

Adelman, Jeremy, and Stephen Aron. "From Borderlands to Borders: Empires, Nation-States, and the Peoples in between in North American History." *American Historical Review* 104, no. 3 (1999): 814–41.

Akizuki Nozomi 秋月望. "Ōryokukō hokugan no tōjun kaishō ni tsuite" 鴨綠江北岸の統巡會哨について. *Kyūshū Daigaku Tōyōshi ronshū* 九州大學東洋史論集 11 (1983): 117–37.

———. "Chō Chū kankai kōshō no hottan to tenkai: Chōsengawano rinento ronri" 中朝勘界交涉の發端と展開: 朝鮮側の理念と論理. *Chōsen gakuhō* 朝鮮學報 132 (1989): 79–108.

———. "Hwa i chilsŏ esŏŭi kyŏnggye chidae wa kukchepŏp chŏk kukkyŏng" 華夷秩序에서의 境界地帶와 國際法的 國境. In *Kŭndae pyŏn'gyŏng ŭi hyŏngsŏng kwa pyŏn'gyŏngmin ŭi sam* 近代 邊境의 形成과 邊境民의 삶, edited by Tongbuga yŏksa chaedan 東北亞歷史財團, 279–316. Seoul: Tongbuga yŏksa chaedan, 2009.

Anderson, Malcolm. *Frontiers: Territory and State Formation in the Modern World*. Oxford: Polity, 1996.

Barfield, Thomas J. *The Perilous Frontier: Nomadic Empires and China*. Cambridge, MA: Blackwell, 1989.

Batten, Bruce L. *To the Ends of Japan: Premodern Frontiers, Boundaries, and Interactions*. Honolulu: University of Hawaii Press, 2003.

Baud, Michel, and Willem van Schendel. "Toward a Comparative History of Borderlands." *Journal of World History* 8, no. 2 (1997): 211–42.

Bello, David. *Across Forest, Steppe, and Mountain: Environment, Identity, and Empire in Qing China's Borderlands*. New York: Cambridge University Press, 2016.

———. "The Cultured Nature of Imperial Foraging in Manchuria." *Late Imperial China* 31, no. 2 (2010): 1–20.

Bohnet, Adam. "Ruling Ideology and Marginal Subjects: Ming Loyalism and Foreign Lineages in Late Chosŏn Korea." *Journal of Early Modern History* 15 (2011): 477–505.

Ch'a Sujŏng 차수정. "Chosŏn hugi insam muyŏk ŭi chŏn'gae wa kwajŏng" 朝鮮後期 人蔘 貿易의 展開와 過程. *Pukhak saron* 北學史論 1 (1989): 139–214.

Chang, Michael G. *A Court on Horseback: Imperial Touring and the Construction of Qing Rule, 1680–1785.* Cambridge, MA: Harvard University Press, 2007.

Chen Hui 陳慧. *Mukedeng bei wenti yanjiu: Qingdai Zhong Chao tumenjiang jiewu kaozheng* 穆克登碑問題研究: 清代中朝圖們江界務考證. Beijing: Zhongyang bianyi chubanshe, 2011.

Chen Jiexian 陳捷先. "Shuo 'Manzhou'" 說滿州. In *Manzhou congkao* 滿洲叢考, 1–24. Taipei: Guoli Taiwan daxue wenxueyuan, 1963.

Cheng Kaihu 程開祜. *Chouliao shuohua* 籌遼碩畫. Shanghai: Shangwu yinshuguan, 1937.

Cho Hyŏng 趙珩. *Ch'wibyŏnggong yŏnhaeng ilgi* 翠屏公燕行日記 [1660]. Vol. 20 of *Yŏnhaengnok chŏnjip* 燕行錄全集, edited by Im Kijung 임기중. Seoul: Tongguk taehakkyo, 2001.

Cho Kwang 조광. "Chosŏn hugi ŭi pyŏn'gyŏng ŭisik" 朝鮮後期의 邊境意識. *Paeksan hakpo* 白山學報 29 (1974): 149–84.

Cho Yŏngnok 조영록. "Ipkwan chŏn Myŏng Sŏn sidae ŭi Manju yŏjiksa" 入關前 明-鮮時代의 滿洲女直史. *Paeksan hakpo* 白山學報 22 (1977): 15–81.

Ch'oe Chongbŏm 崔宗範. *Kando kaech'ŏk pisa: Kangbuk ilgi* 間島開拓秘史: 江北日記. Translated by Ch'oe Kanghyŏn 최강현. Seoul: Sinsŏng ch'ulp'ansa, 2004.

Ch'oe Tŏkchung 崔德中. *Yŏnhaengnok* 燕行錄 [1712]. Vols. 39–40 of *Yŏnhaengnok chŏnjip* 燕行錄全集, edited by Im Kijung 임기중. Seoul: Tongguk taehakkyo, 2001.

Chong Da-ham [Chŏng Taham] 정다함. "Chosŏn ch'ogi yain kwa Taemado e taehan pŏlli, pŏnbyŏng insik ŭi hyŏngsŏng kwa kyŏngch'agwan p'agyŏn" 朝鮮初期 野人과 對馬島에 대한 藩籬, 藩屏認識의 形成과 敬差官 派遣. *Tongbang hakchi* 東方學志 141 (2008): 221–66.

———. "Making Chosŏn's Own Tributaries: Dynamics between the Ming-Centered World Order and a Chosŏn-Centered Regional Order in the East Asian Periphery." *International Journal of Korean History* 15, no. 1 (2010): 29–63.

Chosŏn wangjo sillok 朝鮮王朝實錄. Seoul: Kuksa p'yŏnch'an wiwŏnhoe, 1968. (Order by reign: *T'aejong sillok, Sejong sillok, Sejo sillok, Yŏnsangun ilgi, Chungjong sillok, Myŏngjong sillok, Sŏnjo sillok, Sŏnjo sujŏng sillok, Kwanghaegun ilgi, Injo sillok, Hyŏnjong sillok, Hyŏnjong kaesu sillok, Sukchong sillok, Kyŏngjong sillok, Yŏngjo sillok, Chŏngjo sillok, Kojong sillok*.)

Chun Hae-jong [Chŏn Haejong] 전해종. *Han Chung kwan'gyesa yŏn'gu* 韓中關係史研究. Seoul: Iljogak, 1977.

———. "Sino-Korean Tributary Relations in the Ch'ing Period." In *The Chinese World Order: China's Foreign Relations*, edited by John K. Fairbank, 90–112. Cambridge, MA: Harvard University Press, 1968.

Clark, Donald N. "Sino-Korean Tributary Relations under the Ming." In *The Ming Dynasty, 1368–1644*, 272–300. Vol. 8, part 2, of *The Cambridge History of China*. Edited by Denis Twitchett and Frederick W. Mote. Cambridge, England: Cambridge University Press, 1998.

Cong Peiyuan 叢佩遠. *Dongbei sanbao jingji jianshi* 東北三寶經濟簡史. Beijing: Nongye chubanshe, 1989.

——. *Zhongguo dongbeishi* 中國東北史. Vols. 3–4. Changchun: Jilin wenshi chubanshe, 1998.

Court, William E. *Ginseng: The Genus Panax*. Amsterdam: Harwood Academic, 2000.

Crossley, Pamela K. "Making Mongols." In *Empire at the Margins: Culture, Ethnicity, and Frontier in Early Modern China*, edited by Pamela K. Crossley, Helen F. Siu and Donald S. Sutton, 58–82. Berkeley: University of California Press, 2006.

——. *The Manchus*. Oxford: Blackwell, 2002.

——. "*Manzhou yuanliu kao* and the Formalization of the Manchu Heritage." *Journal of Asian Studies* 46, no. 4 (1987): 761–90.

——. *A Translucent Mirror: History and Identity in Qing Imperial Ideology*. Berkeley: University of California Press, 1999.

Dai Yingcong. *The Sichuan Frontier and Tibet: Imperial Strategy in the Early Qing*. Seattle: University of Washington Press, 2009.

Da Ming huidian 大明會典 [1511]. Edited by Li Dongyang 李東陽. Yangzhou: Guangling shushe, 2007.

Da Ming yitongzhi 大明一統志 [1461]. Edited by Li Xian 李賢. Xian: Sanqin chubanshe, 1990.

Dan Shao. *Remote Homeland, Recovered Borderland: Manchus, Manchoukuo, and Manchuria, 1907–1985*. Honolulu: University of Hawaii Press, 2011.

Dennerline, Jerry. "The Shun-chih Reign." In *The Ch'ing Empire to 1800*, 73–119. Vol. 9, part 1, of *The Cambridge History of China*. Edited by Willard J. Peterson. Cambridge, England: Cambridge University Press, 2002.

Diao Shuren 刁書仁 and Cui Wenzhi 崔文植. "Ming qianqi Zhong Chao dongduan bianjie de bianhua" 明前期中朝東段邊界的變化. *Shixue jikan* 史學集刊 2 (2000): 22–27.

Di Cosmo, Nicola. *Ancient China and Its Enemies*. Cambridge, England: Cambridge University Press, 2002.

——. "Kirghiz Nomads on the Qing Frontier: Tribute, Trade, or Gift Exchange?" In *Political Frontiers, Ethnic Boundaries, and Human Geographies in Chinese History*, edited by Nicola Di Cosmo and Don F. Wyatt, 351–72. London: Routledge Curzon, 2003.

——. "The Manchu Conquest in World-Historical Perspective: A Note on Trade and Silver." *Journal of Central Eurasian Studies* 1 (2009): 43–60.

——. "Qing Colonial Administration in Inner Asia." *International History Review* 20, no. 2 (1998): 287–309.

——. "State Formation and Periodization in Inner Asian History." *Journal of World History* 10, no. 1 (1999): 1–40.

Ding Haibin 丁海斌 and Shi Yi 時義. *Qingdai peidu Shengjing yanjiu* 清代陪都盛京研究. Beijing: Zhongguo shehui kexue chubanshe, 2007.

Ding Yizhuang 定宜莊, and Mark C. Elliott 歐立德. "21 shiji ruhe shuxie Zhongguo lishi: 'Xin Qingshi' yanjiu de yingxiang yu huiying" 21 世紀如何書寫中國歷史: "新清史" 研究的影響與回應. In *Lishixue pinglun* 歷史學評論, vol. 1, edited by Peng Weizhu 彭衛主, 116–46. Beijing: Shehui kexue wenxian chubanshe, 2013.

Edmonds, Richard. "The Willow Palisade." *Annals of the Association of American Geographers* 69, no. 4 (1979): 599–621.

Eggert, Marion. "A Borderline Case: Korean Travelers' Views of the Chinese Border (Eighteenth to Nineteenth Century)." In *China and Her Neighbours: Borders, Visions of the Other, Foreign Policy 10th to 19th Century*, edited by Sabine Dabringhaus et al., 49–78. Wiesbaden: Harrassowitz, 1997.

Elliott, Mark C. "The Limits of Tartary: Manchuria in Imperial and National Geographies." *Journal of Asian Studies* 59, no. 3 (2000): 603–46.

———. *The Manchu Way: The Eight Banners and Ethnic Identity in Late Imperial China*. Stanford, CA: Stanford University Press, 2001.

Fairbank, John K. "A Preliminary Framework." In *The Chinese World Order: China's Foreign Relations*, edited by John K. Fairbank, 1–19. Cambridge, MA: Harvard University Press, 1968.

Fletcher, Joseph. "Sino-Russian Relations, 1800–62." In *Late Ch'ing, 1800–1911*, 318–350. Vol. 10, part 1, of *The Cambridge History of China*. Edited by John K. Fairbank. Cambridge, England: Cambridge University Press, 1978.

Fogel, Joshua A., ed. *The Teleology of the Modern Nation-State, Japan and China*. Philadelphia: University of Pennsylvania Press, 2005.

Foret, Philippe. *Mapping Chengde: The Qing Landscape Enterprise*. Honolulu: University of Hawaii Press, 2000.

Fuma Susumu 夫馬進. "Min Shin Chūgoku no tai Chōsen gaikō ni okeru 'rei' to 'monzai'" 明清中國の對朝鮮外交における禮と問罪. In *Chūgoku Higashi Ajia gaikō kōryūshino kenkyū* 中國東アジア外交交流史の研究, edited by Fuma Susumu 夫馬進, 311–53. Tokyo: Kyōtodaigaku gakujutsu shuppankai, 2007.

Gao Lecai 高樂才. *Jindai Zhongguo dongbei yimin yanjiu* 近代中國東北移民研究. Beijing: Shangwu yinshuguan, 2010.

Gao Shiqi 高士奇. *Hucong dongxun rilu* 扈從東巡日錄. Taipei: Guangwen shuju, 1968.

Giersch, Patterson. *Asian Borderlands: The Transformation of Qing China's Yunnan Frontier*. Cambridge, MA: Harvard University Press, 2006.

Gongzhongdang Yongzhengchao zouzhe: Manwen yuezhe 宮中檔雍正朝奏摺: 滿文月摺. Taiwan: Guoli gugong bowuguan, 1980.

Guan Jixin 關紀新. "Qingdai Manzu zuojia wenxue zhong de Changbaishan qingjie" 清代滿族作家文學中的長白山情結. *Minzu wenxue yanjiu* 民族文學研究 (1997): 72–75.

Haboush, JaHyun Kim. "Contesting Chinese Time, Nationalizing Temporal Space: Temporal Inscription in Late Chosŏn Korea." In *Time, Temporality, and Imperial Transition: East Asia from Ming to Qing*, edited by Lynn A. Struve, 115–41. Honolulu: University of Hawaii Press, 2005.

Hämäläinen, Pekka, and Samuel Truett. "On Borderlands." *Journal of American History* 98, no. 2 (2011): 338–61.

Han Myŏnggi 한명기. *Chŏngmyo, Pyŏngja horan kwa Tong Asia* 丁卯-丙子胡亂과 東아시아. Seoul: P'urŭn yŏksa, 2009.

Han Sŏngju 한성주. "Chosŏn ch'ogi sujik Yŏjinin yŏn'gu" 朝鮮初期 受職女眞人 研究. *Chosŏn sidae sahakpo* 朝鮮時代史學報 36 (2006): 67–108.

———. *Chosŏn chŏn'gi sujik Yŏjinin yŏn'gu* 朝鮮前期 受職女眞人 研究. Seoul: Kyŏngin munhwasa, 2011.

Hatachi Masanori 畑地正憲. "Shinchō to Rishi Chōsen to no chōkō bōeki ni tsuite" 清朝と李氏朝鮮との朝貢貿易について: 特に鄭商の盛衰をめぐって. *Tōyō gakuhō* 東洋學報 62, nos. 3/4 (1981): 70–103.

Heffern, Richard. *The Complete Book of Ginseng*. Millbrae, CA: Celestial Arts, 1976.

Herman, John E. *Amid the Clouds and Mist: China's Colonization of Guizhou, 1200–1700*. Cambridge, MA: Harvard University Press, 2007.

Hevia, James. *Cherishing Men from Afar: Qing Guest Ritual and the Macartney Embassy of 1793*. Durham: NC: Duke University Press, 1995.

Hŏ T'aeyong 허태용. *Chosŏn hugi chunghwaron kwa yŏksa insik* 朝鮮後期 中華論과 歷史認識. Seoul: Ak'anet, 2009.

Hong Taeyong 洪大容. *Tamhŏn yŏn'gi* 湛軒燕記 [1765]. Vol. 42 of *Yŏnhaengnok chŏnjip* 燕行錄全集, edited by Im Kijung 임기중. Seoul: Tongguk taehakkyo, 2001.

Hostetler, Laura. *Qing Colonial Enterprise: Ethnography and Cartography in Early Modern China*. Chicago: University of Chicago Press, 2001.

Hou, Joseph P. *The Myth and Truth about Ginseng*. New York: A. S. Barnes, 1978.

Howell, David. "Ainu Ethnicity and the Boundaries of the Early Modern Japanese State." *Past and Present* 142 (1994): 69–93.

Huang Songyun 黃松筠. *Zhongguo gudai fanshu zhidu yanjiu* 中國古代藩屬制度研究. Changchun: Jilin renmin chubanshe, 2008.

Huang Songyun 黃松筠 and Luan Fan 欒凡. *Jilin tongshi* 吉林通史, vol. 2. Changchun: Jilin renmin chubanshe, 2008.

Hunchun fudutong yamendang 琿春副都統衙門檔. Edited by Zhongguo bianjiang shidi yanjiu zhongxin 中國邊疆史地研究中心 and Zhongguo diyi lishi dang'anguan 中國第一歷史檔案館. Guilin: Guangxi shifan daxue chubanshe, 2007.

Hwang Chiyŏng 황지영. "Yi Sŏngnyang sagŏn ŭl t'onghae pon 17 segi ch'o Yodong chŏngch'aek ŭi pyŏnhwa" 李成梁 事件을 통해 본 17世紀初 遼東政策의 變化. *Chosŏn sidae sahakpo* 朝鮮時代史學報 21 (2002): 5–35.

Hwang, Kyung Moon. *Beyond Birth: Social Status in the Emergence of Modern Korea*. Cambridge, MA: Harvard University Press, 2004.

Im Kaye Soon [Im Kyesun] 任桂淳. *Qingchao baqi zhufang xingshuishi* 清朝八旗駐防興衰史. Beijing: Sanlian shudian, 1993.

Im Kijung 임기중. "Yonhaengnok ŭi tae Chŏng ŭisik kwa tae Chosŏn ŭisik" 燕行錄의 對清意識과 對朝鮮意識. *Yŏmmin hakchi* 淵民學志 1, no. 1 (1993): 117–52.

Imamura Tomo 今村鞆. *Ninjinshi* 人蔘史. 7 vols. Keijō: Chōsen sōtokufu, 1934–40.

Imanishi Shunju 今西春秋. "Jušen koku iiki kō" Jušen 國域考. *Tōhōgaku kiyō* 東方學紀要 2 (1967): 1–172.

Inaba Iwakichi 稻葉岩吉. *Kōkai-kun jidai no Man-Sen kankei* 光海君時代の滿鮮關係. Tokyo: Kokusho kankōkai, 1976.

———. *Manzhou fadashi* 滿洲發達史. Translated by Yang Chengneng 楊成能. Fengtian: Cuiwenzhai shudian, 1939.

Inp'yŏng Taegun 麟坪大君. *Yŏndo kihaeng* 燕途紀行 [1656]. Vol. 22 of *Yŏnhaengnok chŏnjip* 燕行錄全集, edited by Im Kijung 임기중. Seoul: Tongguk taehakkyo, 2001.

Isett, Christopher M. *State, Peasant, and Merchant in Qing Manchuria, 1644–1862*. Stanford, CA: Stanford University Press, 2007.

———. "Village Regulation of Property and the Social Basis for the Transformation of Qing Manchuria." *Late Imperial China* 25, no. 1 (2004): 124–86.

Iwai Shigeki 岩井茂樹. "China's Frontier Society in the Sixteenth and Seventeenth Centuries." *Acta Asiatica* 88 (2005): 1–20.

Jiang Longfan 姜龍範. "Qing zhengfu yimin shibian zhengce yu Zhongguo Chaoxianzu de xingcheng" 清政府移民實邊政策與中國朝鮮族的形成. *Shehui kexue zhanxian* 社會科學戰線 2000, no. 4 (2000): 187–93.

Jiang Zhushan 蔣竹山. *Renshen diguo: Qingdai renshen de shengchan, xiaofei yu yiliao* 人蔘帝國: 清代人蔘的生産, 消費與醫療. Hangzhou: Zhejiang daxue chubanshe, 2015.

Jilin tongzhi 吉林通志. Guangxu 光緒 edition. Shanghai: Shanghai guji chubanshe, 1995.

Junjichu hanwen dangzhe 軍機處漢文檔摺. Taipei: Taiwan Palace Museum.

Junjichu manwen lufu, waijiao lei, Zhong Chao xiang 軍機處滿文錄副, 外交類, 中朝項. Beijing: Beijing First Historical Archive.

Kang Man'gil 강만길. *Chosŏn hugi sangŏp chabon ŭi paldal* 朝鮮後期 商業資本의 發達. Seoul: Koryŏ taehakkyo ch'ulp'anbu, 1973.

Kang Sŏkhwa 강석화. "1712 nyŏn ŭi Cho Chŏng chŏnggye wa 18 segi Chosŏn ŭi pukpang kyŏngyŏng" 1712年의 朝淸 定界와 18世紀 朝鮮의 北方經營. *Chindan hakpo* 震檀學報 79 (1996): 135–61.

———. *Chosŏn hugi Hamgyŏngdo wa pukpang yŏngt'o ŭisik* 朝鮮後期 咸鏡道와 北方領土意識. Seoul: Kyŏngsewŏn, 2000.

Kangxi qijuzhu 康熙起居注. Edited by Zhongguo diyi lishi dang'anguan 中國第一歷史檔案館. Beijing: Zhonghua shuju, 1984.

Kawachi Yoshihiro 河內良弘. *Mindai Joshinshi no kenkyū* 明代女眞史の研究. Kyoto: Dōhōsha, 1992.

Kawakubo Teirō 川久保悌郎. "Shindai Manshū ni okeru *shaoguo* no sōsei ni tsuite" 清代滿洲における燒鍋の簇生について. In *Wada Hakushi koki kinen tōyōshi ronsō* 和田博士古稀記念東洋史論叢, 303–13. Tokyo: Kōdansha, 1960.

Kim Ch'angŏp 金昌業. *Nogajae yŏnhaeng ilgi* 老稼齋燕行日記 [1712]. Vol. 33 of *Yŏnhaengnok chŏnjip* 燕行錄全集, edited by Im Kijung 임기중. Seoul: Tongguk taehakkyo, 2001.

Kim Chŏngmi 김정미. "Chosŏn hugi tae Chŏng muyŏk ŭi chŏn'gae wa muyŏk suseje ŭi sihaeng" 朝鮮後期 對清貿易의 展開와 貿易收稅制의 施行. *Han'guk saron* 韓國史論 36 (1996): 153–217.

Kim Chongwŏn 김종원. *Kŭnse Tong Asia kwan'gyesa yŏn'gu* 近世 東아시아 關係史 研究. Seoul: Hyean, 1999.

Kim Ch'unsŏn 김춘선. "Chosŏn hugi Hanin ŭi Manju roŭi pŏmwŏl kwa chŏngch'ak kwajŏng" 朝鮮後期 韓人의 滿洲로의 犯越과 定着過程. *Paeksan hakpo* 白山學報 51 (1998): 155–95.

———. "Puk Kando chiyŏk Hanin sahoe ŭi hyŏngsŏng kwa t'oji soyu'gwŏn munje" 北間島地域 韓人社會의 形成과 土地所有權 問題. *Chŏnju sahak* 全州史學 6 (1998): 177–91.

Kim Ch'unsŏn 김춘선 and Kim T'aeguk 김태국. "Chosŏn hugi Hanin ŭi pukpang iju wa Manju kaechŏk" 朝鮮後期 韓人의 北方移住와 滿洲開拓. *Han'guksaron* 韓國史論 34 (2002): 159–208.

Kim Han'gyu 김한규. *Han Chung kwan'gyesa* 韓中關係史. 2 vols. Seoul: Munhak kwa chisŏng, 2004.

———. *Yodong sa* 遼東史. Seoul: Munhak kwa chisŏng, 2004.

Kim Hyŏngjong 김형종. "O Taejing kwa 1880 nyŏndae Chŏng Rŏ tongbu kukkyŏng kamgye" 吳大澂과 1880年代 清-러 東部國境勘界. *Chungguk kŭnhyŏndaesa yŏn'gu* 中國近現代史研究 60 (2013): 1–51.

———, trans. *1880 nyŏndae Chosŏn Chŏng kukkyŏng hoedam kwallyŏn charyo sŏnyŏk* 1880년대 朝鮮-清 國境會談 關聯資料 選譯. Seoul: Sŏul taehakkyo ch'ulp'an munhwawŏn, 2014.

———. *1880 nyŏndae Chosŏn Chŏng kukkyŏng hoedam ŭi yŏn'gu* 1880년대 朝鮮-清 國境會談의 研究. Forthcoming.

Kim, Key-Hiuk. *The Last Phase of the East Asian World Order: Korea, Japan, and the Chinese Empire, 1860–1882*. Berkeley: University of California Press, 1980.

Kim Kujin 김구진. "Ch'ogi Morin Orangk'ae yŏn'gu" 初期 毛憐 兀良哈 研究. *Paeksan hakpo* 白山學報 17 (1974): 163–213.

———. "Chosŏn chŏn'gi Yŏjinjok ŭi 2 dae chongjok: orangk'ae wa udik'ae" 朝鮮前期 女眞族의 2大 種族: 오랑캐(兀良哈)와 우디캐(兀狄哈). *Paeksan hakpo* 白山學報 68 (2004): 289–333.

———. "Myŏngdae Yŏjin ŭi Chungguk e taehan kongmuyŏk kwa samuyŏk" 明代 女眞의 中國에 대한 公貿易과 私貿易. *Tongyang sahak yŏn'gu* 東洋史學研究 48 (1994): 1–61.

———. "Oŭmhoe ŭi Alt'ari Yŏjin e taehan yŏn'gu" 吾音會의 알타리 女眞에 대한 研究. *Sach'ong* 史叢 17–18 (1973): 85–122.

Kim Kujin 김구진 and Yi Hyŏnsuk 이현숙. "T'ongmun'gwan chi ŭi p'yŏnch'an kwa kŭ kanhaeng e taehayŏ" 通文館志 編纂과 그 刊行에 대하여. In *T'ongmun'gwan chi* 通文館志, 1:1–30. Seoul: Sejong taewang kinyŏm saŏphoe, 1998.

Kim, Kwangmin. "Korean Migration in Nineteenth-Century Manchuria: A Global Theme in Modern Asian History." In *Mobile Subjects: Boundaries and Identities in the Modern Korean Diaspora*, edited by Wen-hsin Yeh, 17–37. Berkeley, CA: Institute of East Asian Studies, 2013.

———. "Profit and Protection: Emin Khwaja and the Qing Conquest of Central Asia, 1759–1777." *Journal of Asian Studies* 71, no. 3 (2012): 603–26.

Kim Kyŏngch'un 김경춘. "Chosŏnjo hugi ŭi kukkyŏngsŏn e taehan ilgo: muin chidae rŭl chungsim ŭro" 朝鮮朝 後期의 國境線에 대한 一考: 無人地帶를 中心으로. *Paeksan hakpo* 白山學報 29 (1984): 5–32.

Kim Kyŏngnok 김경록. "Chosŏn ŭi tae Chŏng insik kwa oegyo ch'eje" 朝鮮의 對清認識과 外交體制. *Ihwa sahak yŏn'gu* 梨花史學研究 37 (2008): 139–78.

Kim Kyŏngsŏn 金景善. *Yŏnwŏn chikchi* 燕轅直指 [1832]. Vol. 70 of *Yŏnhaengnok chŏnjip* 燕行錄全集, edited by Im Kijung 임기중. Seoul: Tongguk taehakkyo, 2001.

Kim Seonmin [Kim Sŏnmin] 김선민. "Ginseng and Border Trespassing between Qing China and Chosŏn Korea." *Late Imperial China* 28, no. 1 (2007): 33–61.

———. "Insam kwa kangyŏk: Hukŭm Chŏng ŭi kangyŏk insik kwa taeoe kwan'gye ŭi pyŏnhwa" 人蔘과 疆域: 後金-清의 疆域認識과 對外關係의 變化. *Myŏngchŏngsa yŏnggu* 明清史研究 30 (2008): 227–57.

———. "Kŏllyung nyŏn'gan Chosŏn sahaeng ŭi ŭn punsil sagŏn" 乾隆年間 朝鮮使行의 銀 분실사건. *Myŏngchŏngsa yŏnggu* 明清史研究 33 (2010): 139–66.

———. "Nandu: Chŏng Chosŏn chogong kwan'gye ŭi pyŏn'gyŏng chŏk ch'ŭkmyŏn" 欄頭: 清-朝鮮 조공관계의 변경적 측면. *Taegu sahak* 大邱史學 96 (2009): 1–37.

———. "Ongjŏng Kŏllyung nyŏn'gan Manguch'o sagŏn kwa Chŏng Chosŏn kukkyŏng chi-dae" 雍正-乾隆年間 荞牛哨사건과 清-朝鮮 國境地帶. *Chungguksa yŏn'gu* 中國史研究 71 (2011): 69–97.

———. "Ongjŏngje wa Sŏnggyŏng chiyŏk t'ongch'i" 雍正帝와 盛京地域 統治. *Myŏngch'ŏngsa yŏn'gu* 明清史研究 34 (2010): 143–77.

Kim Yongguk 김용국. "Paektusan ko" 白頭山考. *Paeksan hakpo* 白山學報 8 (1970): 254–98.

Kolossov, Vladimir, and James Scott. "Selected Conceptual Issues in Border Studies." *Belgeo* 1 (2013): https://belgeo.revues.org/10532.

Ku Pŏmjin 구범진. "19 segi Sŏnggyŏng tongbyŏnoe sanjang ŭi kwalli wa Cho Chŏng kong-dong hoech'o" 19世紀 盛京 東邊外 山場의 管理와 朝清 公同會哨. *Sarim* 史林 32 (2009): 261–300.

———. "Chŏng ŭi Chosŏn sahaeng insŏn kwa Tae Chŏng cheguk ch'eje" 清의 朝鮮使行 人選과 大清帝國體制. *Inmun nonch'ong* 人文論叢 59 (2008): 1–50.

Ku Sŏnhŭi 구선희. *Han'guk kŭndae tae Chŏng chŏngch'aeksa yŏn'gu* 韓國近代 對清政策史研究. Seoul: Hye'an, 1999.

Kwŏn Naehyŏn 권내현. *Chosŏn hugi P'yŏngando chaejŏng yŏn'gu* 朝鮮後期 平安道 財政研究. Seoul: Chisik sanŏpsa, 2004.

Kye Seung B. [Kye Sŭngbŏm] 계승범. *Chosŏn sidae haeoe p'abyŏng kwa HanChung kwan'gye* 朝鮮時代 海外派兵과 韓中關係. Seoul: P'urŭn yŏksa, 2009.

———. "Huddling under the Imperial Umbrella: A Korean Approach to Ming China in the Early 1500s." *Journal of Korean Studies* 15, no. 1 (2010): 41–66.

———. "Imjin waeran kwa Nurŭhach'i" 壬辰倭亂과 누르하치. In *Imjin Waeran: Tong Asia samguk chŏnjaeng* 壬辰倭亂: 東아시아 三國戰爭, edited by Chŏng Tuhŭi 정두희 and Yi Kyŏngsun 이경순, 355–84. Seoul: Humanist, 2007.

Larsen, Kirk. *Tradition, Treaties, and Trade: Qing Imperialism and Chosŏn Korea, 1850–1910.* Cambridge, MA: Harvard University Press, 2008.

Lattimore, Owen. *Inner Asian Frontiers of China.* Boston: Beacon, 1940.

———. *Manchuria: Cradle of Conflict.* New York: Macmillan, 1932.

Ledyard, Gari. "Cartography in Korea." In *Cartography in the Traditional East and Southeast Asian Societies*, 235–344. Vol. 2, book 2, of *The History of Cartography*. Edited by J. B. Harley and David Woodward. Chicago: University of Chicago Press, 1987.

———. "Hong Taeyong and His 'Peking Memoir.'" *Korean Studies* 6 (1982): 63–103.

———. "Korean Travelers in China over Four Hundred Years, 1488–1887." *Occasional Papers on Korea* 2 (1974): 1–42.

———. "Yin and Yang in the China-Manchuria-Korea Triangle." In *China among Equals: The Middle Kingdom and Its Neighbors*, edited by Morris Rossabi, 313–53. Berkeley: University of California Press, 1983.

Lee, Peter H. *Songs of Flying Dragons: A Critical Reading.* Cambridge, MA: Harvard University Press, 1975.

Lee, Robert H. G. *The Manchurian Frontier in Ch'ing History.* Cambridge, MA: Harvard University Press, 1970.

Lewis, James B. *Frontier Contact between Chosŏn Korea and Tokugawa Japan.* London and New York: RoutledgeCurzon, 2003.

Li, Gertraude Roth. "State Building before 1644." In *The Ch'ing Empire to 1800*, 9–72. Vol. 9, part 1, of *The Cambridge History of China*. Edited by Willard J. Peterson. Cambridge, England: Cambridge University Press, 2002.

Li Huazi 李花子. "Chaoxian wangchao de Changbaishan renshi" 朝鮮王朝的長白山認識. *Zhongguo bianjiang shidi yanjiu* 中國邊疆史地研究 17, no. 2 (2007): 126–35.

———. *Cho Chŏng kukkyŏng munje yŏn'gu* 朝清國境問題研究. Seoul: Chipmundang, 2008.

———. *Han Chung kukkyŏngsa yŏn'gu* 韓中國境史研究. Seoul: Hye'an, 2011.

Li Shizhen 李時珍. *Bencao gangmu* 本草綱目. Vol. 143 of *Guoxue jiben congshu* 國學基本叢書. Taipei: Shangwu yinshuguan, 1968.

Li Zhiting 李治亭, ed. *Dongbei tongshi* 東北通史. Zhengzhou: Zhongzhou guji chubanshe, 2003.

Lian Songxin 廉松心. "Qingdai dui Yalujiang bei'an Chaoxian yimin de zhengce" 清代對鴨綠江北岸朝鮮移民的政策. *Shehui kexue zhanxian* 社會科學戰線 2009, no. 8 (2009): 156–62.

Lin Shih-hsuan [Lin Shixuan] 林士鉉. *Qingji dongbei yimin shibian zhengce zhi yanjiu* 清季東北移民實邊政策之研究. Taipei: Guoli zhengzhi daxue lishi xuexi, 2001.

Liu Wei 劉為. "Qingdai Chaoxian shituan maoyi zhidu shulüe" 清代朝鮮使團貿易制度述略. *Zhongguo bianjiang shidi yanjiu* 中國邊疆史地研究 12, no. 4 (2002): 36–47.

———. "Qingdai Zhong Chao zongfan guanxi xia de tongshi wanglai" 清代中朝宗藩關係下的通使往來. *Zhongguo bianjiang shidi yanjiu* 中國邊疆史地研究 10, no. 3 (2000): 25–36.

Liu Xiaomeng 劉小萌. *Manzu cong buluo dao guojia de fazhan* 滿族從部落到國家的發展. Beijing: Zhongguo shehui kexue chubanshe, 2007.

———. *Manzu de shehui yu shenghuo* 滿族的社會與生活. Beijing: Beijing tushuguan chubanshe, 1998.

Liu Yongzhi 劉永智. *Zhong Chao guanxishi yanjiu* 中朝關係史研究. Shenyang: Zhongzhou guji chubanshe, 1995.

Manbun rōtō 滿文老檔. Translated by Manbun rōtō kenkyūkai 滿文老檔研究會. Tokyo: Tōyō bunko, 1955–63.

Mancall, Mark. "The Ch'ing Tribute System: An Interpretative Essay." In *The Chinese World Order: China's Foreign Relations*, edited by John K. Fairbank, 63–89. Cambridge, MA: Harvard University Press, 1968.

Man'gi Yoram 萬機要覽. Seoul: Minjok munhwa ch'ujin wiwŏnhoe, 1971.

Matsuura Akira 松浦章. *Kinsei Chūgoku Chōsen kōshōshi no kenkyū* 近世中國朝鮮交涉史の研究. Kyoto: Shibunkaku shuppan, 2013.

———. "Minshin jidai Pekin no kaidōkan" 明清時代北京の會同館. In *Shinchō to Higashi Ajia: Kanda Nobuo Sensei koki kinen ronshū* 清朝と東アジア: 神田信夫先生古稀記念論集, 359–79. Tokyo: Yamakawa shuppansha, 1992.

Matsuura Shigeru 松浦茂. *Shinchō no Amūru seisaku to shōsū minzoku* 清朝のアムール政策と少數民族. Kyoto: Kyōto daigaku gakujutsu shuppankai, 2006.

Millward, James A. *Beyond the Pass: Economy, Ethnicity, and Empire in Qing Central Asia*. Stanford, CA: Stanford University Press, 1998.

———. "'Coming onto the Map': 'Western Regions' Geography and Cartographic Nomenclature in the Making of Chinese Empire in Xinjiang." *Late Imperial China* 20, no. 2 (1999): 61–98.

———. "New Perspectives on the Qing Frontier." In *Remapping China: Fissures in Historical Terrain*, edited by Gail Hershatter et al., 113–29. Stanford, CA: Stanford University Press, 1996.

Mingshi 明史. Beijing: Zhonghua shuju, 1974.

Ming shilu 明實錄. Taipei: Zhongyang yanjiuyuan lishi yuyan yanjiusuo, 1962; Zhongwen chubanshe, 1984. (Order by reign: *Taizong shilu, Shenzong shilu.*)

Mun Sunsil 文純實. "Hakutōzan teikaihi to jūhasseiki Chōsen no kyōikikan" 白頭山定界碑と十八世紀朝鮮の疆域觀. *Chōsenshi kenkyūkai ronbunshū* 朝鮮史研究会論文集 40 (2002): 39–66.

Nakami Tatsuo 中見立夫. "Chiiki gainen no seijisei" 地域概念の政治性. In *Ajia kara kangaeru: Kōsakusuru Ajia* アジアから考える: 交錯するアジア, 273–96. Tokyo: Tokyo daigaku shuppankai, 1993.

———. "Nihonteki Tōyōgaku no keisei to kōzu" 日本的東洋學の形成と構圖. In *Teikoku Nihon no gakuchi* 帝國日本の學知, vol. 3, *Tōyōgaku no Jiba* 東洋學の磁場, edited by Kishimoto Mio 岸本美緒, 13–97. Tokyo: Iwanami shoten, 2006.

Nam Ŭihyŏn 남의현. *Myŏngdae Yodong chibae chŏngch'aek yŏn'gu* 明代遼東支配政策研究. Ch'unch'ŏn: Kangwŏn taehakkyo ch'ulp'anbu, 2008.

Nishijima Sadao 西島定生. *Chūgoku kodai kokka to Higashi Ajia sekai* 中國古代國家と東アジア世界. Tokyo: Tokyo daigaku shuppankai, 1983.

No Kisik 노기식. "Myŏngdae Monggol kwa Manju ŭi kyoch'e" 明代 몽골과 滿洲의 交替. *Sach'ong* 史叢 59 (2004): 45–72.

Norman, Jerry. *A Comprehensive Manchu-English Dictionary*. Cambridge, MA: Harvard University Press, 2013.

O Toil 吳道一. *Pyŏngin yŏnhaeng ilsŭng* 丙寅燕行日乘 [1686]. Vol. 29 of *Yŏnhaengnok chŏnjip* 燕行錄全集, edited by Im Kijung 임기중. Seoul: Tongguk taehakkyo, 2001.

Okamoto Takashi 岡本隆司. *Sekai no naka no Nisshin-Kan kankeishi: Kōrin to zokkoku, jishu to dokuritsu* 世界のなかの日清韓關係史: 交隣と屬國, 自主と獨立. Tokyo: Kōdansha, 2008. Translated by Kang Chin'a 강진아 as *Miwan ŭi kihoek, Chosŏn ŭi tongnip* 未完의 企劃, 朝鮮의 獨立. Seoul: Sowadang, 2009.

Pae Usŏng 배우성. *Chosŏn hugi kukt'ogwan kwa chŏnhagwan ŭi pyŏnhwa* 朝鮮後期 國土觀과 天下觀의 變化. Seoul: Ilchisa, 1998.

———. *Chosŏn kwa Chunghwa* 朝鮮과 中華. Seoul: Tolbegae, 2014.

Pak Chiwŏn 朴趾源. *Yŏrha ilgi* 熱河日記 [1780]. Vol. 53 of *Yŏnhaengnok chŏnjip* 燕行錄全集, edited by Im Kijung 임기중. Seoul: Tongguk taehakkyo, 2001.

Pak Wŏnho 박원호. *Myŏngch'o Chosŏn kwan'gyesa yŏn'gu* 明初朝鮮關係史研究. Seoul: Iljogak, 2002.

Pang Tongin 방동인. *Han'guk ŭi kukkyŏng hoekchŏng yŏn'gu* 韓國의 國境劃定研究. Seoul: Iljogak, 1997.

Parker, Bradley J., and Lars Rodseth. "Introduction: Theoretical Considerations in the Study of Frontiers." In *Untaming the Frontier in Anthropology, Archaeology, and History*, edited by Bradley J. Parker and Lars Rodseth, 3–21. Tucson: University of Arizona Press, 2005.

Perdue, Peter C. "Boundaries, Maps, and Movement: Chinese, Russian, and Mongolian Empires in Early Modern Central Eurasia." *International History Review* 20, no. 2 (1998): 263–86.

————. *China Marches West: The Qing Conquest of Central Eurasia*. Cambridge, MA: Harvard University Press, 2005.

————. "From Turfan to Taiwan: Trade and War on Two Chinese Frontiers." In *Untaming the Frontier in Anthropology, Archaeology, and History*, edited by Bradley J. Parker and Lars Rodseth, 27–51. Tucson: University of Arizona Press, 2005.

————. "A Frontier View of Chineseness." In *The Resurgence of East Asia: 500, 150, and 50 Year Perspectives*, edited by Giovanni Arrighi, Takeshi Hamashita, and Mark Selden, 51–77. London: Routledge, 2003.

Pibyŏnsa tŭngnok 備邊司謄錄. Seoul: Kuksa p'yŏnch'an wiwŏnhoe, 1959.

Qi Meiqin 祁美琴. "Lun Qingdai changcheng biankou maoyi de shidai tezheng" 論清代長城邊口貿易的時代特徵. *Qingshi yanjiu* 清史研究 3 (2007): 73–86.

————. *Qingdai Neiwufu* 清代內務府. Beijing: Zhongguo renmin daxue chubanshe, 1998.

Qinding Da Qing huidian shili 欽定大清會典事例. Shanghai: Shanghai guji chubanshe, 1995.

Qinding Manzhou yuanliu kao 欽定滿洲源流考. Jindai Zhongguo shiliao congkan 近代中國史料叢刊. Taipei: Wenhai chubanshe, 1967.

Qingdai Zhong Chao guanxi dang'an shiliao xubian 清代中朝關係檔案史料續編. Edited by Zhongguo diyi lishi dang'anguan 中國第一歷史檔案館. Beijing: Zhongguo dang'an chubanshe, 1998.

Qingji Zhong Ri Han guanxi shiliao 清季中日韓關係史料. Taipei: Zhongyang yanjiuyuan jindaishi yanjiusuo, 1972.

Qingshigao 清史稿. Beijing: Zhonghua shuju, 1977.

Qing shilu 清實錄. Beijing: Zhonghua shuju, 1986. (Order by reign: *Manzhou shilu, Taizu shilu, Taizong shilu, Shengzu shilu, Shizong shilu, Gaozong shilu, Wenzong shilu, Dezong shilu*.)

Rawski, Evelyn S. *Early Modern China and Northeast Asia: Cross-Border Perspectives*. Cambridge, England: Cambridge University Press, 2015.

————. *The Last Emperors: A Social History of Qing Imperial Institutions*. Berkeley: University of California Press, 1998.

Reardon-Anderson, James. *Reluctant Pioneers: China's Expansion Northward, 1644–1937*. Stanford, CA: Stanford University Press, 2005.

Reid, Anthony. "Introduction: Negotiating Asymmetry: Parents, Brothers, Friends and Enemies." In *Negotiating Asymmetry: China's Place in Asia*, edited by Anthony Reid and Zheng Yangwen, 1–25. Honolulu: University of Hawaii Press, 2009.

Robinson, Kenneth R. "From Raiders to Traders: Border Security and Border Control in Early Chosŏn, 1392–1450." *Korean Studies* 16 (1992): 94–115.

————. "Residence and Foreign Relations in the Peninsular Northeast during the Fifteenth and Sixteenth Centuries." In *The Northern Region of Korea: History, Identity, and Culture*, edited by Sun Joo Kim, 18–36. Seattle: University of Washington Press, 2010.

Rossabi, Morris, ed. *China among Equals: The Middle Kingdom and Its Neighbors*. Berkeley: University of California Press, 1983.

Sadae mun'gwe 事大文軌. Edited by Han Myŏnggi 한명기 and Yi Sanghun 이상훈. Vol. 7 of *Imjin waeran saryo ch'ongsŏ: Tae Myŏngoegyo* 壬辰倭亂史料叢書: 對明外交. Chinju: Kungnip Chinju pangmulgwan, 2002.

Schlesinger, Jonathan. "The Qing Invention of Nature: Environment and Identity in Northeast China and Mongolia, 1750–1850." PhD diss., Harvard University, 2012.

Schmid, Andre. *Korea between Empires, 1895–1919.* New York: Columbia University Press, 2002.

———. "Tributary Relations and the Qing-Chosŏn Frontier on Mountain Paektu." In *The Chinese State at the Borders,* edited by Diana Lary, 126–50. Vancouver: University of British Columbia Press, 2007.

Serruys, Henry. *Sino-Jürčed Relations during the Yung-Lo Period, 1403–1424.* Wiesbaden: Harrassowitz, 1955.

Shengjing shenwu dang'an shiliao 盛京蔘務檔案史料. Translated by Liaoningsheng dang'anguan 遼寧省檔案館. Shenyang: Liaohai chubanshe, 2003.

Shengjing tongzhi 盛京通志 [1778]. Shenyang: Liaohai chubanshe, 1997.

Sŏ Hosu 徐浩修. *Yŏnhaenggi* 燕行記 [1790]. Vol. 50 of *Yŏnhaengnok chŏnjip* 燕行錄全集, edited by Im Kijung 임기중. Seoul: Tongguk taehakkyo, 2001.

Sŏ Munjung 徐文重. *Yŏnhaeng illok* 燕行日錄 [1690]. Vol. 24 of *Yŏnhaengnok chŏnjip* 燕行錄全集, edited by Im Kijung 임기중. Seoul: Tongguk taehakkyo, 2001.

Song Di 宋抵 and Wang Xiuhua 王秀華, eds. *Qingdai dongbei shenwu* 清代東北蔘務. Jilin: Jilin wenshi chubanshe, 1991.

Song Miryŏng 송미령. "Chŏng Kanghŭije tongsun ŭi mokchŏk kwa ŭimi" 清康熙帝 東巡의 目的과 意味. *Myŏngchŏngsa yŏn'gu* 明清史研究 24 (2005): 228–42.

Soongsil [Sungsil] Taehakkyo Hanguk Kidokkyo Pangmulgwan 숭실대학교 한국기독교 박물관 ed. *Yŏnhaengdo* 燕行圖: *Paintings of the Korean Envoys to Beijing during the Joseon Dynasty.* Seoul: Sungsil taehakkyo Hanguk Kidokkyo Pangmulgwan, 2009.

Spence, Jonathan D. "The K'ang-hsi Reign." In *The Ch'ing Empire to 1800,* 120–82. Vol. 9, part 1, of *The Cambridge History of China.* Edited by Willard J. Peterson. Cambridge, England: Cambridge University Press, 2002.

Standen, Naomi. *Unbounded Loyalty: Frontier Crossings in Liao China.* Honolulu: University of Hawaii Press, 2007.

Sun Chunri 孫春日. *Zhongguo Chaoxianzu yiminshi* 中國朝鮮族移民史. Beijing: Zhonghua shuju, 2009.

Sun Zhe 孫喆. *Kang Yong Qian shiqi yutu huizhi yu jiangyu xingcheng yanjiu* 康雍乾時期興圖繪制與疆域形成研究. Beijing: Zhongguo renmin daxue chubanshe, 2003.

Sŭngjŏngwŏn ilgi 承政院日記. Seoul: Kuksa p'yŏnch'an wiwŏnhoe, 1961–77.

Symons, Van Jay. "Ch'ing Ginseng Management: Ch'ing Monopolies in Microcosm." *Arizona State University Center for Asian Studies Occasional Paper,* no. 13 (March 1981).

Tamanoi, Mariko Asano. "Introduction." In *Crossed Histories: Manchuria in the Age of Empire,* edited by Mariko Asano Tamanoi, 1–24. Honolulu: University of Hawaii Press, 2005.

Tanaka, Stefan. *Japan's Orient: Rendering Pasts into History.* Berkeley: University of California Press, 1993.

Tao Mian 陶勉. "Qingdai fengji Changbaishan yu paiyuan tacha Changbaishan" 清代封祭長白山與派員踏查長白山. *Zhongguo bianjiang shidi yanjiu* 中國邊疆史地研究 1996, no. 3 (1996): 66–84.

Teng, Emma J. *Taiwan's Imagined Geography: Chinese Colonial Travel Writing and Pictures, 1683–1895.* Cambridge, MA: Harvard University Press, 2004.

Teng Shaozhen 滕紹箴. "Mingdai Jianzhou Nüzhenren" 明代建州女眞人. In *Mingdai Nüzhen yu Manzhou wenshi lunji* 明代女眞與滿洲文史論集, 3-16. Shenyang: Liaoning minzu chubanshe, 2012.

———. "Ruguan qian Manzhou shehui jingji gailun" 入關前滿洲社會經濟概論, in *Mingdai Nüzhen yu Manzhou wenshi lunji* 明代女眞與滿洲文史論集, 52-64. Shenyang: Liaoning minzu chubanshe, 2012.

———. "Shilun Houjinguo de xingcheng, xingzhi ji qi tedian" 試論後金國的形成, 性質及其特點. In *Mingdai Nüzhen yu Manzhou wenshi lunji* 明代女眞與滿洲文史論集, 129-72. Shenyang: Liaoning minzu chubanshe, 2012.

Terauchi Itarō 寺內威太郎. "Mansenshi kenkyū to Inaba Iwakichi" 滿鮮史研究と稻葉岩吉. In *Shokuminchi shugi to rekishigaku: Sono manazashi ga nokoshita mono* 植民地主義と歷史學: そのまなざしが殘したもの, 19-70. Tokyo: Tōsui Shobō, 2004.

Tong Yonggong 佟永功. "Qingdai Shengjing shenwu huodong shulüe" 清代盛京蔘務活動述略. *Qingshi yanjiu* 清史研究 2000, no. 1 (2000): 42-49.

T'ongmun'gwan chi 通文館志. 4 vols. Seoul: Sejong taewang kinyŏm saŏphoe, 1998.

Tongmun hwigo 同文彙考. 4 vols. Seoul: Kuksa p'yŏnch'an wiwŏnhoe, 1978.

Torbert, Preston M. *The Ch'ing Imperial Household Department: A Study of Its Organization and Principal Functions, 1662-1796*. Cambridge, MA: Harvard University Press, 1977.

Tsukase Susumu 塚瀨進. "Chūgoku tōhoku tōchi no henyō: 1860-80 nendai no kitsurin o chūshinni" 中國東北統治の變容: 1860-80 年代の吉林を中心に. In *Kindai Tōhoku Ajia no tanjō: Kokyōshi e no kokoromi* 近代東北アジアの誕生: 跨境史への試み, edited by Sakon Yukimura 左近幸村, 269-94. Sapporo: Hokkaidō daigaku shuppankai, 2008.

———. *Manchuria shi kenkyū: Manshū600nen no shakai henyō* マンチュリア史研究: 滿洲600年の社會變容. Tokyo: Yoshikawa kōbunkan, 2014.

Wada Sei 和田清. "Manshū shobu no ichi ni tsuite" 滿洲諸部の位置について. In *Tōashi kenkyū: Manshū hen* 東亞史研究: 滿洲篇, 566-81.Tokyo: Tōyō Bunko, 1955.

———. "Minmatsu ni okeru Ōryokukō hōmen no kaitaku" 明末に於ける鴨綠江方面の開拓. In *Tōashi kenkyū: Manshū hen* 東亞史研究: 滿洲篇, 503-65. Tokyo: Tōyō Bunko, 1955.

———. "Minsho no Manshū keiryaku: ge" 明初の滿洲經略: 下. In *Tōashi kenkyū: Manshū hen* 東亞史研究: 滿洲篇, 337-477. Tokyo: Tōyō Bunko, 1955.

———. "Minsho no Manshū keiryaku: jō" 明初の滿洲經略: 上. In *Tōashi kenkyū: Manshū hen* 東亞史研究: 滿洲篇, 260-336. Tokyo: Tōyō Bunko, 1955.

Wakeman Jr., Frederic. *The Great Enterprise: The Manchu Reconstruction of Imperial Order in Seventeenth-Century China*. 2 vols. Berkeley: University of California Press, 1985.

Waley-Cohen, Joanna. "The New Qing History." *Radical History Review* 88 (2004): 193-206.

Wang Dongfang 王冬芳. "Guanyu Mingdai Zhong Chao bianjie xingcheng de yanjiu" 關于明代中朝邊界形成的研究. *Zhongguo bianjiang shidi yanjiu* 中國邊疆史地研究 1997, no. 3 (1997): 54-62.

Wang Fenling 王玢玲. "Renshen yuanliu kao" 人蔘原流考. In *Renshen wenhua yanjiu* 人蔘文化研究. Changchun: Shidai wenyi chubanshe, 1992.

Wang Jingze 王景澤. "Dui Qingdai fengjin dongbei zhengce de zai renshi" 對清代封禁東北政策的再認識. *Dongbei shida xuebao* 東北師大學報 166 (1997): 48-54.

Wang Peihuan 王佩環. "Qingdai dongbei caishenye de xingshuai" 清代東北采蔘業的興衰. *Shehui kexue zhanxian* 社會科學戰線 1982, no. 4 (1982): 189-92.

———. *Qingdi dongxun* 清帝東巡. Shenyang: Liaoning daxue chubanshe, 1991.

Wang Xuemei 王雪梅. "Qingdai Dasheng Wula zongguan yamen yanjiu" 清代打牲烏拉總管衙門研究. PhD diss., Zhongyang minzu daxue, 2006.

Wang Yanjie 王燕杰. "Qingchao qianqi yu Chaoxian bianwu jiaoshe yu hezuo yanjiu: Yi Chaoxianren yuejing fanzui anjian de shenli wei zhongxin" 清朝前期與朝鮮邊務交涉與合作研究: 以朝鮮人越境犯罪案件的審理爲中心. PhD diss., Shandong University, 2012.

Wang Zhonghan 王鍾翰. "Guanyu Manzu xingcheng zhong de jige wenti" 關于滿族形成中的幾個問題. In *Manzushi yanjiuji* 滿族史研究集, 1–16. Beijing: Zhongguo shehui chubanshe, 1988.

Wei Zhijiang 魏志江. *Zhong Han guanxishi yanjiu* 中韓關係史研究. Guangzhou: Zhongshan daxue chubanshe, 2006.

Winichakul, Thongchai. *Siam Mapped: A History of the Geo-Body of a Nation*. Honolulu: University of Hawaii Press, 1994.

Xu Wanmin 徐萬民. *Zhong Han guanxishi* 中韓關係史. Beijing: Shehui kexue wenxian chubanshe, 1996.

Yamamoto Susumu 山本進. *Daishin teikoku to Chōsen keizai: kaihatsu, kahei, shin'yō* 大清帝國と朝鮮經濟: 開發, 貨幣, 信用. Fukuoka: Kyūshū Daigaku Shuppankai, 2014.

Yang T'aejin 양태진. *Han'guk kukkyŏngsa yŏn'gu* 韓國國境史研究. Seoul: Pŏpkyŏng ch'ulp'ansa, 1992.

Yang Zhaoquan 楊昭全 and Sun Yumei 孫玉梅. *Zhong Chao bianjieshi* 中朝邊界史. Changchun: Jilin wenshi chubanshe, 1993.

Yee, Cordell D. K. "Reinterpreting Traditional Chinese Geographical Maps." In *Cartography in the Traditional East and Southeast Asian Societies*, 35–70. Vol. 2, book 2, of *The History of Cartography*. Edited by J. B. Harley and David Woodward. Chicago: University of Chicago Press, 1994.

Yi Chiyŏng 이지영. "19 segi mal Chŏngjo ŭi tae Kando Chosŏnin chŏngch'aek: Wŏlgan Hanin ŭi chiwi munje wa kwallyŏn hayŏ" 19世紀末 清朝의 對間島 朝鮮人 政策: 越墾 韓人의 地位問題와 관련하여. *Myŏngchŏngsa yŏn'gu* 明清史研究 32 (2009): 257–80.

Yi Hongryŏl 이홍렬. "Samdogu sagŏn kwa kŭ sŏnhuch'aek" 三道溝事件과 그 善後策. *Paeksan hakpo* 白山學報 5 (1968): 155–212.

Yi Hun 이훈. "Chŏng ch'ogi Changbaeksan t'amsa wa hwangjegwŏn" 清初期 長白山 探査와 皇帝權. *Tongyang sahak yŏn'gu* 東洋史學研究 126 (2014): 235–75.

———. "Chŏngdae Kŏllyunggi Manjujok ŭi kŭnbon chi chi mandŭlgi: kyŏngsa kiin ŭi iju wa Manju ŭi ponggŭm ŭl chungsim ŭro" 清代 乾隆期 滿洲族의 根本之地 만들기: 京師 旗人의 移住와 滿洲의 封禁을 中心으로. *Sach'ong* 史叢 72 (2011): 267–305.

Yi Hyŏnhŭi 이현희. "Chosŏn wangjo sidae ŭi pukp'yŏnggwan yain" 朝鮮王朝時代의 北平館 野人. *Paeksan hakpo* 白山學報 11 (1971): 107–48.

Yi Inyŏng 이인영. *Han'guk Manju kwan'gyesa ŭi yŏn'gu* 韓國滿洲關係史의 研究. Seoul: Ŭryu munhwasa, 1954.

Yi Sŏnggyu 이성규. "Chunghwa cheguk ŭi p'aengch'ang kwa ch'ukso" 中華帝國의 膨脹과 縮小. *Yŏksa hakpo* 歷史學報 186 (2005): 87–133.

Yongbi ŏch'ŏn'ga 龍飛御天歌. Vol. 1 of *Han'guk kojŏn ch'ongsŏ* 韓國古典叢書. Seoul: Taejegak, 1973.

Yongzhengchao manwen zhupi zouzhe quanyi 雍正朝滿文硃批奏摺全譯. Translated by Zhongguo diyi lishi dang'anguan 中國第一歷史檔案館. 2 vols. Hefei: Huangshan shuju, 1998.

Yu Pongyŏng 유봉영. "Paektusan chŏnggyebi wa kando munje" 白頭山 定界碑와 間島問題. *Paeksan hakpo* 白山學報 13 (1972): 73–134.

Yu Sŭngju 유승주. "Chosŏn hugi tae Chŏng muyŏk i kungnae sanŏp e mich'in yŏnghyang" 朝鮮後期 對清貿易이 國內 産業에 미친 影响. *Asea yŏn'gu* 亞細亞研究 37, no. 2 (1994): 1–27.

Yu Sŭngju 유승주 and Yi Chŏlsŏng 이철성. *Chosŏn hugi Chungguk kwa ŭi muyŏksa* 朝鮮後期 中國과의 貿易史. Seoul: Kyŏngin munhwasa, 1999.

Yu T'aejong 유태종. *Uri mome choŭn insam kwa hongsam* 우리 몸에 좋은 人蔘과 紅蔘. Seoul: Ak'ademibuk, 2000.

Yun Uk 윤욱. "Cho Chŏng kwan'gyesa yŏn'gu e issŏsŏ manmun saryo ŭi chungyosŏng e kwanhan siron" 朝清關係史 研究에 있어서 滿文史料의 重要性에 관한 試論. *Yŏksa hakpo* 歷史學報 218 (2013): 341–79.

Zhang Cunwu 張存武. *Qing Han zongfan maoyi, 1637–1894* 清韓宗藩貿易, 1637–1894. Taipei: Taiwan zhongyang yanjiuyuan, 1978.

———. *Qingdai Zhong Han guanxi lunwenji* 清代中韓關係論文集. Taipei: Taiwan shangwu yinshuguan, 1987.

Zhang Jie 張杰. "Liutiaobian, yinpiao yu Qingchao dongbei fengjin xinlun" 柳條邊, 印票與清朝東北封禁新論. *Zhongguo bianjiang shidi yanjiu* 中國邊疆史地研究 9, no. 1 (1999): 78–85.

———. "Qing qianqi dui Yalujiang fengjinqu de guanxia" 清前期對鴨綠江封禁區的關轄. *Zhongguo bianjiang shidi yanjiu* 中國邊疆史地研究 14, no. 4 (2004): 52–61.

Zhang Jie 張杰 and Zhang Danhui 張丹卉. *Qingdai dongbei bianjiang de Manzu, 1644–1840* 清代東北邊疆的滿族, 1644–1840. Shenyang: Liaoning minzu chubanshe, 2005.

Zhang Shizun 張士尊. *Qingdai dongbei yimin yu shehui bianqian, 1644–1911* 清代東北移民與社會變遷, 1644–1911. Changchun: Jilin renmin chubanshe, 2003.

Zhang Yongjiang 張永江. *Qingdai fanbu yanjiu: Yi zhengzhi bianqian wei zhongxin* 清代藩部研究: 以政治變遷爲中心. Haerbin: Heilongjiang jiaoyu chubanshe, 2001.

GLOSSARY

Abang kangyŏkko 我邦疆域考
Aihe 靉河
Amnok 鴨綠
Andong duhufu 安東都護府

Baishan 白山
bajia junfen 八家均分
bao 堡
baoren 保人
baqi 八旗
baqi shengji wenti 八旗生計問題
beile 貝勒
beise 貝子
Bencao gangmu 本草綱目
Bencao jing jizhu 本草經集注
bian 鞭
bian 邊
bianjiang 邊疆
bianjin 邊禁
bianmen 邊門
bianmen zhangjing 邊門章京

205

bianqiang 邊墻
bianwai 邊外
bianzhen 邊鎭

Caohe 草河
Ch'aengmun 柵門
ch'aji anch'i 借地安置
Changbaishan 長白山
Changbaishan zhi 長白山誌
Chaoxian difang 朝鮮地方
Chaoxianzu 朝鮮族
chaso 字小
chengshouwei 城守衛
chin 鎭
chishu 勅書
Chogong 朝貢
chŏmsa 僉使
Chŏngch'ae yokkuk 清債辱國
chŏngsa 正使
Chŏng Yagyong 丁若鏞
chŏnjo 天朝
Chōsen shōtokufu 朝鮮總督府
Choyangmun 朝陽門
Chuanchang 船廠
ch'ujing 推徵
Chunggang 中江
chungin 中人
chwaŭijŏng 左議政

daguo 大國
Daldangga 達爾當阿, 達勒黨阿
Da Ming huidian 大明會典
Da Ming yitongzhi 大明一統志
Da Qing yitongzhi 大清一統志
Dasheng Wula zongguan 打牲烏喇總管
dasheng zhuangding 打牲壯丁

diling 地靈
Döen 朵顔
Dong bazhan 東八站
Dongbei 東北
Donghai woji 東海窩集
Dong sansheng 東三省
Dong sansheng liu'an 東三省六案
dongxun 東巡
dudu 都督
Duyusi 都虞司
duzhihuishi 都指揮使

Elmin 額爾敏, 厄爾敏
E-lu-te 厄魯特

fanfeng 藩封
fanguo 藩國
fangwu 方物
fanshu 藩屬
Fatha 法特哈
faxiang zhi ben 發祥之本
faxiang zhi di 發祥之地
faxiang zhongdi 發祥重地
feng'en jiangjun 奉恩將軍
fengguo jiangjun 奉國將軍
Fenghuangcheng 鳳凰城
fengjiang yaoyuan 封疆要員
fengjin 封禁
fudutong 副都統
fuguogong 輔國公
fuguo jiangjun 輔國將軍
fuyin 府尹

Jianchang 醶廠, 鹼敞
Gaogouli 高句麗
gaoliang jiu 高粱酒

genben zhi di 根本之地
geshou fengjiang 各守封疆
gezu renmin 各族人民
guandong 關東
Guanshenju 管蔘局
guanwai 關外
Guo Lianjin 郭連進

Haeran'gang 海闌江
Hailanhe 海闌河
Halmin 哈爾敏
Hamgyŏng 咸鏡
han'gu 閑區
hanjun baqi 漢軍八旗
Hanmin 韓民
Higashi Ajia sekairon 東アジア世界論
Hoeryŏng 會寧
hogye 胡界
hoin 胡人
hoji 胡地
hongpiao 紅票
Hongt'osan su 紅土山水
Hongtushan shui 紅土山水
hosi 互市
hua 華
Huamin 華民
Huangyu quanlan tu 皇輿全覽圖
huguo jiangjun 護國將軍
hulie zongguan 護獵總管
hŭngwang ŭi chi 興王의 地
Hŭrha 虎爾哈
hwangjo 皇朝
hyŏngjo ch'amŭi 刑曹參議

Jiandao 間島
jiang 疆

jiangjun 將軍

Jianzhou dengchu difang guowang Tong 建州等處地方國王佟

Jianzhou zuowei 建州左衛

jierang difang 接壤地方

Ji Han tongshangju 吉韓通商局

jin 斤

Jinguo/Houjin 金國/後金

jinshan zhaopiao 進山照票

junwang 郡王

kaho 假胡

Kaiyuan tushuo 開原圖說

Kando 間島

Kangbuk ilgi 江北日記

kanggye 疆界

kangyŏk 疆域

Kapsan 甲山

ki 氣

Ko Chosŏn 古朝鮮

Koguryŏ 高句麗

kou 口

kŭmsu 禽獸

kun 郡

kŭn 斤

kun'gwan 軍官

kunsu 郡守

kut'al 甌脫

kwanch'alsa 觀察使

Kyaon Mŏngge t'emul 갸온명거터물

Kyŏngwŏn 慶源

lantou 欄頭

Le-chu 勒楚

li 里

liang 兩

Liaodong duzhihui shisi 遼東都指揮使司

Liaodong zhaomin kaiken ling 遼東招民開墾令
Liaoxi 遼西
Liaozuo 遼左
Lifanyuan 理藩院
Liji 禮記
lingcui 領催
liutiaobian 柳條邊
longhu jiangjun 龍虎將軍
longxing zhi di 龍興之地
luyin 路引

Mangniushao 莽牛哨
Mansenshi 滿鮮史
Manzhou shilu 滿洲實錄
Manzhou yuanliu kao 滿洲源流考
Maolian 毛憐
mashi 馬市
mashiguan 馬市官
Mengtemu 孟特穆
mu 畝
muin chidae 無人地帶
Mu-ke-deng 穆克登
mushi 木市

naebok 內服
Nasutu 那蘇圖
neidi 內地
neidi chenmin 內地臣民
Neiwufu 內務府
no 虜
Nurgan duzhihui shisi 奴兒干都指揮使司

Odori 斡朶里, 吾都里
oebŏn 外藩
oeji 外地

Ollyanghap 兀良哈
Orangk'ae 오랑캐
Oŭmhoe 吾音會
outuo 甌脫

Paektusan 白頭山
Paektusan chŏnggyebi chido 白頭山定界碑地圖
Paektusan pi pon'guk kyŏngnae 白頭山非本國境內
p'aldo 八道
p'alp'o 八包
Parhae 渤海
peidu 陪都
p'o 包
pŏlli 藩籬
pŏmwŏl 犯越
pŏnbyŏng 藩屏
ponggang 封疆
pŏnho 藩胡
Pugak 北岳
pukpŏl 北伐
Pukp'yŏnggwan 北平館
pungmun 北門
pusa 副使
puyun 府尹
pyŏn'gŭm 邊禁
pyŏn'gye 邊界
pyŏnji 邊地
P'yesagun 廢四郡
P'yesagundo 廢四郡圖

qianhu 千戶
Qinghe 清河
Qing Taizu shilu 清太祖實錄
qinwang 親王
qiren 旗人

ren 人
renshen 人蔘
ru bantu 入版圖

sadae 事大
sagun 四郡
Sahwan 士還
samchŏlli 三千里
Samguk yusa 三國遺事
Sandaogou 三道溝
Sanfan 三藩
sangguk 上國
sanghogun 上護軍
Sanhaegwan tongnasŏng 山海關東羅城
Sanxing 三姓
Sayŏgwŏn 司譯院
Sejong sillok chiri chi 世宗實錄地理志
Shangsanqi 上三旗
Shanhaiguan 山海關
shaoguo puhu 燒鍋鋪戶
shencao 神草
Shengjing fu 盛京賦
Shengjing Neiwufu 盛京內務府
Shengjing quantu 盛京全圖
Shengjing Shangsanqi baoyi zuoling 盛京上三旗包衣佐領
Shengjing tongzhi 盛京通志
Shengjing xi wo Manzhou genben zhi di 盛京係我滿洲根本之地
shenshan 蔘山
shibian 實邊
shilang 侍郎
Shilu 使鹿
Shiquan 使犬
Shiyishui 石乙水
shizi 世子
Sirhak 實學

sobang 小邦
Sŏbuk kyedo 西北界圖
Sŏbuk p'ia yanggye malli illam chido 西北彼我兩界萬里一覽地圖
Sŏgŭlsu 石乙水
sŏjanggwan 書狀官
Sok taejŏn 續大典
Song Erdazi 宋二達子
Suifenhe 綏芬河
suo 所

taeguk 大國
Taehan cheguk 大韓帝國
Taihedian 太和殿
talja 獺子
tallyŏnsa 團練使
Tangin 唐人
tianchao 天朝
T'omun 土門
T'omun'gang chŭk hwaŭm Tuman'gang 土門江卽華音豆滿江
Tong Maengga Chŏmmoga 童猛哥帖木兒
tu 徒
tujing 土精
Tuman 豆滿
Tumen 土門, 圖們
Tumenjiang Zhong Han jiewu tiaokuan 圖們江中韓界務條款
Tumun goronbori 투문고론보리

Udike 兀狄哈
Ŭiju 義州

waifan 外藩
waiguo 外國
wangdao 王道
Warka 瓦爾喀
wei 衛

weichang 圍場

Wiwŏn 渭原

Wu Dacheng 吳大澂

wu jiang bianjie chaming laizou 務將邊界查明來奏

Wula zongguan 烏喇總管

Wuliangha 兀良哈

wuren didai 無人地帶

xiang 晌

xiaobang 小邦

xiashan zhaopiao 下山照票

xieling 協領

yain muyŏkso 野人貿易所

Yalu 鴨綠

yapiao 押票

yeren 野人

yimin shibian 移民實邊

yi Zhongguo zhi kuangtu, ju Zhongguo zhi minren, li zhi suozai 以中國之曠土, 居中國之民人, 利之所在

Yŏjin yain 女眞 野人

Yongbi ŏchŏn'ga 龍飛御天歌

yŏngŭijŏng 領議政

Yongzheng huangzhi 雍正皇旨

Yŏnhaengdo 燕行圖

Yong-fu 永福

youshen 有神

yukchin 六鎭

zhang 杖

zhangzi 長子

zhaokenju 招墾局

zhenguogong 鎭國公

Zhongguo difang 中國地方

Zhongguo suoshu difang 中國所屬地方

Zhongguo zhi min 中國之民
Zhongjiang 中江
zhufang xieling 駐防協領
Zongli yamen 總理衙門
zuoling 佐領

INDEX

CPSIA information can be obtained
at www.ICGtesting.com
Printed in the USA
LVHW06s1944290618
582001LV00007B/4/P